From Electronic
to Mobile
Government

Vincent Homburg • Thomas J. Lampoltshammer •
Mihkel Solvak

Editors

From Electronic
to Mobile
Government

 Springer

Editors
Vincent Homburg 🄳
Johan Skytte Institute of Political Studies
University of Tartu
Tartu Linn, Estonia

Thomas J. Lampoltshammer 🄳
Center for E-Governance
University for Continuing Education Krems
Krems an der Donau, Austria

Mihkel Solvak 🄳
Johan Skytte Institute of Political Studies
University of Tartu
Tartu Linn, Estonia

ISBN 978-3-031-64470-2   ISBN 978-3-031-64471-9   (eBook)
https://doi.org/10.1007/978-3-031-64471-9

This publication is supported by the mGov4EU project (grant agreement No 959072) and ECePS ERA Chair project (grant agreement No 857622), both funded from the European Union's Horizon 2020 research and innovation programme.
Views and opinions expressed are however those of the author(s) only and do not necessarily reflect those of the European Union or European Research Executive Agency. Neither the European Union nor the granting authority can be held responsible for them.

This Springer imprint is published by the registered company Springer Nature Switzerland AG
The registered company address is: Gewerbestrasse 11, 6330 Cham, Switzerland

If disposing of this product, please recycle the paper.

Preface

Over the past decades, E-Government has transitioned from an admittedly voguish, futurist derivate of digital dreams to a day-to-day reality of how citizens, businesses, and governments worldwide interact. For many individual citizens and business representatives, electronic access to government services has not only been realised, but it has also become the default way of requesting services, submitting documents, and interacting with civil servants. If we look at the current situation, it is tempting to conclude that E-Government is reaching maturity about 25 years after it was first discussed.

There are, however, at least two developments that force us to rethink the phenomenon of E-Government.

The first one is that whereas E-Government is sometimes called 'wired government', many citizens and business representatives nowadays use mobile devices to access all kinds of services, creating new expectations of government services being accessible anytime from anywhere, with appropriate levels of security. E-Government is in the day-to-day practice not so much a wired but rather a wireless government.

The second one is that in the European Union, policymakers and technologists have increasingly abandoned the idea of electronic services provided within national boundaries. The Digital Single Market is a reality that urges us to think about how information can be shared across national boundaries and how services can be provided seamlessly across national borders. In the 2009 Malmö Declaration, the 2010 Digital Agenda, the 2017 Tallinn Declaration, and in E-Government Action Plans, the European Commission and the Member States identified the need and necessity to allow for the delivery of services across national borders. The eIDAS regulation (allowing for authentication and identification of citizens across Europe) was passed in 2014. In 2017, the European Integration Framework came into force to facilitate information integration across sovereign states, and in 2018, the Single Digital Gateway Regulation (SDGR) came into effect, facilitating individuals' and businesses' access to information and EU rules, rights, and procedures. These policy developments signal that E-Government is more and more taking shape in the form of cross-border digital services.

In 2021, the mGov4EU research project started with the idea that the future of E-Government is likely to be mobile and should or should not be restricted to the boundaries of sovereign European Member States. mGov4EU brought together ten academic institutions and business partners from five countries to push forward the practical use of safe, resilient, and sustainable mobile technologies to deliver public services across European countries' borders. The project aimed to bridge eIDAS and the Single Digital Gateway and develop an open ecosystem with actual mobile cross-border services that could be designed, implemented, and tested in practice. In doing so, the mGov4EU partners did not only reflect on policy developments related to cross-border services and identify management. Rather, it was the express intention of mGov4EU to develop, implement, and evaluate digital cross-border mobile public services, taking into account information security and data protection rules and regulations. In doing so, mGov4EU explicitly attempted to identify possibilities and limitations of available infrastructural components and existing digital public services. The consortium demonstrated the potential of current technologies, with a specific emphasis on the aspect of digital wallets, via three distinct pilots, i.e. electronic voting, smart mobility, and mobile signature. With this book, the results of these research and engineering endeavours are made available to an audience of policymakers, software developers, academics, businesses, and citizens interested in finding out what mobile cross-border digital public service delivery looks like, what its promises are, and also what legal, architectural, and policy-related challenges have to be dealt with.

With the results now available in a series of conference papers, journal articles, and chapters presented in this book, mGov4EU has been an interesting and truly interdisciplinary endeavour. Working in mGov4EU brought occasional transdisciplinary and intercultural challenges, but it also demonstrated the legal, political, and engineering realities behind European E-Government action plans and Ministerial Declarations. With the results, the participants in mGov4EU hoped to have paved the way for digital public services that can seamlessly and safely transcend national borders.

All of this, of course, would not have been possible without the efforts, encouragement, and relentless support of various individuals and organisations. Therefore, we would like to express our gratitude to the external reviewers of the project and organisations that have participated in the pilots in which ideas and solutions were tested. A final word of thanks goes to the European Commission, which funded the research reported in this book under its Horizon 2020 research and innovation programme under grant agreement number 959072.

Tartu, Estonia   Vincent Homburg
Krems an der Donau, Austria   Thomas J. Lampoltshammer
Tartu, Estonia   Mihkel Solvak
January 2024

Contents

Introduction

Thomas J. Lampoltshammer (iD), **Mihkel Solvak** (iD), and **Vincent Homburg** (iD)

Abstract This chapter introduces some technological and policy developments that are at the heart of the mGov4EU project. In the mGov4EU project, various pilots implement and validate enhanced infrastructure services for electronic voting, smart mobility and mobile signing, using mobile devices most of us nowadays naturally expect as a default way of accessing services. The pilots aimed to demonstrate the feasibility of providing cross-border information to enhance cross-border mobility and cross-border collaboration in the European Union. The pilots also demonstrated how enhanced electronic identities and trust services (eIDAS) and Single Digital Gateway Regulation (SDGR) layers can accommodate once-only, digital-by-default and mobile-first principles.

For this to result in user-centric, user-friendly mobile public services, stakeholders' roles (including but not limited to end users' experiences and requirements) have to be identified, architecture core building blocks have to be assembled, implementations have to align with EU eIDAS and SDG regulations and, with the eSignature interoperability system and the Digital Wallet System, ethics, security and privacy requirements have to be taken into account and evaluated. The long-term viability has to be ensured. This first chapter briefly introduces all these relevant angles and describes how the various chapters will focus on how specific challenges were tackled and what lessons learnt could be drawn.

Keywords Mobile government · Pilots · eIDAS · SDG · Once-only

T. J. Lampoltshammer
University for Continuing Education Krems, Krems an der Donau, Austria
e-mail: thomas.lampoltshammer@donau-uni.ac.at

M. Solvak · V. Homburg (✉)
University of Tartu, Tartu, Estonia
e-mail: mihkel.solvak@ut.ee; vincent.homburg@ut.ee

© The Author(s) 2025
V. Homburg et al. (eds.), *From Electronic to Mobile Government*,
https://doi.org/10.1007/978-3-031-64471-9_1

1 Mobile Cross-border Government Services for Europe

It is almost a bit of a cliché to note that governments around the world provide public services more frequently through electronic means. The phenomenon of electronic public service delivery has existed for decades. The topic has brought academics from various fields together to form a mature academic discipline that studies the development, use and impacts of electronic public services at local and national levels of government. Political and technological trends have converged for a couple of years, resulting in new research puzzles, engineering challenges and questions for policymakers.

The first trend is mobile and wireless communication technologies within government administrations. The use of mobile technologies in public service delivery can be seen as either an extension or a subset of electronic public service delivery [1, 2], and it has inspired experts and academics to coin the term mobile government (or m-government). Reviews of literature on mobile government [1, 3] have traced the origins of mobile government to the beginning of the millennium, with mobile government being defined as a strategy and its implementation involving the use of mobile and wireless technologies for the delivery of public services to citizens, business and all government units [1, 2, 4, 5], including but not limited to location-based services [6]. For about two decades, a stream of academic publications has focused mainly on explaining mobile government use intentions and behaviours [1]. Gaps in the literature include a lack of attention to the impact of user-friendliness on the adoption of mobile government, negligence of service providers' technological conditions and capabilities and questions regarding how mobile government initiatives align (or fail to do so) with existing administrative procedures and public policies, for instance, about security requirements, privacy concerns and information ethics [1, 3].

A second trend in developing e-government in Europe is that more and more, electronic public services are open to more than just local [7, 8] or national [9] contexts. For countries in the European Union, the emergence of the European Single Market and Digital Single Market has underlined the importance of digital public services that are provided across national borders or require information exchange across national jurisdictions [10–12]. These services are commonly referred to as cross-border digital public services. An example of a cross-border digital public service is an electronic prescription, a service that, during the COVID crisis, proved to be of vital importance for medication-dependent citizens who contracted COVID and had to self-isolate while in transit. Developing and implementing cross-border services requires levels of legal, organisational, semantic and technical interoperability that are hard to realise in the real world. It has been observed that the academic literature underreports the challenges of developing services in a cross-border context [10, 11, 13].

A third trend is related to developing policy initiatives in the European Union. One relevant initiative in this context is the Single Digital Gateway Regulation. To further develop the European Union's Digital Single Market, the Single Digital

Gateway Regulation (SDGR) was adopted in 2018 by the European Parliament. The regulation allows for developing a network of national portals in EU member states and the four European Free Trade Association countries (Iceland, Norway, Switzerland and Liechtenstein), with the Once Only Technical System (OOTS) being the underlying platform. A driving idea behind this policy initiative is that OOTS will become a trusted tool and a pillar of the Digital Single Market, allowing European citizens and businesses to provide their data only once while carrying out administrative procedures across the EU and the EFTA countries. Another relevant policy initiative is regulating electronic identities and trust services (eIDAS). eIDAS regulation marks an important milestone toward electronic identification and e-transactions across EU borders by enabling e-signatures across European Union authorities and companies that provide public services. eIDAS is, therefore, considered a foundation for securing cross-border transactions in Europe. eIDAS has been updated and is still part of an ongoing revision initiated by the European Commission. Part of the revisions is mandating the implementation of a European Union Digital Identity Wallet (EUDI Wallet or EUDIW) to member states. EUDI Wallets complement physical ID documents such as identity cards, driving licenses, passports, payment cards, transport cards and travel passes. They are meant to facilitate online identity verification.

The abovementioned trends may be seen as converging into a new electronic public service delivery form in a European Digital Single Market. This new image emphasises user-centric, user-friendly mobile public services that are efficient in their use by citizens, governments and businesses, allow for inclusivity and non-discrimination and boost security and privacy protection levels. With the Single Digital Gateway Regulation in place, electronic identities and trust services and digital wallets being developed, European flagship policy initiatives are well under-way, and the prospects of realising visions of seamless, 24/7, location-independent public services are thought-provoking. At the same time, it must be observed that there are many uncertainties and challenges to overcome at the time of writing. Currently, various member states in the European Union are providing public services accessible using smartphones. However, a fair assessment also is that mobile government is still in its infancy. This is the point of departure of the Horizon 2020 project mGov4EU. This multidisciplinary project was funded by the European Commission and brought together ten partners from five countries to develop an open ecosystem for providing secure mobile cross-border electronic government services using the eIDAS and SDGR foundations. This book presents the main findings, outcomes, lessons learned and policy recommendations developed during the project.

2   The mGov4EU Project

The mGov4EU project took place between January 2021 and December 2023 and had at its core the ambition to unlock the full potential of mobile cross-border services, the Single Digital Gateway and updated eIDAS regulations. The project's final results were presented during an international symposium held on the 4th of December 2023, at the Permanent Representation of Estonia to the European Union in Brussels.

In the mGov4EU project, it is acknowledged that digital transformation and the challenges of providing seamless, user-centric, secure and privacy-preserving public services require practice and academia. Within each of those realms, various disciplines work hand in hand. It is not uncommon to claim that understanding digital public service delivery (either or not using mobile technologies) requires bringing together insights from disciplines ranging from computer science to law, political science, public administration and organisation studies. However sympathetic this may sound, it must not be underestimated that important epistemological differences exist between social sciences and engineering disciplines and practice and academia. Traditionally, social science has committed itself to answering 'questions and striving for theories of high generality, where the epistemology of the engineering discipline (including but not limited to computer science), the practical question "what works" drives much of the research' [14]. Experiences in the mGov4EU project showed that.

To bridge the gap between epistemological differences and make sure to lift mobile cross-border public services to new levels, mGov4EU has committed itself to implement and validate three pilots:

- An internet voting pilot with which an identification mechanism and SDG layer are integrated into a remote online voting system. This solution was implemented and tested during University Council elections at the University of Tartu in Estonia.
- A mobile signing pilot with which electronic signatures were implemented and validated in the mGov4EU workflows and business processes, which requires cross-border information exchange because signatories use electronic ID means from various European Member States.
- A smart mobility pilot with which an eIDAS authentication backend, an eIDAS node, an SDG backend and a reconfigured Passenger App were used to allow German and Austrian test users to use their national test eIDs for using the state-subsidised FiftyFifty taxi service that operates in German rural areas.

The abovementioned pilots served not only as testbeds for realising technological solutions but also as providers of valuable data with which users' responses could be theorised and improved understanding of development activities and users' evaluation could be realised.

3   Outline of the Book

Insights from pilots are documented in various chapters, which are the core of this book. The contents of various chapters are summarised below.

In the chapter 'User Journey, User Experience', Rachelle Selling and Thomas J. Lampoltshammer discuss user experience design literature and explain how various pilots' user experience was considered to develop mobile electronic public services so that users of mobile government experience better public services. The chapter provides the reader with good practices for appropriately designing mobile government services and lessons learned throughout from these various pilots.

In the chapter titled 'Stakeholders', Rachelle Sellung and Thomas Lampoltshammer provide an overview of the mobile government ecosystem and discuss roles performed by various stakeholders that populate the ecosystem, using qualitative studies that were conducted with mobile government stakeholders in Estonia and Austria.

The chapter 'Design and Architecture of Mobile Cross-Border Services Building Blocks', authored by Blaž Podgorelec, Thomas Zefferer and Andreea Corici, discusses the eID interoperability system, the SDG interoperability system, the eSignature interoperability system and the Digital Wallet system as core building blocks of a technical architecture that serves as the foundation for mobile government applications. The assemblage of these building blocks makes it possible to design secure ways for citizens to identify themselves electronically, develop cross-border solutions that make efficient use of user-authorization access points, allow for trust to emerge among users by the generation of electronic signatures and provide a user-friendly platform (a wallet) that allows citizens to manage credentials and evidence of transactions. The chapter provides technical details of each component and discusses current and future applications of the architecture in European mobile government initiatives.

In 'Implementation and Systems Integration', Bernd Prünster, Andreea Corici, Roland Czerny, Tobias Wich and Thomas Zefferer discuss how more or less traditional focus on uses of Web browsers on desktop computers needs to be reconsidered when services are delivered through smartphones, as the latter have different characteristics, capabilities and also other limitations. The chapter provides specific solutions to technical mobile government challenges.

Jordi Cucurull, Polina Toropova and Andreea Corici describe the Internet voting pilot in their chapter, 'An i-Voting Pilot in the eIDAS and SDG Context'. The authors describe transitioning a laboratory proof of concept to a real-world application and discuss voters' experiences.

The chapter 'Ethics and Privacy' provides Hans Graux's elaboration of the relevance of the General Data Protection Regulation (GDPR), the Single Digital Gateway Regulation (SDGR) and ongoing revisions of the eIDAS Regulation for mobile government applications. Hans Graux also reflects on how regulations interact, what ethics principles underlie these regulations, how legal rules impact mGov4EU and how mGov4EU addresses known legal and ethics issues.

Lucy Temple and Gregor Eibl focus on transdisciplinary research at the heart of the MGov4EU project. In 'Evaluation and Transdisciplinarity', the authors reflect on the needs, promises and challenges of truly transdisciplinary research and develop and apply an evaluation framework with which the relevance of digital government projects—including mobile government initiatives—can be assessed.

An important issue with mobile government is security, which is the topic of Thomas Zefferer's chapter titled 'Security'. Mobile devices introduce new security challenges, like their vulnerability to theft and loss, while their 'always on'- characteristic paves the way for new attack vectors. Thomas Zefferer describes a security-evaluation model that helps ensure mobile government solutions' security during design and implementation. The feasibility of the model describes the results of its application to software components and applications developed in the mGov4EU project.

Sustainability is a core area of attention of the mGov4EU project, and Carsten Schmidt, Stefan Dedović, Bogdan Romanov and Thomas J. Lampoltshammer reflect on MGov4EU's lasting impact in their chapter, 'Sustainability'. The authors discuss the project's outcomes and deliverables and critically examine whether and, if so, how, the involvement of stakeholders and focus on take-up, flexibility and interoperable solutions and continuity have contributed to results that are likely to extend beyond MGov4EU's life span.

The chapter titled 'Relevant Business Models and Patterns' discusses the results of an expert analysis of business model patterns for the eID interoperability system, the eSignature interoperability system, the SDG interoperability system and the Digital Wallet. In this chapter, authors Thomas J. Lampoltshammer and Rachelle Sellung also reflect on the sustainability of these mGov4EU components beyond the project's end date.

In 'Future Outlook, Research Ideas', Herbert Leithold, Carsten Schmidt, Thomas Zefferer and Thomas J. Lampoltshammer synthesise main results and findings discussed in the abovementioned chapters into a road map of research that is needed to reap the benefits of eIDAS, SDG, the Once-Only Technical System and the European Digital Identity Wallet. The authors provide a governance outlook, a privacy and data protection outlook, an electronic services outlook and a mobile technologies outlook.

In this book's final chapter, 'Summary', Carsten Schmidt, Thomas Lampolt- shammer and Vincent Homburg look over all the contributions and lessons learnt and try to regain a bigger picture of the European mobile government's past, present and future.

References

1. Wirtz, B.W., Balzer, I., Schmitt, D.: Mobile government: research development and research perspectives. Int. J. Public Adm. **46** (2023). https://doi.org/10.1080/01900692.2021.1993910
2. Kushchu, I., Kuscu, M.H.: From E-government to M-government: Facing the Inevitable. Proceedings of the 3rd European conference on eGovernment. (2004)

3. Albesher, A.S., Stone, R.T.: Current state of m-government research: Identifying future research opportunities. Int J Electron Gov. **8** (2016). https://doi.org/10.1504/IJEG.2016.078118

4. Kim, Y., Yoon, J., Park, S., Han, J.: Architecture for implementing the mobile government services in Korea. Lecture Notes in Computer Science (including subseries Lecture Notes in Artificial Intelligence and Lecture Notes in Bioinformatics). **3289** (2004). https://doi.org/10.1007/978-3-540-30466-1_55

5. Eibl, G., Lampoltshammer, T., Temple, L.: Towards identifying factors influencing mobile government adoption: an exploratory literature review. eJ. eDemocr. Open Gov. **14** (2022). https://doi.org/10.29379/jedem.v14i1.693

6. Wirtz, B.W., Birkmeyer, S.: Mobile government services: an empirical analysis of mobile government attractiveness. Int. J. Public Adm. **41** (2018). https://doi.org/10.1080/01900692.2017.1390583

7. Pittaway, J.J., Montazemi, A.R.: Know-how to lead digital transformation: the case of local governments. Gov. Inf. Q. **37** (2020). https://doi.org/10.1016/j.giq.2020.101474

8. Budding, T., Faber, B., Gradus, R.: Assessing electronic service delivery in municipalities: determinants and financial consequences of e-government implementation. Local Gov. Stud. **44** (2018). https://doi.org/10.1080/03003930.2018.1473768

9. Scupola, A., Mergel, I.: Co-production in digital transformation of public administration and public value creation: the case of Denmark. Gov. Inf. Q. **39** (2022). https://doi.org/10.1016/j.giq.2021.101650

10. Dedović, S., Homburg, V.: Cross-border digital public services in the European Union: a systematic literature review. Int. J. Electron. Gov. **16**(1), (2024). https://doi.org/10.1504/IJEG.2024.138457

11. Criado, J.I.: Interoperability of eGovernment for building intergovernmental integration in the European Union. Soc. Sci. Comput. Rev. **30**, 37–60 (2012). https://doi.org/10.1177/0894439310392189

12. Schmidt, C., Krimmer, R., Lampoltshammer, T.J.: "When need becomes necessity" - The single digital gateway regulation and the once-only principle from a European point of view. In: Lecture Notes in Informatics (LNI). Proceedings - Series of the Gesellschaft fur Informatik (GI). (2021)

13. Klievink, B., Janssen, M.: Realizing joined-up government - Dynamic capabilities and stage models for transformation. Gov. Inf. Q. **26**, 275–284 (2009). https://doi.org/10.1016/j.giq.2008.12.007

14. Orlikowski, W.J., Barley, S.R.: Technology and institutions: what can research on information technology and research on organizations learn from each other? MIS Q. **25**, 145–165 (2001)

User and Design Research of Digital Government

Rachelle Sellung (iD) **and Lennart Kiss** (iD)

Abstract User experience (UX) and design research are pivotal in developing mobile and e-government services. As digital governance evolves, it faces the challenge of meeting citizens' expectations for intuitive, accessible, and efficient online interfaces. The primary challenge is the need for standardised design approaches and insufficient user involvement in developing digital government services. This has led to interfaces that often fail to meet users' diverse needs and preferences, impacting the effectiveness and accessibility of government services. The focus of this chapter is an in-depth exploration of these challenges within the context of the mGov4EU project. Through comprehensive desk research and analysis of user interfaces in digital government, this chapter evaluates existing design practices and user involvement strategies. The analysed evidence includes case studies and empirical methods, including surveys, interviews, and brain activity analysis. The results reveal significant insights into the effectiveness of current design practices and highlight the diverse approaches required to cater to different user groups. The study demonstrates how the mGov4EU project successfully addressed the challenges through established best practices and lessons learned in user-centric design. The chapter concludes with a forward-looking perspective, emphasising the importance of ongoing research and innovation in UX for digital governance. It suggests that future efforts should focus on enhancing user participation in design processes and standardising UX approaches to ensure the development of more effective and accessible government services.

Keywords User experience (UX) · Design research · User centricity · Public sector innovation · Standardization · mGov4EU

R. Sellung (✉) · L. Kiss
Fraunhofer IAO, Stuttgart, Germany
e-mail: rachelle.sellung@iao.fraunhofer.de; lennart.kiss@iao.fraunhofer.de

© The Author(s) 2025
V. Homburg et al. (eds.), *From Electronic to Mobile Government*,
https://doi.org/10.1007/978-3-031-64471-9_2

1 Introduction

As societies increasingly rely on digital platforms for governmental transactions, the significance of creating user-friendly experiences should be noticed. The user experience (UX) and usability of digital governance services play a crucial role in shaping citizens' interactions with public services. This chapter explains the research motivations and the importance of UX and usability in mGovernment (mGov) and eGovernment (eGov) applications. It draws attention to the challenges one faces when developing governmental services and presents lessons learned from the mGov4EU project.

The increase of mobile and eGovernment applications has impacted the engagement of citizens with public services. Typical use cases are, e.g. to access critical information or conducting transactions. Prior research has shown that the design patterns used while developing a mGov application greatly impact the users' perception of that service [1]. Citizens expect intuitive, accessible, and efficient interfaces that align with their needs and preferences. To emphasise the relevance of this topic, one can reflect on instances where m/eGov applications fell short due to a lack of emphasis on good UX. The case of the German eID serves as a stirring example. Users who adopt this service face challenges, including complicated applications and inadequate citizen involvement [2]. Due to low adoption rates and general complications around the German eID, it became a cautionary example in digital governance. This points towards the critical need for a comprehensive understanding of UX principles and user involvement in the development process of governmental services.

Even though prior research has already explored the topic of UX and usability in m/eGov services, substantial challenges endure [3–5]. The initial sections of this chapter elaborate on these challenges. Challenges include diverse mobile user interfaces, lack of standardised design approaches, and insufficient user involvement. This places a considerable hurdle in front of governmental developers.

This chapter specifically serves as a comprehensive evaluation of the mGov4EU project's progress in addressing complexities of UX and usability in digital governance. It showcases in detail how the project addresses existing challenges. Additionally, it presents good practices established through the project's work and the lessons learned.

2 Challenges in User Experience Research of Digital Government Services

This section reflects on the challenges in the user experience of digital government services. In the project's first year, desk research resulted in a summary of challenges in designing mGov Services, which was later published in [6].

Table 1 Challenges of designing mGovernmental services [7]

	Challenges of designing mGov services	Source
1	Different smartphones and mobile interfaces require different approaches for developing mGov applications	[4, 8]
2	No standardised approaches (principles, frameworks, or best practices) address the usability requirements of mGov services	[4, 5, 9]
3	Most mGov developers and designers use approaches concentrating on developing functioning mobile applications. Most of these developers aim to achieve good working applications more than mGov applications that address users' usability requirements	[4, 10]
4	The most impactful factors on the usability of mGov services are considering technology familiarity, demographics, trust, political status, and the nature of the service provided. This makes developing standardised approaches more challenging	[4, 5, 9–12]
5	Most mGovernmental solutions lack the inclusion of citizens in the development process, which makes it more challenging to address the usability requirements	[5, 12]

Table 1 summarises challenges learned from mGovernmental-related literature. This section will review each challenge and present reflections and learnings from the mGov4EU project.

Challenge 1: Different Smartphones and Mobile Interfaces Require Different Approaches for Developing mGov Applications
This challenge was addressed by adding relevant usability and economic requirements that encourage pilots and developing components to be aware of these challenges throughout the project's technical development. These requirements were derived on research and work shown in Deliverable 1.3 Specification of System Requirements in the mGov4EU Project [13].

Usability requirement	Adaptive user interface
	The user interface for the mGov4EU project must be adaptive so that the content shows well on small and large screens

Economic requirement	Platform independence
	Various platforms are used in both the consumer and business environment. To maximise the potential user base, mGov4EU SHOULD be designed to be deployed regardless of the platforms used by end users, service providers, etc.

From a user perspective, users expect their service to be used across devices, whether with their phone or laptop. For this reason, it is important that any service or application can be easily used on various types of screens with smaller differences between types of cell phones or larger differences such as different-sized monitors or tablets. Different sizes should maintain the service to users.

From an economic perspective, platform independence can help counter this challenge by ensuring that components consider multiple platforms in the development process when developing different pilots. This helps ensure independence and enable greater opportunities for the product. This allows for a higher-potential user base.

Together, these two challenges help address how it is perceived visually by the user with an adaptive user interface and more economic opportunities by allowing platform independence and flexibility for service providers and options or greater accessibility.

Challenge 2: No Standardised Approaches (Principles, Frameworks, or Best Practices) Address the Usability Requirements of mGov Services
The project addressed this challenge in various ways—the first months of the project dedicated effort to establishing an inventory and interdisciplinary requirements. There was a dedicated requirement category for user experience, where principles, frameworks, and best practices were considered in establishing the requirements. For example, requirements consider the following references [14–20].

The usability requirement created to address this challenge was "Established Usability Guidelines and Principles" [13].

Established Usability Guidelines and Principles
The User Interface MUST consider established Usability Guidelines and Principles to ensure an easy-to-use product and overall Usability.

This principle helped emphasise the importance of considering these guidelines and principles throughout development.

The requirement helped keep accountability and to consider usability in the pilots and components of the project. While it helped move the development toward considering usability guidelines, it was a learning process to realise how best to apply and balance other technical requirements.

Challenge 3: Technical Functionality Not Meeting Expectations of User Experience Requirements
This challenge points out the disconnect that can happen with implementing a solution that technically meets requirements or expectations but not user experience.

To help address this challenge, the following requirements were created for components and pilots to consider in their development and implementation [13].

High usability

Usability and understanding of services and applications *must* be a main benefit to end users. Given that end users may have a wide range of competence with this technology, it is important to make it as simple and usable as possible.

User centricity

User centricity *should* place effort in putting the user of the product at the centre of product development. The user's needs and requirements guide the design and development of the Web site or Web application.

The following expectations *should* be considered: a multi-channel service delivery approach, a single point of contact should be made available to users, and user feedback should be collected and evaluated to improve existing Web sites or applications.

User acceptance

The Web site/applications *should* be designed to meet users' requirements. The user decides whether the Web site/application meets their requirements or not. An example would be User Acceptance Testing (UAT), which focuses on user testing, not the developer. By testing the accessibility, the product quality can be checked and adjusted if necessary.

Co-creation

The project *should* involve methods and practices of co-creation throughout the project's duration. This implies that creating solutions for mGov4EU should involve the insights of stakeholders, especially end users.

These requirements were considered and applied in user testing completed by the pilots and components. Throughout these user tests, all components and pilots gained valuable insight from the user experience perspective to help address this challenge and develop the user experience of the solutions built into the mGov4EU project.

Challenge 4: Creating Standard Approaches That Fulfil a Diversified Set of Users

This challenge emphasises the lack of standardised approaches that include the perceptions of a diversified set of users. For example, this can include users that vary in political status, familiarity with technology, demographics, etc. The following requirements were developed to address that [13].

High usability

Usability and understanding of services and applications *must* be a main benefit to end users. Given that end users may have a wide range of competence with this technology, it is important to make it as simple and usable as possible.

Learnability
Learnability is an important usability design principle. In this case, it is even more important because most users have little knowledge of the topic. So first, they have to learn how the system works. Learnability *must* be considered in the UI.

Commonality of language
Ensure that global language requirements are considered, including languages that use special characters. In mGov4EU, tools *must* have a commonality of language.

Easy-to-grasp metaphors
Security software often uses metaphors that are not easily understood or even misunderstood (e.g. the metaphor for public and private keys). Easier to understand and grasp metaphors would help users understand the whole concept of the topic on a high level. There *should* be easy-to-grasp metaphors for users to understand.

Accessibility (1): Service Availability
The tools and solutions created in mGov4EU *must* support Accessibility Services that meet current standards, such as the Web Content Accessibility Guidelines (WCAG), the Authoring Tool Accessibility Guidelines (ATAG), and the User Agent Accessibility Guidelines (UAAG). They should be the foundation for accessibility service guidelines and can serve in developing accessible Web sites/applications. For example, explain how to make Web content accessible for people with disabilities and address text, images, forms, sounds, videos, and other Web site or Web application content.

Accessibility (2): Digital Inclusion
mGov4EU solutions *must* be as barrier-free as possible in providing digital accessibility. There MUST be support for all users in various situations, including those with disabilities. To maximise the user base, there must be no exclusion of a specific user group.

These requirements were created to help ensure that as many users as possible would have the understanding, through terminology and language used, accessibility of service or digital inclusion and that the user is using a product with a high level of learnability.

While these requirements are hard to perfect, having them encourages greater inclusion of these topics in developing solutions during the project and post-project reaction throughout development.

This challenge states the importance of co-creating solutions with users. To help address this challenge, the following requirements were made [13].

Co-creation
The project *should* involve methods and practices of co-creation throughout the project. This implies that creating solutions for mGov4EU should involve the insights of stakeholders, especially end users.

User centricity
User centricity *should* place effort in putting the user of the product at the centre of product development. The user's needs and requirements guide the design and development of the Web site or Web application.
The following expectations *should* be considered: a multi-channel service delivery approach, a single point of contact should be made available to users, and user feedback should be collected and evaluated to improve existing Web sites or applications.

These requirements emphasised the need to consider co-creation and to practice user-centricity in the development process. The co-creation activities established to meet these requirements in the project, like workshops or user tests, gave key feedback that led to further idea creation, higher usability, and higher understanding of the users' needs.

3   Good Practices and Lessons Learned

This section offers an overview of the good practices, examines their impact on perceived UX, and reports on lessons learned in the sense of the mGov4EU project. In prior research from [6], ten good practices were established to provide guidance and serve as a development toolkit for designing user-friendly mobile government and e-government services. These practices include aspects such as learnability, minimalistic and simple design, feedback structures, and error handling. The underlying goal of these good practices was to contribute to the gap of not having any good practices for UX and design for governmental services. However, the validation of the good practices and their positive relationship with UX and usability has not yet been addressed in the research. Table 2 summarises each good practice with a shortened description from [6].

This section highlights some good practices and provides examples of design solutions that fulfil these requirements or showcase where improvements can be considered. The second good practice advocates a minimalistic and simple design to improve usability and UX. This good practice states that a cluttered user interface has the potential to divert the user from their goals or impede their ability to locate the necessary functionalities. To develop a design that fits these criteria, one has to be certain about the main functionalities of their specific use case. For example, a mobile banking app aiming for a minimalistic and simple design might prioritise displaying key features such as balance inquiry prominently on the home screen. Therefore, users can reach their goals efficiently and effectively by avoiding unnecessary visual clutter and simplifying the navigation. Figure 1 shows an extracted screen from the Smart Mobility Pilot. Initially, this UI section appeared straightforward, yet numerous users reported difficulties and uncertainty. This goes hand in hand with another good practice: placement of information. While the simplified navigation structure and the general positioning of information

Table 2 Good practices of user experience and design [6]

	Good practices of user experience and design	Description
1	Learnability	[18, 19] defines learnability as how the user can easily learn, use, and remember
2	Minimalistic and simple design	Minimalistic and simple designs allow users to focus on what is most important for them to understand. Having a minimalistic design can also increase accessibility
3	Language	The language should be simple and offer the ability to be understood by a broad user group
4	User-readable terminology	Users should understand the terminology used despite their demographics or technology familiarity
5	Help and feedback	Multiple avenues of help and feedback should be offered to users. Multiple methods should be applied to offer users strong support
6	Error handling	If an error occurs, the user needs to be informed of what they can do to fix or restart their action
7	Search and filter	One of six interaction design patterns defined by Hoober and Berkman is the search and filter design pattern [11, 21]. Offering a way for the user to search for certain information, data, or functionality through a search engine implemented in the application can be very helpful to users
8	Operability	According to [4, 8], operability stands for (a) suitability of the device and (b) conformity of the device with user expectations. Independently of the definition, the developer must ensure that the service can be accessed through any device
9	Placement of information	Research by [1, 3, 4, 8, 22] has shown in their works that having a straightforward layout and supporting users with instructions is critical for the usability of a service. In addition, information should be given to users in easy-to-understand ways, with simple and straightforward text
10	Use of colours	[3, 12] has conducted case studies and empirical studies that reflected the importance of colour usage. The colours used can impact how a user perceives the look and feel of an application and how user-friendly it is perceived

Fig. 1 Selecting the type of eID in the Smart Mobility Pilot

contributed positively to users' comprehension, the length, description structure, and button labels were confusing. Users were unsure what button was meant for their specific user story. Version A was supposed to use their German eID, while users that tested version B were supposed to use "eIDAS AT". However, in the user story, they were only told that they were either German or Austrian citizens residing in Germany. The cause for the confusion lies in the missed connection between one's citizenship and which type of eID one must use. Some users also tried the third button option, indicating that they either do not know that their eID is already set up or that they misunderstood or completely missed the information in the description above. These reports highlight the importance of the placement of information and the depth of provided information a user needs to achieve their goals.

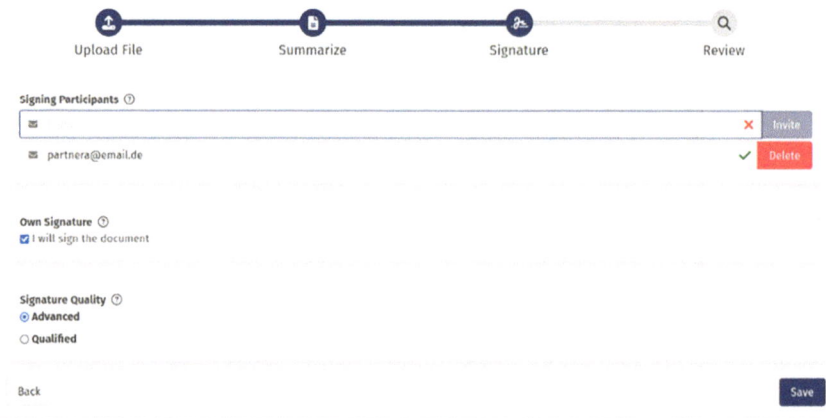

Fig. 2 Adjacent question mark icons in the E-Signature Pilot

Another example of this good practice is found in the E-Signature Pilot. This user-centric practice also highlights the importance of prioritising order when presenting information and instructions. Consequently, one has to be certain about the type and depth of information a user needs to achieve their goals in a specific use case to present the information according to its relevance. Additionally, it is important not to flood the user with information not directly required to proceed. A practical workaround for displaying optional information is to offer users readily accessible means to inform themselves about the topic in question when they opt to do so. Figure 2 shows one of the pilots' solutions for this practice. By using adjacent question mark icons, the UI elements indicated that more information can be accessed by clicking on them.

When a diverse user group engages with a system, the likelihood of errors increases. Whether these errors originate from user actions or technical issues, how they are handled directly impacts the perceived usability of the system. The good practice of error handling suggests that users should not only be informed about the occurrence of an error but also be provided with guidance to resolve the issue or start anew. Especially the aspect of informing users about the error state aligns with yet another good practice, emphasising their interdependence. While working with the pilots, users encountered several instances of unclear system status. This resulted in some assuming that an error has occurred while others stating that this process lacks technical security or feels incomprehensible—these findings back the good practice of help and feedback structures and the practice of error handling.

This section offers an overview of the conducted UX evaluation and presents the lessons learned and recommendations derived from them. As part of the mGov4EU project, all three developed pilots were subject to a comprehensive UX evaluation. The evaluation employed a mixed-methods approach consisting of quantitative questionnaires like the System Usability Scale (SUS) and the User

Experience Questionnaire (UEQ), as well as qualitative post-task and post-test questions encouraging users to report on perceived difficulty, suggestions, and general feedback along with additional use case specific questions. Although none of the questions directly targeted the fulfilment of specific good practices, the gathered qualitative user feedback extensively touched upon most good practices. It is important to note that most questions were phrased primarily to encourage users to report on things that negatively impacted task completion. In addition, users were asked about unfulfilled needs and preferences and suggestions for the future state of the pilot. This resulted mostly in feedback that inadvertently addressed the lack of good practices much more than the presence or fulfilment of those. Lessons learned from the UX evaluation and the user feedback are the following:

Firstly, emphasise the importance of user involvement and testing throughout each development stage. Iterative testing and feedback loops contribute to a better understanding of potential UX problems and help reduce the workload towards the end of the development stages.

Secondly, have the capability to test pilots in a working state with enough time to fix emerged problems and subsequent post-launch monitoring.

The third lesson learned is about effective communication between cross-functional teams. Through this, a feeling of cohesion and efficient project execution can be achieved.

Fourthly, be truly aware of error-prone conditions, not only from a technical standpoint but also from the user perspective—a proactive approach to error handling and resolution results in a robust and user-centric system with promising UX.

These lessons emphasise the importance of iterative development, communication, error awareness, and user involvement. Considering the good practices and the lessons learned during the design process, it is anticipated to result in a more user-friendly and usable governmental service.

4   Conclusion

This chapter summarises the inventory or desk research conducted at the start of the project about the current research and experiences of UX and Usability in mGov and eGov Services. It then continues to observe what challenges were identified from the findings and how the mgov4EU project addressed those challenges throughout the project duration. Lastly, the chapter highlights the good practices that were published and some lessons learned in our user tests and those practices.

Overall, one of the many lessons learned from this project and the integration of UX and usability is that it should have been given a clear task or workflow throughout the project. This is a key element in promising user centricity, and having a dedicated task or work package would have helped fulfil it.

In summary, many opportunities exist to improve the user experience of mobile governmental and e-government services. This project established good practices to assist in accomplishing that. These good practices will continue to be evaluated and adapted as further research is conducted.

References

1. Da Silva, L.F., Freire, A.P.: An investigation on the use of interaction design patterns in Brazilian government mobile information systems. In: XVI Brazilian symposium on information systems, pp. 1–8. ACM, São Bernardo do Campo Brazil (2020). https://doi.org/10.1145/3411564.3411651
2. Sellung, R., Kubach, M.: Research on user experience for digital Identity wallets: state-of-the-art and recommendations (2023). https://doi.org/10.18420/OID2023_03
3. Chang, D., Li, F., Huang, L.: A user-centered evaluation and redesign approach for E-Government APP. In: 2020 IEEE international conference on industrial engineering and engineering management (IEEM), pp. 270–274. IEEE (2020)
4. Isagah, T., Wimmer, M.A.: Addressing requirements of M-government services: empirical study from designers' perspectives. In: ICEGOV '18, Galway (2018). https://doi.org/10.1145/3209415.3209469
5. Lönn, C.-M., Uppström, E., Nilsson, A.: Designing an M-government solution: enabling collaboration through citizen sourcing. In: ECIS 2016. p. 68, Turkey (2016)
6. Sellung, R., Hölscher, M., Burgstaller-Hochenwarter, L.: Good practices of user experience and design research for mobile and electronic governmental services. In: Kő, A., Francesconi, E., Kotsis, G., Tjoa, A.M., Khalil, I. (eds.) Electronic government and the information systems perspective, pp. 138–149. Springer International Publishing, Cham (2022). https://doi.org/10.1007/978-3-031-12673-4_10
7. mGov4EU Project: D2.1 Business Model and Stakeholder Ecosystem Development, https://www.mgov4.eu/community/public-deliverables, last accessed 2024/01/17
8. Isagah, T., Wimmer, M.A.: Mobile government applications: challenges and needs for a comprehensive design approach. In: ICEGOV. pp. 423–432. New Delhi (2017)
9. Chang, D., Li, F., Huang, L.: A user-centered evaluation and redesign approach for E-government APP. (2020)
10. Kureerung, P., Ramingwong, L.: A framework for usability design to promote awareness of information disseminated via mobile government applications (2019)
11. da Silva, L.F., Freire, A.P.: An investigation on the use of interaction design patterns in Brazilian government mobile information systems. In: Brazilian symposium on information systems, pp. 3–6. Brazil (2020)
12. Kő, A., Molnar, T., Matyus, B.: A user-centred design approach for mobile-government systems for the elderly, Hungary (2018)
13. Public Deliverables, https://www.mgov4.eu/community/public-deliverables, last accessed 2024/01/22
14. DIN EN ISO 9241-11:2018–11, Ergonomie der Mensch-System-Interaktion_- Teil_11: Gebrauchstauglichkeit: Begriffe und Konzepte (ISO_9241-11:2018); Deutsche Fassung EN_ISO_9241-11:2018. Beuth Verlag GmbH. https://doi.org/10.31030/2757945
15. Garfinkel, S.: Design principles and patterns for computer systems that are simultaneously secure and usable, http://dspace.mit.edu/bitstream/handle/1721.1/33204/67550192.pdf?sequence=1&origin=publication_detail (2005)
16. Hassenzahl, M.: User experience (UX): towards an experiential perspective on product quality. In: Proceedings of the 20th international conference of the association francophone d'Interaction Homme-Machine (2008)

17. Jaferian, P., Hawkey, K., Sotirakopoulos, A., Beznosov, K.: Heuristics for evaluating IT security management tools. In: Human-computer interaction. pp. 1633–1638 (2011)
18. Nielsen, J.: Usability 101: introduction to usability (2012)
19. Whitten, A., Tygar, J.D.: Why Johnny can't encrypt: a usability evaluation of PGP 5.0. In: Usenix Security (1999)
20. Yee, K.-P.: Aligning security and usability. IEEE Secur. Priv. 2, 48–55 (2004)
21. Hoober, S., Berkman, E.: Designing mobile interfaces: patterns for interaction design (2011)
22. Kureerung, P., Ramingwong, L.: A framework for usability design to promote awareness of information disseminated via mobile government applications. In: 2019 IEEE 10th international conference on awareness science and technology (iCAST). pp. 1–6. IEEE (2019)

M-Government Services: A Multi-country Stakeholder Analysis

Rachelle Sellung ⓘ and Thomas J. Lampoltshammer ⓘ

Abstract Despite the rapid advancement of digital technologies in governance, there remains a significant gap in understanding the complex interplay between various stakeholders and the actual needs of end users. This disconnect poses a challenge in designing and implementing effective, user-centric digital government services. This chapter provides an in-depth exploration of the evolving landscape of mGovernment and eGovernment, primarily through the lens of stakeholder dynamics and end-user perspectives. It situates its inquiry within the broader context of the mGov4EU project, emphasising the growing importance of digital governance in modern public administration. The core focus of this chapter is to dissect and analyse the roles, challenges, and expectations of diverse stakeholders in the mGovernment and eGovernment domains. Simultaneously, it prioritises end-user experience, stressing its vital role in the success of digital governance initiatives. Case studies from Austria, Estonia, and Germany provide practical insights into these dynamics. The key findings comprise the necessity for nuanced stakeholder analysis in digital governance projects and the imperative of a user-centric approach in service design. It reveals how stakeholder engagement and user satisfaction are pivotal for the adoption and effectiveness of mGovernment and eGovernment services. Concluding with a forward-looking perspective, the chapter advocates for continuous adaptation and innovation in digital governance. It calls for more inclusive and participatory frameworks that accommodate evolving stakeholder needs and enhance end-user experiences, thereby setting a roadmap for future research and practice in digital government.

Keywords Stakeholder research · Stakeholder ecosystem · mGovernment · eGovernment

R. Sellung (✉)
Fraunhofer IAO, Stuttgart, Germany
e-mail: rachelle.sellung@iao.fraunhofer.de

T. J. Lampoltshammer
University for Continuing Education Krems, Krems an der Donau, Austria
e-mail: thomas.lampoltshammer@donau-uni.ac.at

1 Introduction

Understanding the stakeholder ecosystem assists in understanding the actors involved in the later adoption of new technology or solutions. It is key to know which stakeholders have an active role in the success of adoption. Identifying and being aware of these dynamics and actors early on can help in the development process and include requirements that could be much more time-consuming or costly to incorporate after the fact.

This chapter first provides an overview of the stakeholder ecosystem identified in the mGov4EU project. It describes the types of active and enabling stakeholders involved and briefly their relationship dynamics. The following two sections discuss some key results gained from end users. As there are two types of end users, service providers and citizens, both will be elaborated on in their respective sections. The service provider end users will be described in Sect. 3, which will highlight qualitative results that were conducted in Austria and Estonia on service providers' perceptions of single digital gateway (SDG) and once-only principle (OOP), cross-border aspects, mobile and digital services, and eID, eIDAS, and identity management topics.

Section 4 will build on desk research that was done at the start of the project that highlights non-technical challenges found in research for end users and showcases some results from the pilot user tests that were conducted and how it reflects with a subset of the challenges mentioned in related research.

Overall, this chapter gives insight into the stakeholder ecosystem and a deeper dive into the mGov4EU project results on perceptions from end users at varying project stages.

2 Stakeholder Ecosystem

The stakeholder ecosystem is identified for the mGov4EU project and considers which stakeholders are relevant for mGovernment and eGovernment services and use cases. To understand the involved stakeholders in the ecosystem, it's important to have an overview of the existing environment or market. Within the mGov4EU project, an extensive market overview was conducted at the start of the project [1]. The market overview summarised desk research that contributed to market trends, opportunities, and challenges but also relevant topics for the project, such as European eID schemes or EU cross-border e-governmental and m-governmental services.

The stakeholder ecosystem identified in the mGov4EU project results from a multi-step process. First, the term stakeholder was defined according to the project context. Second, a review of various stakeholder group categorisation approaches was conducted, which included [2–4]. Although the named categorisation approaches individually have their gaps, they were used as a starting point along with related literature to define the stakeholder groups in the ecosystem. In addition, this ecosystem was built on ongoing work on various identity management ecosystems found in [5, 6].

There are two main groups of stakeholders that have been identified. The first are the active stakeholders directly participating in the ecosystem. The second group are the enabling stakeholders. These are indirect participants but still have an impact on the ecosystem.

2.1 Active Stakeholders

The active stakeholders can be seen in Fig. 1. Users and ID/credential/trust providers are divided into two main types.

2.1.1 ID/Credential/Trust Providers

These stakeholders provide key components necessary for this ecosystem to function. They provide digital IDs or trust-related services that users need for services.

With that in mind, there are various types of organisations and interests between these providers. These stakeholders have a key interest in being the catalyst of a successful business model or a thriving ecosystem. One reason for this is their need for compensation for the costs and effort needed in their products of an ID/trust ecosystem.

Figure 1 shows the types of organisations that could take on the role of these stakeholders. ID/credential/trust providers could be seen as government/administration ID providers; IT platform ID providers, ID consortia, traditional credential providers, alternative ID providers, trust service providers, or other credential providers.

2.1.2 Users

The users are the second subgroup of active stakeholders. They are split into two types of users of mobile governmental services: end users and service providers or relying parties.

End Users

The end users are the users who would be using the digital services, e.g., citizens. The types of end users are the following: end user/consumers, with no special features; end users in government administrative entities or service providers, e.g.

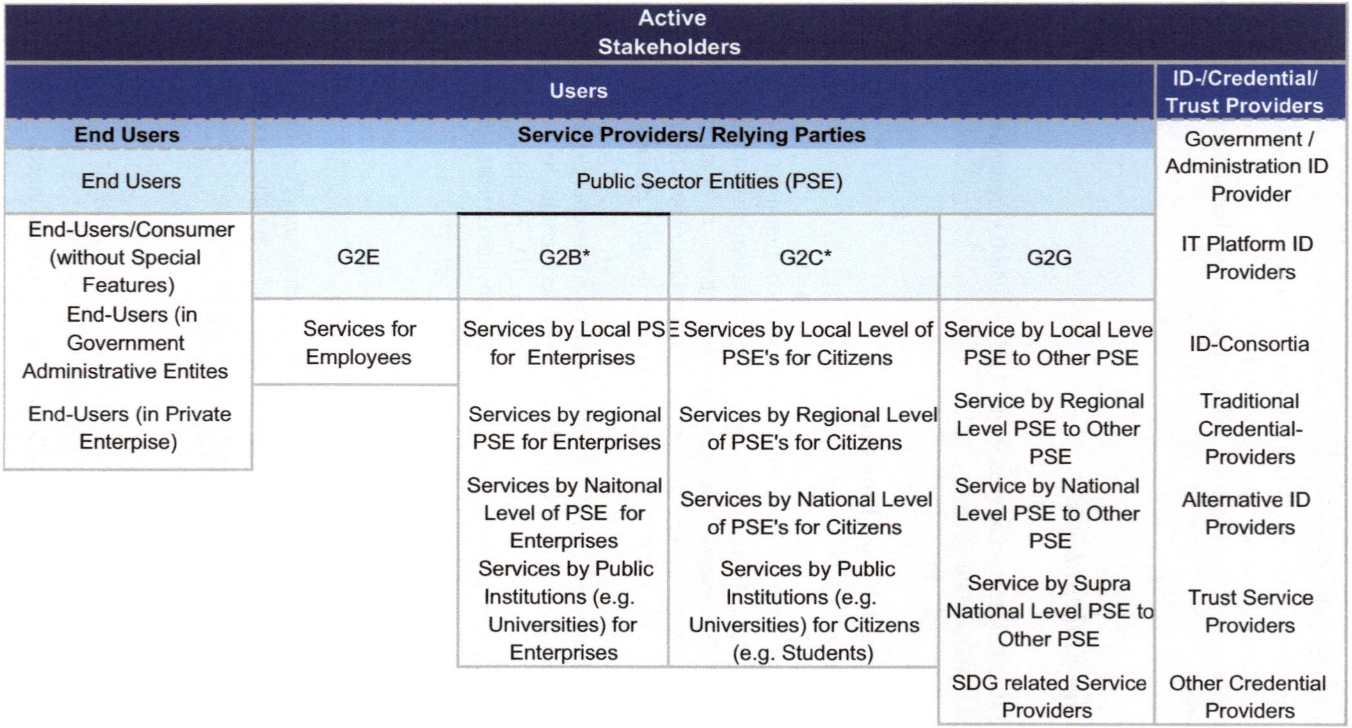

Active Stakeholders					
Users					**ID-/Credential/ Trust Providers**
End Users	**Service Providers/ Relying Parties**				
	Public Sector Entities (PSE)				
End Users	G2E	G2B*	G2C*	G2G	
End-Users/Consumer (without Special Features)	Services for Employees	Services by Local PSE for Enterprises	Services by Local Level of PSE's for Citizens	Service by Local Level PSE to Other PSE	Government / Administration ID Provider
End-Users (in Government Administrative Entites)		Services by regional PSE for Enterprises	Services by Regional Level of PSE's for Citizens	Service by Regional Level PSE to Other PSE	IT Platform ID Providers
End-Users (in Private Enterprise)		Services by Naitonal Level of PSE for Enterprises	Services by National Level of PSE's for Citizens	Service by National Level PSE to Other PSE	ID-Consortia
		Services by Public Institutions (e.g. Universities) for Enterprises	Services by Public Institutions (e.g. Universities) for Citizens (e.g. Students)	Service by Supra National Level PSE to Other PSE	Traditional Credential-Providers
				SDG related Service Providers	Alternative ID Providers
					Trust Service Providers
					Other Credential Providers

Fig. 1 mGov4EU Ecosystem—Active Stakeholders [1]

as employees; or end users in private enterprises as service providers, e.g. as employees.

The end users' goals are to be able to use their services for their private use, to be able to register their new address, or to place their vote. On the other hand, end users could be working for service providers and use these services for their jobs.

The service providers/relying parties are the users who would be integrating components of mGov4EU into their existing services to enhance their services to end users. Figure 1 shows what types of service providers are relevant for mGov4EU. It was identified that public sector entities are the main service providers relevant to this project. The public sector entities can be divided into different relations: government to employee (G2E), government to business (G2B), government to citizen (G2C), and government to government (G2G) (see [7]).

The goals for these stakeholders are to enhance their services and provide a better product for their end users. In addition, they are assuming the roles of data consumers and providers, which places them in the position to be key stakeholders in a data exchange.

Service Providers: The Public Sector Entities

This is an example of who could be the service provider to the end user. The service provider would take on the role of providing a product or a service to the end user or the citizen. For many of the components and use cases developed in the mGov4EU project, the service provider is the end user for their products. This is who would buy or use the component in their existing services to enhance their product for their end users, the citizens.

As mGov4EU focuses on the public sector, the service provider groups within the public sector entities are examples. Four different roles are identified: G2E (Government to Employees), G2B (Government to Business), G2C (Government to Consumer/Citizen), and G2G (Government to Government).

2.2 Enabling Stakeholders

These stakeholders do not have a direct role in the ecosystem, but what they do can influence the active stakeholders indirectly (see Fig. 2). For overall success, it is key to understand how these stakeholders can impact the active stakeholders. They have been divided into two enabling types: developing and framing stakeholders.

2.2.1 Developing Stakeholders

These stakeholders are developing the technology and standards required for the ecosystem. These stakeholders are interested in the success of technology and are

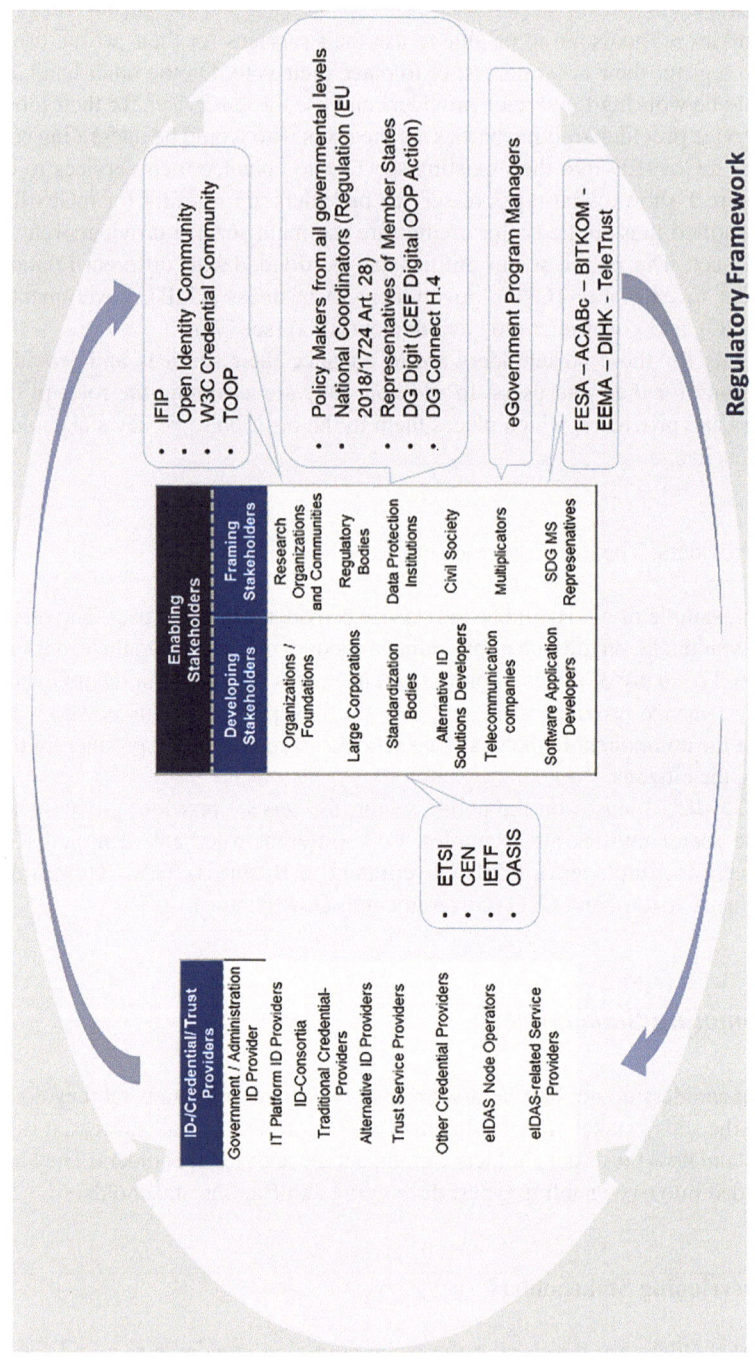

Fig. 2 mGov4EU Ecosystem—Enabling Stakeholders [1]

motivated to generate revenue to balance costs for research and development. For mGov4EU, the key developing stakeholders could be standardisation bodies like IETF, ETSI, CEN, or OASIS who work on standards that have a direct impact on mobile governmental services and stakeholders who are involved.

2.2.2 Framing Stakeholders

Concerning framing stakeholders, these actors have the role or impact to set framework conditions for identity management systems. They are not typically active in using or developing the actual technology or components but have a motivation for their success. Framing stakeholders in the context of mGov4EU could be research organisations and communities, regulatory bodies, data protection institutions, civil society, multiplicators (e.g. eGovernment program managers), or single digital gateway (SDG) Member State representatives (e.g. FESA, BITKOM, EEMA, etc.) The research organisations impact by developing basic technologies and diving into potential changing innovation opportunities. Regulatory bodies have a key role in creating a regulatory framework. Multiplicators and the civil society have the position to be able to influence legislative processes or public discussions.

Figure 2 shows the relation or impact that the enabling stakeholders can have on active stakeholders like ID/credential/trust providers. For example, these providers are held accountable to adapt to standards created by standardisation bodies like ETSI or IETF. In addition, the policies created by framing stakeholders, like regulatory bodies, also impact their product.

3 Insights from End Users: Service Providers

3.1 *Methodology*

In this section, the methodology and results of the empirical evaluation of the findings of relevant stakeholders for the mGov4EU project are presented, particularly focusing on the perspective of service providers. It is the active stakeholders that are at the centre of the assessment. This is because they are directly involved in the operation of the solution that is the result of the project and are thus most relevant for its long-term success without being directly involved within the project itself.

A qualitative research methodology was chosen to understand the goals, needs, resources, constraints, and experiences of these institutional/organisational stakeholders. The selected approach allowed for the provision of valuable answers using fewer semi-structured interviews within our target group. Respondents were recruited through the network of the project consortium.

The qualitative stakeholder research is structured according to the following process:

1. Based on the initial stakeholder analyses of relevant stakeholders in Sect. 2, the target group for the qualitative analysis was identified.
2. A semi-structured questionnaire was constructed based on the market overview and previous research.
3. A pre-test of the semi-structured questionnaire with experts recruited from the project was conducted. The analysis of the results and the associated learnings were used for refining the questionnaire.
4. The recruitment of respondents from relevant stakeholders for the mGov4EU context was achieved through the network of the consortium partners.
5. Interviewers were briefed to ensure equal quality of the interviews.
6. The semi-structured interviews were led by at least one instructed interviewer, either supported by an assistant who notes down the answers or recorded for later transcription by an assistant.
7. Interpretation of the answers through software-supported analysis.

The qualitative research approach follows that of [8, 9]. The interviewer's role is to listen, prompt, encourage, and guide the conversation. Overall, the more comfortable the atmosphere of the interview is and the more the stakeholders are willing to open up and talk, the better the results that can be expected.

Semi-structured interviews were used for the surveys. Such interviews use some prepared questions, but there is no strict obligation to follow a particular set of questions or order. Improvisation by the interviewer is encouraged and necessary as new questions can arise anytime during the interview. However, this form of interviewing also ensures consistency across all interviews, as the interviewer usually starts with a similar basic set of questions.

This type of interview allows a framework to be followed while leaving enough room for improvisation. The prepared questions maintain a certain focus while allowing the interviewee to add important insights and findings as the interview progresses.

3.2   Sampling, Data Collection, and Analysis

The focus was set on service providers, which could be IT service providers offering their services to government digital services or the government service providers themselves. The government service providers could be from any level of government (national, regional, or local). Interviews were conducted to get deeper and more dynamic insights or viewpoints directly from the experts who work closely with or provide these services.

As mGov4EU is an EU project, including more than one country perspective was important. Therefore, a multi-country analysis of Austria and Estonia was conducted. These countries provide greater insight into the differences between countries of different sizes, structures, cultural differences, and digital progress.

A purposive sampling strategy was applied. This means experts were selected who represent a specific location as a key criterion. A total of 14 experts were interviewed. Of these experts, eight were interviewed in Austria and six in Estonia:

- Austrian experts

The eight experts interviewed comprised three experts from federal ministries, one expert from a municipality, one expert from the Rundfunk und Telekoms Regulierung GmbH, and one expert from IT Kommunal, the main IT service provider for Austrian eGov portals and online forms. In addition, two government agencies were interviewed regarding different parts of the federal eGov services.

Of the interviewees in Austria representing either eGovernment portals and services at municipal or national level, four provide both G2C and G2B services, two only G2C and two only G2B. Two of the eight respondents (25%) offer a mobile application, while six (75%) do not. Meanwhile, seven out of eight offered a mobile Web site. Half of the respondents indicated that it is possible to log in to their portal with a user account. Two (25%) out of eight respondents stated that it is possible to identify oneself with eIDAS/eID. All but one respondent, for whom no information was provided, stated that administrative services on their Web sites are fully online.

- Estonian experts

Of the interviewees in Estonia, four belong to the Estonian government, specifically the National Information Agency providing eID services, the Data Protection Agency, and the Centre of Registers and Information Systems providing e-business services. One interviewee belongs to a non-profit organisation providing support and development of the national core data exchange infrastructure X-Road and one to a private company providing national identity solutions to the Estonian government.

The interviewees who were invited from Estonia and participated in the data collection process were mainly located and involved in some core Estonia digitalisation processes. They were not involved in specific service provisions such as G2C and G2B (except one) but in the core infrastructure technology that is a foundation for Estonian services, such as Information System Agency, X-Road, and Business Register. Most interviewees were mainly involved in the services aimed at G2G, such as providing data exchange software (X-Road) or identification and authentication services for PSE. In contrast, one interviewee was involved as a technology director in the Data Protection Agency with a special focus on GDPR issues in technology.

The expert interviews were largely conducted online using MS Teams or Webex. Interviews were conducted in either English or German. The German interviews were then translated into English in preparation for analysis. However, as the interviewers were bilingual, it is possible that some meaning was lost in translation. The interviews were conducted between August and November 2021. The interviewers asked the interviewees to be recorded to ensure the transcriptions' accuracy. In addition, the interviewers followed the instructions of the project's

Data Protection Officer and informed the interviewees about their rights around data collected during the interview and their processing.

The expert interviews were transcribed and processed using MAXQDA, a qualitative research tool. A coding taxonomy was created to analyse the transcriptions. This coding taxonomy was framed around key themes relevant to the project. This coding taxonomy was refined and adapted to suit the content of the interviews to ensure comparison and summarisation of content (see Appendix).

In line with the SCOT theory (Social Construction of Technology) [10], this research has provided insights into the first element, 'interpretive flexibility'. This is the step where the technological artefacts (e.g. this could be 'technologies' such as eIDAS or SDG) are interpreted. The qualitative research helped gain the necessary insights on these four key points:

1. eID/eIDAS
2. Cross borders
3. SDG/OOP (once-only principle)
4. Mobile services

The interviews sought a better understanding from the service providers' perspective of their general understanding, perceived importance, challenges, or impact on the different points.

3.3   Summary of the Results

This section describes interviewees' impressions of their awareness of Single Digital Gateway Regulation (SDGR) and OOP in general, their perceived impact, the effort required for implementation, and other comments they made on the subject.

3.3.1   SDGR

Among the Austrian stakeholder group, all respondents had at least heard of the SDGR, and most had a basic understanding of it. Most could not specify how their services could be implemented to meet the SDGR. However, one mentioned their concern about the high costs associated with implementation. Another felt it would take a "medium effort" to adapt their services.

Within the Estonian group, most respondents were aware of the SDGR. One challenge mentioned about the SDGR implementation is the issues related to identity matching and how to solve this challenge. Another interviewee mentioned that implementing it must be decided at the national level first; then, they can estimate better.

3.3.2 Once-Only Principle

Most Austrian respondents had a basic understanding of what the OOP was intended to do but could not explain in detail how it would affect them. Only one in eight respondents did not know what the OOP was. In comparison, all Estonian interviewees were well aware of OOP. Some challenges for implementing the OOP in a cross-border context were mentioned. Implementing the OOP in Estonia in the national context was very mature and successful. Still, in the cross-border context, there was a general doubt about how the implementations could look and be used in practice. The DPO mentioned that there is a good idea, but the current legislation doesn't support it.

3.3.3 Cross-border Aspects

From the Austrian perspective, the interviewees were also mostly positive about the relevance of cross-border use cases. However, some still did not see a big benefit or need for cross-border services. Those who found cross-border services relevant stated this was mainly due to eIDAS-compliant identification. Another stated that they believed cross-border use cases would become even more important because of the increasing need for digital transfer and exchange between other EU countries. A similarly mixed opinion was also found about the expected future impact of cross-border use cases. Many believed that cross-border use cases would increase in demand and relevance. There was a suggestion that infrastructure could be a key enabler of cross-border use cases if they were digitally delivered. Regarding foreign users, most respondents stated that they had few or very few foreign users.

Concerning Estonia, interviewees favoured cross-border use cases and further implementation. Some interviewees mentioned that as long as the country has a notified eID from the EU, it is possible to use most of their services. All interviewees seemed to agree that cross-border use cases will continue to have an increasing impact. One reason was that these services must work for large companies, as their headquarters are often outside Estonia. Of course, creating the right infrastructure and building blocks for cross-border data exchange was mentioned as one of the challenges in achieving this increase in demand.

3.3.4 Mobile and Digital Services

Concerning Austria, of the respondents that had mobile services, the majority offered them online with a mobile-configured Web site with a responsive design, meaning that it could be used for a smartphone. Overall, respondents gave the impression that there was a focus on mobile-friendliness and mobile-first services. In terms of importance, many interviewees emphasised the importance of offering mobile services. One interviewee explained that this is becoming increasingly important due to the overall increase in the use of mobile devices and the need to meet the market's growing demand for mobile services.

Concerning Estonia, in terms of importance, one of the respondents mentioned that a mobile-configured Web site is more scalable. Given that it is more scalable, this is a key reason for choosing it over offering a mobile app. Overall, respondents seemed to feel that offering online services with a mobile-configured or responsive Web site suitable for smartphones is important.

3.3.5 eID, eIDAS, and Identity Management

Overall, the Austrian interviewees were very supportive of eID in Austria and emphasised the importance of its development. One interviewee mentioned that there are three types of eIDs in Austria, depending on the services you want to access: citizen card, mobile signature, and ID Austria. One interviewee highlighted the demand and advantages of the Austrian mobile signature, especially in the current COVID-19 pandemic at the time of the interview, there was a much higher demand for mobile signatures due to increased digital processes and transactions. Another interviewee talked about the next generation, ID Austria, which is in a pilot phase, where the authentication and signature function can be used with the same service.

In addition, there is a high level of eIDAS compatibility with all notified countries. Overall, there seems to be much support for foreign eID compatibility. One of the respondents mentioned that this year (until August 2021), they had 730,000 visits from EU countries to their services, two-thirds of which were from Germany.

Regarding eIDAS, the Estonian interviewees that discussed this topic, their services were compatible with eIDAS by enabling and establishing eIDAS infrastructure such as eIDAS connectors and eIDAS receiving nodes. Thus, eIDAS-notified eID schemes are enabled to identify and authenticate Estonian e-services. In Estonia, six eID schemes are notified under eIDAS regulation: ID card, Digi-ID card, e-residency card, Mobil-ID, and diplomatic ID card. Thus, holders of these provided eID means should be able to consume and use e-services across borders in the EU.

Regarding identity management, the Austrian interviewees stressed the following aspects:

- User Authentication—Overall, the interview partners showed a high importance in using the Austrian eID for their services. There are, of course, low trust level ways to authenticate for users trying to complete some services, where a higher level is unnecessary. However, the Austrian eID overall has a positive impression from service providers.
- User self-management—One of the four interviewees who elaborated on the importance of user self-management stated that they found it important for users

to self-manage. Other interview partners depicted a more sceptical impression, stating that it could lead to disadvantages like a lack of data quality.

• Attribute-based credential—There were mixed impressions on the relevance of attribute-based credentials. One interviewee saw a need for verifying the attribute-based credentials of users, while others saw no need. It did not appear that use cases for attribute-based credentials have been implemented.

Regarding identity management, the Estonian interviewees stressed the following aspects:

• User self-management—One interviewee expressed uncertainty about users' perceptions of trust and trust in general when interacting with different data transactions. One interviewee stated that they thought concepts such as SSI were a good option for people to maintain their data. However, they felt that people might not be ready for this responsibility or understand all the implications of sharing some data or information. According to one interviewee, another challenge with user self-management is that some users may not be tech-savvy enough. Some interviewees expressed strong support and interest in using SSI solutions and following its future development. However, respondents mentioned that while new functionality could benefit, processes and development of a working solution are expected to present many challenges.

• Attribute-based credentials—The respondent who discussed this topic was supportive and felt that there could be value in having use cases for attribute-based credentials.

• Digital wallets—One interviewee elaborated on how a digital wallet or SSI could theoretically be good for the user. However, many other complications in using these technologies could interfere with their intention. For example, they highlighted the challenges of privacy and data protection. It could also happen that because of these privacy and data protection requirements, some information or items could become untraceable or unfindable in times of need. Another major challenge would be if someone stole the wallet or identity and how to return it to the rightful owner, if possible.

3.4 Service Provider Insights and Key Takeaways

3.4.1 SDGR/OOP

Most service providers interviewed, regardless of the country, were aware of SDGR or OOP. Understandably, given the centralised approach of Estonia and the interviewees, SDGR and OOP are seen as a very important issue with a high impact. In Austria, however, there seemed to be a general uncertainty about the direct impact or how it would be implemented. This could be due to the decentralised approach and the different roles of these service providers within this ecosystem.

3.4.2 Cross-border Services

This topic gave a wide range of impressions across the different countries surveyed. In Estonia, the respondents have focused on borders and are actively looking for solutions to meet their potential demand for these use cases. On the other hand, the respondents from Austria gave very mixed responses regarding the use of cross-border use cases and the future of cross-border services.

3.4.3 Mobile and Digital Services

Regardless of country, most service providers emphasise that their services are provided online with a mobile-configured Web site. In Estonia, one service provider mentioned that it is more scalable and, therefore, they prefer to stay with a mobile-configured Web site. Despite the preference for a mobile-configured Web site over a mobile application, most service providers indicated that mobile services are important for the future and that there is an overall growing demand.

3.4.4 eID and eIDAS

Overall, most service providers from each country indicated that their services were eIDAS compliant. The Austrian sample of service providers showed a greater integration of eIDs into their services by having multiple types of eIDs nationally supported. Estonia's service provider interviews didn't focus as much on eIDs and eIDAS. Still, the interviews that did were compatible, and overall, Estonia is an example of how well eIDs can be integrated into services.

4 Insights from End Users: Citizens

Literature in mGovernment and eGovernmental services has pointed out many technical and non-technical challenges for the market and the development of mobile governmental services. Figure 3 summarises the non-technical challenges found in the literature. They can be divided into five categories: economic/strategic, cultural, legal/political, end users' perception of services, and end user-related challenges.

In the mGov4EU project, user tests were conducted on the pilots and components implemented within the project. All of these working together provide a service to end users. This section gives insight into some of the "Users Perception of Services" challenges mentioned in Fig. 3. As stated in the literature, [19] highlights that the citizens' or users' perception of service has a key role in adopting mobile services. They emphasise how citizens or end users perceive a service differently than the

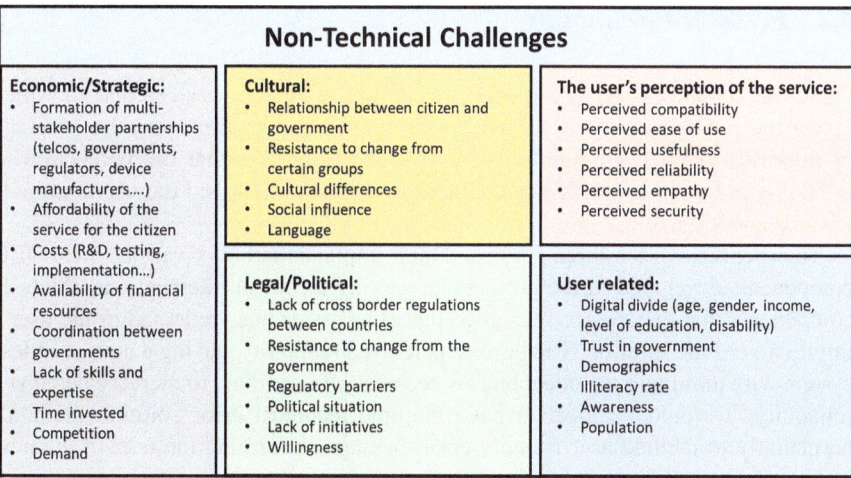

Fig. 3 Non-technical challenge of cross-border public services [7, 11–22]

governments or service providers. In addition, the differences in perception could be about the service's security, reliability, and usefulness.

The user tests conducted followed a mixed-methods approach. It was a mix of both qualitative and quantitative methods that were used. Users completed varying pilots' tasks, where they were asked to "think out loud" and to answer a set of post-task questions each step and at the end. In addition, users completed quantitative surveys that are commonly used in user experience research: SUS and UEQ. They also completed a post-questionnaire that asked them about other aspects of their overall experience.

With these results, the following impressions can be compared or validated with the list of perceptions by [19]. This chapter highlights three perceptions: perceptions of security, ease of use, and reliability.

4.1 Perceived Ease of Use

Consumers naturally adopt any system that's easy to interact with and use [23, 24]. Users desire to have an effortless user experience. If there is any effort, it should be deemed useful to the user.

The user experience tests conducted at the end of the project of the pilots and components gave an overall positive impression with ease of use. However, users often suggested incorporating colour and other visuals to improve their ease of use and comprehension of the pilots. In addition, the user interface can make a large impact on the impressions users have. Pilots or components with a more modern design often create a more positive impression on the user.

4.2   Perceived Reliability

Perceived reliability refers to users' perception of mGov services and to which extent the product or service providers meet their expectations and the accuracy of promises given [19]. Emphasis by [25, 26] elaborates that the perception of reliability is key in adopting any technology-related system and the users' attitude towards adoption.

The user tests of the three pilots and their implementation of various mGov4EU components developed in the project had varying technical interruptions. Pilots or components that experienced fewer technical errors or bugs reflected in the user's impression of the solution. To optimise perceived reliability, having a near-seamless system with minimum technical bugs is necessary. In addition, to increase perceived reliability, it would be ideal to have multiple technical error solution methods, particularly to include user-friendly error messages informing the user of the next step. Understandably, technical interruptions or errors can occur when developing a new pilot with multiple new and developing components. However, this should be prevented and perceived if the user is informed of how to resolve problems.

4.3   Perceived Security

According to [19], perceived security refers to users' confidence that any information they disclose through the mGov channel will not be shared with unauthorised parties. In addition, users expect that the system should have sufficient social and technological protection to protect their data.

The user tests showed how perceived security can greatly impact the outcome of the user test. If a user has one instance where they feel the situation is not secure, it is reflected throughout the results. For example, in one of the pilot user tests, the user saw the processing of the screens instead of a waiting screen. Many users felt that the pilot was potentially not secure or created doubt.

5   Conclusion

The mGov4EU project aimed to identify the stakeholder ecosystem essential for the success of mGovernment and eGovernment services. A comprehensive market overview was conducted at the project's start to explore market trends, opportunities, challenges, and key issues such as European eID systems and EU cross-border eGovernment and mGovernment services. Following this, a definition of a stakeholder ecosystem was established. This ecosystem consisted of both active and enabling stakeholders. To consider requirements economic, requirements were established for the components and pilots to consider throughout development.

Throughout the project, this chapter highlights two studies that took place of end users. There are two types of end users: service providers and citizens; they were tested separately as they have different requirements and attributes. A qualitative study was conducted with service providers from Austria, Estonia, and Germany. The results from the Austrian and Estonian service providers were highlighted in this chapter, along with their views on key relevant topics regarding SDG/OOP, eDIAS/eIDs, mobile services, and cross borders.

In addition, the citizen perspective was elaborated by first showcasing market research conducted at the start of the project and highlighting the perception of service challenges identified in the research summary of end users. The citizen reflections were extracted from user tests conducted by the mGov4EU pilots at the end of the project.

Overall, it was found that stakeholder research provided vital insight into the development and results of the components and pilots. It would be recommended to complete more stakeholder research and to reflect this further throughout developing mGovernmental and eGovernmental services. This can help ensure that key requirements and understanding of the services are met for end users.

Appendix

Coding Taxonomy

This is the Coding Taxonomy of what was coded in the Qualitative Research.

1. **Demographics**
   These are basic demographics of the interviewees.

   - Interviewee position
   - Country
   - Type of organisation
   - Services provided
   - Structure
   - Services availability
     - Online
     - Offline
     - Hybrid
     - Planned changes

2. **Regulations**
   This is about the awareness of SDGR and OOP and their perception of these topics.

   - SDGR
     - Known
     - Unknown

- Implementation
- Timeline
- Impact
- OOP
  - Known
  - Unknown
  - Implementation
  - Timeline
  - Impact
  - OZG

3. **Cross-border services**
   This is about the perception of cross-border service efforts among governmental services.

   - Cross-border services development
     - Relevant
     - Irrelevant
     - Timeline
   - Foreign customers currently
     - Relevant
     - Irrelevant
   - Cross-border services—others
   - Cross-border future impact

4. **Services Availability**
   About the discussion of the availability of services provided by the government.

   - Mobile
   - Offline
   - Online
   - Hybrid model
   - Planned changes
   - Service channel usage

5. **Mobile Services**
   Codes that are about mobile services in present and future contexts.

   - Importance
   - Opportunities
   - Challenges
   - Benefits
   - Availability level
     - Pilot
     - Mobile configured Web site
     - Mobile application
     - None
     - Planned changes

6. **eID and eIDAS**
   Codes about eID and eIDAS in present and future contexts.

   - eID capability
     - Yes
     - No
   - eIDAS compatibility
     - Yes
     - No
   - Planned changes
   - Foreign eID compatibility
   - eIDAS
   - eSignature

7. **Identity Management**
   Codes about identity management topics and the interviewee's perception of various aspects of identity

   - Challenges
   - Drivers
   - Change(s)
     - Most beneficial improvement
     - No need for change
     - Felt need
     - Type of change
   - User authentication
     - eID
     - Username Password
     - Other
   - User self-management
     - Yes
     - No
   - Outsourcing
     - Yes
     - No
   - Digital Wallet

8. **Digital and Mobile Services**
   This code group is about digital and mobile services. This could be when they are talking about a specific service example they offer digitally or mobile. This could also be about these services in a broader context relating to challenges, drivers, hurdles, etc.

   - (Un)Success
     - Most successful
     - Least successful

- Technical challenges/barriers
- Drivers for adoption of services/products
- Hurdles for adoption of services/products

References

1. mGov4EU Project: D2.1 Business Model and Stakeholder Ecosystem Development, https://www.mgov4.eu/community/public-deliverables, last accessed 2024/01/17
2. Cotterell, M., Hughes, B.: Software project management. International Thomson Computer Press (1995)
3. Sharp, H., Finkelstein, A., Galal, G.: Stakeholder identification in the requirements engineering process. In: Proceedings. Tenth international workshop on database and expert systems applications. DEXA 99. pp. 387–391 (1999). doi:https://doi.org/10.1109/DEXA.1999.795198
4. Sillitti, A., Succi, G.: Requirements engineering for agile methods. In: Engineering and managing software requirements, pp. 309–326. Springer (2005)
5. Kubach, M., Sellung, R.: On the market for self-sovereign identity: structure and stakeholders. In: Roßnagel, H., Schunck, C.H., Mödersheim, S. (eds.) Open identity summit 2021, pp. 143–154. Gesellschaft für Informatik e.V, Bonn (2021)
6. Zibuschka, J., Roßnagel, H.: Stakeholder economics of identity management infrastructures for the web. In: Proceedings of the 17th Nordic workshop on secure IT systems (NordSec 2012). Karlskrone (2012)
7. Falch, M., Williams, I., Tadayouni, R.: Cross-border provision of e-Government business registration services. In: ITS Online Event. pp. 8–10 (2020)
8. Myers, M.D.: Qualitative research in business and management. Sage, London (2009)
9. Myers, M.D., Newman, M.: The qualitative interview in IS research: examining the craft. Inf. Organ. **17**, 2–26 (2007)
10. Cozzens, S.: The social construction of technological systems: new directions in the sociology and history of technology by Bijker, W. E., Hughes, T. P., Pinch, T. Technology and culture. 30, 705–707 (1989)
11. Alonazi, M., Beloff, N., White, M.: MGAUM—towards a mobile government adoption and utilization model: the case of Saudi Arabia. Int. J. Hum. Soc. Sci. **12**, 459–463 (2018)
12. Alssbaiheen, A., Love, S.: Mobile government in Saudi Arabia: challenges and opportunities. Int. J. Mob. Hum. Comput. Int. **8**, 20–24 (2016)
13. Kalvet, T., Toots, M., Van Veenstra, A.F., Krimmer, R.: Cross-border e-Government Services in Europe: expected benefits, barriers and drivers of the once-only principle. Presented at the ICEGOV '18: Proceedings of the 11th international conference on theory and practice of electronic governance, New York, NY (2018)
14. Kureerung, P., Ramingwong, L.: A framework for usability design to promote awareness of information disseminated via mobile government applications (2019).
15. Müller, P.A., Gil-Garcia, J.R., Tirelli, C.: The impact of political, technological and social variables on the development of local E-Government: lessons from Brazil. Presented at the Proceedings of the 11th international conference on theory and practice of electronic governance. Galway (2018). https://doi.org/10.1145/3209415.3209440
16. Munyoka, W., Manzira, M.F.: From E-Government to M-Government – challenges faced by Sub-Saharan Africa. In: Proceedings of the international conference on computing technology and information management. pp. 88–91. Dubai (2014)
17. Rakotonirina, V., Raoelson, H.: E-government: factor of public administration efficiency and effectiveness. Case of the Ministry of Higher Education and Scientific Research in Madagascar. In: ICEGOV '18, pp. 166–170. Galway (2018). doi:https://doi.org/10.1145/3209415.3209432

18. Rosenbaum, J., Zepic, R., Schreieck, M., Wiesche, M., Krcmar, H.: Barriers to mobile government adoption: an exploratory case study of an information platform for refugees in Germany. Technical University of Munich, München
19. Shareef, M.A., Dwivedi, Y.K., Laumer, S., Archer, N.: Citizens' adoption behavior of mobile government (mGov): a cross-cultural study. In: Information Systems Management (2016)
20. Talukder, S., Chiong, R., Corbitt, B., Bao, Y.: Critical factors influencing the intention to adopt m-Government services by the elderly. J. Glob. Inf. Manag., 74–78 (2020)
21. Williams, I., Falch, M., Tadayouni, R.: Internationalization of e-government services (2018)
22. Schmidt, C., Krimmer, R., Lampoltshammer, T.J.: "When need becomes necessity"-the single digital gateway regulation and the once-only principle from a European point of view. Open Identity Summit 2021 (2021)
23. Deci, E.L., Ryan, R.M.: Conceptualizations of intrinsic motivation and self-determination. In: Intrinsic motivation and self-determination in human behavior. pp. 11–40. Springer US, Boston, MA (1985). doi:https://doi.org/10.1007/978-1-4899-2271-7_2
24. Deci, E.L., Ryan, R.M.: The general causality orientations scale: self-determination in personality. J. Res. Pers. **19**, 109–134 (1985)
25. Chai, L., Pavlou, P.: Customer relationship management.com: a cross-cultural empirical investigation of electronic commerce (2002)
26. Baškarada, S., Koronios, A.: A critical success factor framework for information quality management. Inf. Syst. Manag. **31**, 276–295 (2014)

Design and Architecture of Mobile Cross-Border Services Building Blocks

Blaž Podgorelec ⓘ, Roland Czerny ⓘ, Thomas Zefferer ⓘ, Bernd Prünster ⓘ, Andreea Ancuta Corici ⓘ, Tobias Wich ⓘ, and Detlef Hühnlein ⓘ

Abstract The growing trend of mobile services usage compared to desktop services necessitates the development of mobile-accessible e-government to cater to citizens' growing digital needs. Secure and efficient solutions for strong authentication and cross-institutional data exchange are crucial in this context, particularly within the eID (electronic Identification) and SDG (Single Digital Gateway) domains. This work presents an advanced technical architecture developed as part of the H2020 mGov4EU project, which addresses these challenges by offering a comprehensive set of mobile-tailored building blocks that could serve as a basis when using e-Government. The proposed architecture consists of four building blocks: (1) eID Interoperability System, enabling mobile-based cross-border authentication; (2) Digital Wallet System, providing a user-friendly platform for citizens to manage their eID credentials and (SDGR) evidence; (3) SDG Interoperability System, enabling efficient cross-border data exchange and user-authorization access point; and (4) eSignature Interoperability System, ensuring secure and efficient creation of electronic signatures. Integrating these building blocks, the mGov4EU project enhances the baseline of e-Government in a mobile environment.

Keywords eGovernment · eIDAS · SDGR · Mobile · Interoperability

B. Podgorelec (✉) · R. Czerny
Institute of Applied Information Processing and Communications (IAIK), Graz University of Technology, and Secure Information Technology Center Austria (A-SIT), Graz, Austria
e-mail: blaz.podgorelec@iaik.tugraz.at; roland.czerny@iaik.tugraz.at

T. Zefferer · B. Prünster
A-SIT Plus GmbH, Wien, Austria
e-mail: thomas.zefferer@a-sit.at; bernd.pruenster@a-sit.at

A. A. Corici
Fraunhofer FOKUS Institute, Berlin, Germany
e-mail: andreea.ancuta.corici@fokus.fraunhofer.de

T. Wich · D. Hühnlein
ecsec GmbH, Michelau, Germany
e-mail: tobias.wich@ecsec.de; detlef.huehnlein@ecsec.de

V. Homburg et al. (eds.), *From Electronic to Mobile Government*,
https://doi.org/10.1007/978-3-031-64471-9_4

1 Introduction

The Mobile Cross-Border Government Services for Europe (mGov4EU) project is dedicated to enhancing mobile government services within the European Union (EU). It addresses the digital shift from desktop to mobile platforms, adopting a "mobile-first" approach and focusing on critical e-government services. This project also aims to refine and integrate existing technical solutions from the Electronic Identification, Authentication, and Trust Services (eIDAS) and the Single Digital Gateway Regulation (SDGR). Such integration is vital to fulfil mobile-based e-government requirements. The mGov4EU project prioritizes user-centric procedures in cross-border contexts. To tackle challenges in mobile-first implementation, secure cross-border user authentication, and efficient cross-border data exchange, and based on a survey of related works results [1], mGov4EU offers an enhanced technical architecture. This architecture incorporates improvements to eIDAS and SDGR components. The chapter outlines these enhancements within the mGov4EU ecosystem, consisting of four key components: the eID Interoperability System for mobile cross-border authentication, the SDG Interoperability System for seamless cross-border data exchange, the eSignature Interoperability System for secure electronic signatures, and the Digital Wallet System, a user-friendly platform for managing eID credentials and SDGR-related information. Each building block in this architecture is an autonomous, reusable unit, designed to be applicable across various domains. The methodology used in crafting the mGov4EU technical architecture employs the C4 model [2], which uses hierarchical abstractions of software systems, containers, components, and code. This model is represented in architectural diagrams, including C4-Level 1: System Context, C4-Level 2: Containers, C4-Level 3: Components, and C4-Level 4: Code. Considering the project's timeline, a distributed approach was adopted for designing the technical architecture. Initially, different building blocks were identified, each with a designated lead architect. The backbone architecture was developed through C4 Level 1 and Level 2 diagrams, defining the static structure and detailing interfaces and interdependencies among the building blocks. The C4 model facilitated streamlined design processes, ensuring alignment in vocabulary and abstraction levels despite the distributed nature of development. Detailed designs of the mGov4EU ecosystem's building blocks were concurrently executed by research teams, leading to the creation of C4 Level 3 Component diagrams. Generated architectural design of building blocks served as a basis for the project's implementation activities.

This chapter provides a high-level overview of the mGov4EU ecosystem's building blocks, avoiding deep technical details. It is organized as follows: Sects. 2 and 3 introduce the primary domains of eIDAS and SDGR. Section 4 discusses the mGov4EU ecosystem, highlighting the interplay between its building blocks. Sections 5 to 8 delve into the architectural design of each building block, and Sect. 9 concludes the chapter.

2 eIDAS-Related Services: Secure Digital Identity and Trust

The eIDAS Interoperability Architecture, as detailed in [3] and depicted in Fig. 1, is implemented via the eIDAS-Network. This network comprises various connection points, known as eIDAS-Nodes, which are essential for enabling secure cross-border authentication. This system involves two main components: the eIDAS-Connector and the eIDAS-Service. The eIDAS-Connector initiates the cross-border authentication request, while the eIDAS-Service responds to it. The eIDAS-Service is further divided into two categories: the eIDAS-Proxy-Service, managed by the Sending Member State, and the eIDAS-Middleware-Service, handled by the Receiving Member State using middleware provided by the Sending Member State. All eIDAS-Services, with the exception of the German eID, operate as eIDAS-Proxy-Services and are controlled in the citizen's country, or MS User. The Receiving Member State, in contrast, is referred to as the Service Provider (SP) country or MS SP.

The eIDAS-Network facilitates user authentication with an SP in a different country using their national eID system. The authentication process starts with the SP generating a request, which is sent to the MS SP eIDAS-Node. This node then generates a Security Assertion Markup Language (SAML) AuthnRequest, redirecting it to the eIDAS-Node of the MS User. Each Member State processes this request according to its specific eID system. Regardless of these variations, the MS User eIDAS-Node formulates a SAML assertion response, which is forwarded to the MS SP eIDAS-Node. The SP then receives and processes the authentication data.

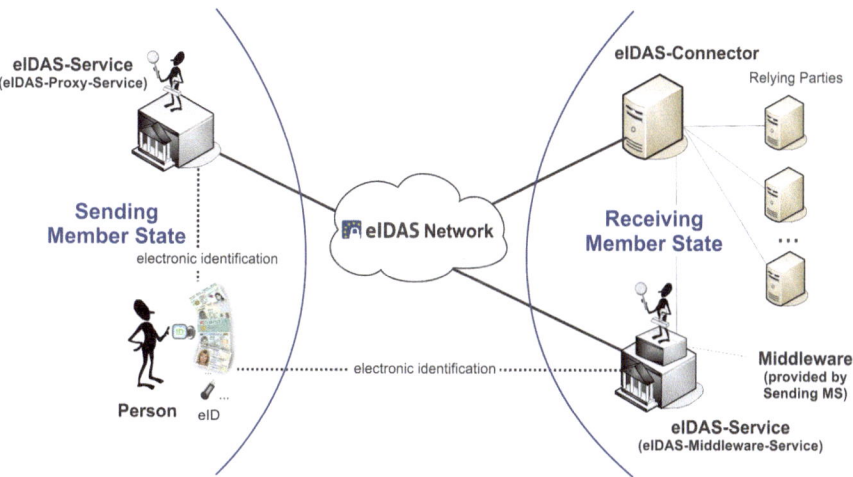

Fig. 1 eIDAS Interoperability Architecture [4]

SAML [5], a standard for exchanging authentication data between an SP and an Identity Provider (IdP), faces challenges in mobile use cases, as it was originally designed for Web applications with server backends. The digital signing mechanism, crucial for message integrity between SP and IdP, becomes complex in mobile contexts due to the difficulty in securely managing SP private keys on mobile devices. Furthermore, SAML's reliance on back channels and HTTP POST poses challenges in terms of response size and configuration data sharing in mobile applications. Consequently, many organizations are transitioning to alternatives like OpenID Connect (OIDC) and Open Authorization (OAuth), which are more suited for mobile scenarios [6].

OIDC [7], built on OAuth 2.0 [8], supports various client types, including Web, mobile, and JavaScript clients, to acquire information about authenticated sessions and end users. It improves upon SAML by offering additional features such as encryption, identity data signing, and provider discovery. OIDC, employing JavaScript Object Notation (JSON) instead of SAML's Extensible Markup Language (XML), results in lighter data exchanges, ideal for front-channel transmission. Moreover, OIDC enables dynamic client registration and discovery, facilitating trusted interactions between an SP and IdP [6].

Conversely, recent advancements in identity management systems, influenced by Self-Sovereign Identity (SSI) and the World Wide Web Consortium (W3C) Verifiable Credentials (VC) data model [9], often involve digital wallets. In this model, where the digital wallet is central, there are three additional actors: the user, who acquires, stores, and manages the data in the digital wallet; the issuer, who attests and issues VCs to the user's wallet; and the SP, who accepts and verifies Verifiable Presentations (VPs) from the user's wallet [10].

3   Facilitating Access to European Cross-Border Digital Public Services

The Single Digital Gateway Regulation (SDGR) for cross-border digital public services [11] originates from the Once-Only Principle (OOP) and the eDelivery framework [12]. The OOP is a concept designed to ensure that citizens, institutions, and companies need to provide specific standard information to authorities and administrations only once. Under this principle, communication systems should exchange the necessary information with the consent of the information owner. The eDelivery framework for cross-border data exchange adheres to standards set by the Organization for the Advancement of Structured Information Standards (OASIS), including:

- The Applicability Statement 4 (AS4) Profile of the Electronic Business using eXtensible Markup Language (eBXML) [13], facilitating secure and payload-agnostic exchange. AS4 Gateways act as intermediary nodes, ensuring technical interoperability among different Member States' data exchange infrastructures.

- The Service Metadata Protocol (SMP) [14], used for dynamically discovering nodes' capabilities. SMP can locate the specific server storing a particular document type from a country.

The EU Commission has also completed the first technical specification for the Once-Only Technical System (OOTS) [15]. The system's main goal is to reduce administrative load on citizens and businesses by enabling efficient cross-border document/evidence exchange. The OOTS architecture (see Fig. 2) includes the Procedure Portal, which acts as the communication endpoint for the Evidence Requester (citizen or business). It utilizes the OOTS infrastructure to obtain citizen evidence from an Evidence Provider (EP), situated at the national authority issuing the evidence. In the mGov4EU project, applying the access-right type defined by the General Data Protection Regulation (GDPR) [16] means that citizens should be able to preview and retrieve their evidence from their local or another EU Member State. From an access control perspective, these operations correspond to the read right. While not yet incorporated in the OOTS architecture, the SDGR suggests that citizens should also be able to authorize third parties to access their evidence, eliminating the need for manual transfers (e.g., via email). From a technological standpoint, the Open Authorization (OAuth) 2.0 framework [17], extended by the User Managed Access (UMA) [18] from the Kantara initiative, appears as a suitable solution. This framework allows a third-party agent to obtain an OAuth 2.0 access token, such as JSON Web Tokens (JWT) [19], from an Authorization Server to access a protected resource. The server issues the access token based on the access policies set by the evidence owner, thus embodying the owner's consent. If no matching access policy exists, the process operates asynchronously: only after the owner updates the access policies can an access token be issued for the requesting party.

4 mGov4EU Reference Architecture

Based on the motivations and methodology outlined in Sect. 1, the mGov4EU project developed multiple generic building blocks for mobile usage within the eIDAS and SDGR domains. These building blocks not only enhanced the existing ecosystem but were also designed as decoupled units to maximize reusability in other domains.

The initial phase involved the isolated design of various mGov4EU building blocks. Subsequently, these blocks were integrated to form a comprehensive solution that addressed the requirements of both the eIDAS and SDGR domains, along with related components. This integration led to the creation of a cohesive ecosystem of software building blocks, interacting and complementing each other through well-defined interfaces. The result was the mGov4EU reference architecture, utilizing the C4 modelling technique, as illustrated in Fig. 3.

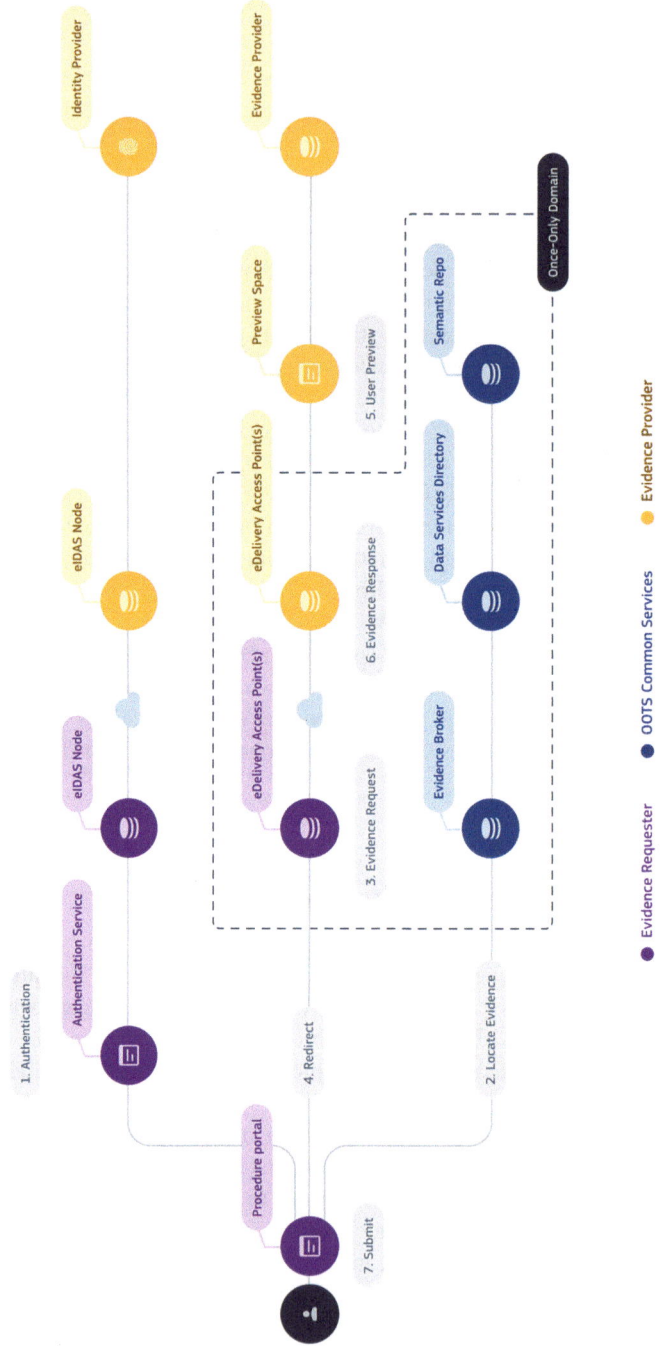

Fig. 2 Once-Only Technical System architecture [20]

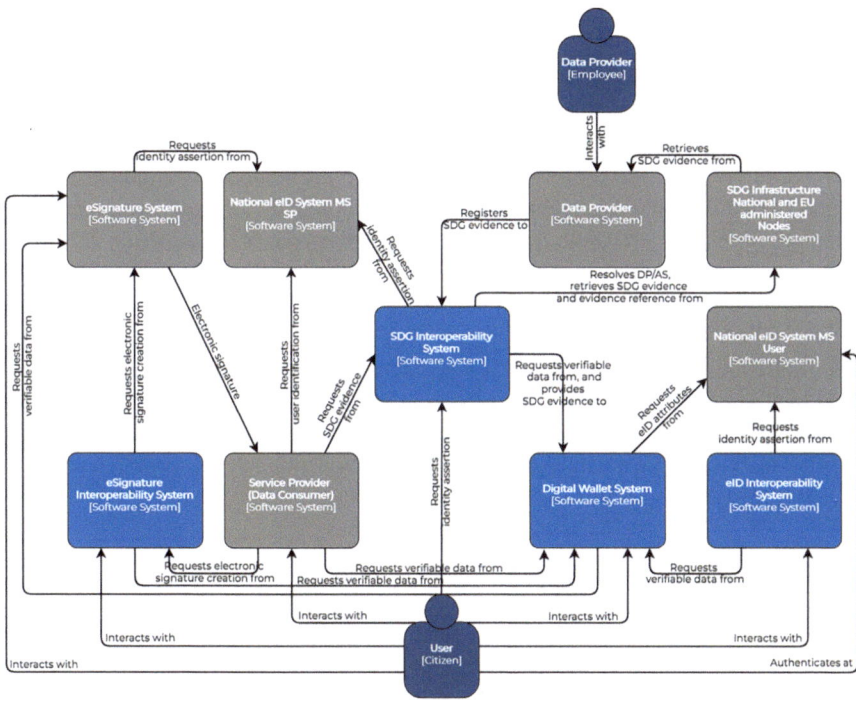

Fig. 3 Technical architecture of mGov4EU ecosystem (C4 landscape diagram)

This reference architecture outlines each building block (identified as a Software System and highlighted in blue, following the C4 modelling methodology) and their interactions. As shown in Fig. 3, the mGov4EU ecosystem comprises the following key building blocks (Software Systems), elaborated further in this work:

- The eSignature Interoperability System
- The SDG Interoperability System
- The eID Interoperability System
- The Digital Wallet System

Additionally, as Fig. 3 indicates, the mGov4EU building blocks interact with existing components (termed External Software Systems, marked in gray following the C4 methodology). A key external component is the SP Software System, which represents any technical system that leverages the mGov4EU building blocks. For instance, in the mGov4EU project, these blocks are demonstrated through various pilot applications acting as SPs, with further details available in Chapter X. The figure also showcases other External Software Systems, including national eIDAS- and SDG-related technical infrastructure like national eSignature solutions, eIDAS-compliant national eID systems, SDG-compliant data providers, and national SDG infrastructure components.

The eID Interoperability System acknowledges the existing eIDAS infrastructure, particularly the operational eIDAS-Nodes, as external software components. With the proposed European Digital Identity Wallet (EUDIW) infrastructure in the eIDAS revision, mGov4EU has been closely monitoring the toolbox process led by the eIDAS Expert Group to ensure compatibility. At the time of the mGov4EU architecture design, the protocols for EUDI were undecided. Preliminary analysis of the Expert Group's Architecture Reference Framework suggests alignment with mGov4EU's approach, although definitive conclusions are premature due to its technology-neutral status.

Similarly, mGov4EU has been keeping abreast of developments in the SDG OOTS. While designing the mGov4EU SDG-related building blocks, the OOTS draft Implementing Act was under SDG Committee review. The modifications to the working assumptions, based on the Once-Only Principle Project (TOOP) outcomes, were minor and included user consent at the EP and a re-authentication option for identity matching. These changes had minimal impact on the mGov4EU concepts.

5 Architectural Design of eID Interoperability System

This section details the architectural design of the eID Interoperability System within the mGov4EU ecosystem.

As depicted in Fig. 4, the eID Interoperability System is designed in two distinct forms, the App-based and SDK-based variants, to accommodate the diverse needs of Service Providers (SPs) and the evolving technology landscape. While both are designed to facilitate eIDAS-compliant cross-border user authentication within mobile applications, they utilize slightly different strategies to achieve this common objective.

The system connects with a citizen's national eID System either through eIDAS-Nodes (App-based variant) or via an Identity Management Service (IMS, SDK-based variant). Uniquely, the App-based variant also includes a direct connection to the Digital Wallet System, enabling the request and retrieval of user identity attributes as Verifiable Credentials (VC).

Country selection is a critical component of eIDAS-specific cross-border authentication, particularly in mobile user flows [6]. It is a common feature across different authentication workflows, unlike other functionalities that are specific to the SP or the eID system. A standardized procedure for country selection involves exchanging essential data, such as a protocol identifier for compatibility, a list of supported countries with readable names and two-letter identifiers, and, optionally, country flags. A target Uniform Resource Locator (URL) and a free-form data field are also included for transmitting the selected country. This standardized approach centralizes country selection, enhancing cross-border authentication efficiency. The country selection process can be integrated within the national eID framework (App-based variant) or through an independent IMS (SDK-based variant).

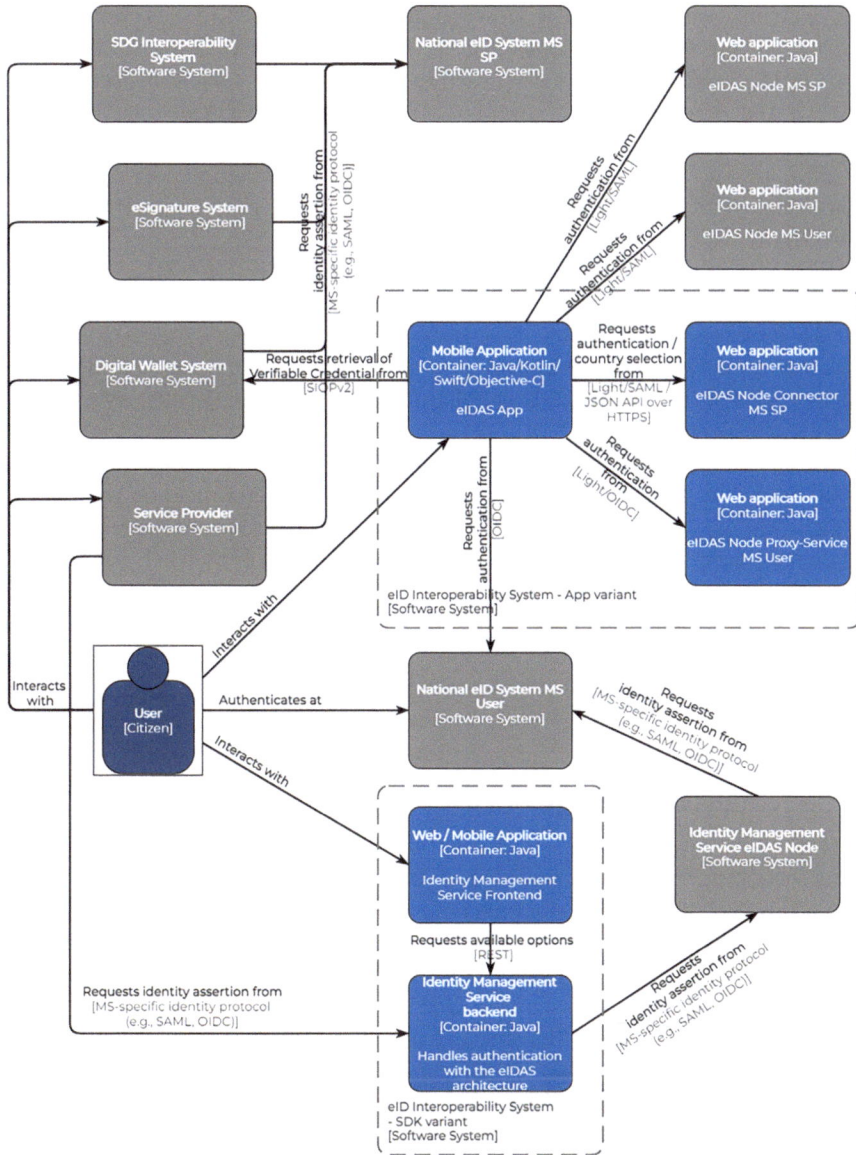

Fig. 4 Technical architecture of mGov4EU eID Interoperability System (C4 component diagram)

Key components in the App-based variant include the eIDAS-Connector MS SP, which links the eIDAS App with the national eID System of MS SP and the eIDAS-Node MS SP. This connector, crucial for initiating cross-border authentication, includes an OIDC protocol handler to improve functionality in mobile workflows and a country selection handler. However, the interface module connecting with the eIDAS-Node remains unchanged. The eIDAS-Proxy-Service MS User is another significant component, facilitating user authentication by interfacing between the eIDAS App, the national eID System of MS User, and the eIDAS-Node MS User. It also includes an OIDC handler and a unique mapping between OIDC and the eIDAS SAML2 profile. The eIDAS App, central to user interaction, effectively manages the interfacing with the eIDAS-Connector, eIDAS-Proxy-Service, and eIDAS-Nodes [6, 21].

The SDK-based variant, designed to simplify the process for SPs, includes the IMS, which handles country selection and relieves SPs from technical details. The IMS consists of a Frontend and a Backend, connected through a specified interface, facilitating access to authentication options and transmitting user selections. For mobile user scenarios, an SDK-based IMS Frontend, implemented as a web or mobile app, is recommended.

In the SDK-based approach, the specific eIDAS-Connector's responsibility shifts from the SP to the IMS. SPs make a standard authentication request to the IMS, which then interfaces with the eIDAS infrastructure. This setup requires only one implementation of the specific eIDAS-Connector at the IMS level, streamlining the process. The IMS, independent of any member state, connects to a singular eIDAS-Connector node, termed the IMS eIDAS-Node. This configuration simplifies the infrastructure for cross-border authentication, reducing the need for multiple national eIDAS-Connector nodes across member states.

6 Architectural Design of Digital Wallet System

This section presents the architectural design of the Digital Wallet System within the mGov4EU ecosystem, which incorporates Self-Sovereign Identity (SSI), i.e., Digital Wallet principles and the W3C Verifiable Credentials (VC) data model [9].

As depicted in Fig. 5, the Digital Wallet System interacts with external systems such as the national eID System (MS User), the SDG Interoperability System, and other data sources, acting as "Issuers" in the W3C VC data model context [9]. These Issuers provide verifiable data, including the user's eID attributes and SDG-related evidence, which are stored as VCs within the Mobile Digital Wallet Application.

As in detail described in [21], the VC Provisioning Service is a central component of the Digital Wallet System and is responsible for issuing and storing verifiable data. It comprises a Web application (VC Provisioning Service Frontend), a backend service (VC Provisioning Service Backend), a storage component (VC Provisioning Service Database), and a security module (VC Provisioning Service Security Module). This service is crucial for issuing VCs to the Digital Wallet Application, which in turn facilitates the presentation (i.e., usage in the form of Verifiable Presentations, VPs) of stored VCs. External systems, including the eSignature System, eID Interoperability System, and SPs, can request and retrieve

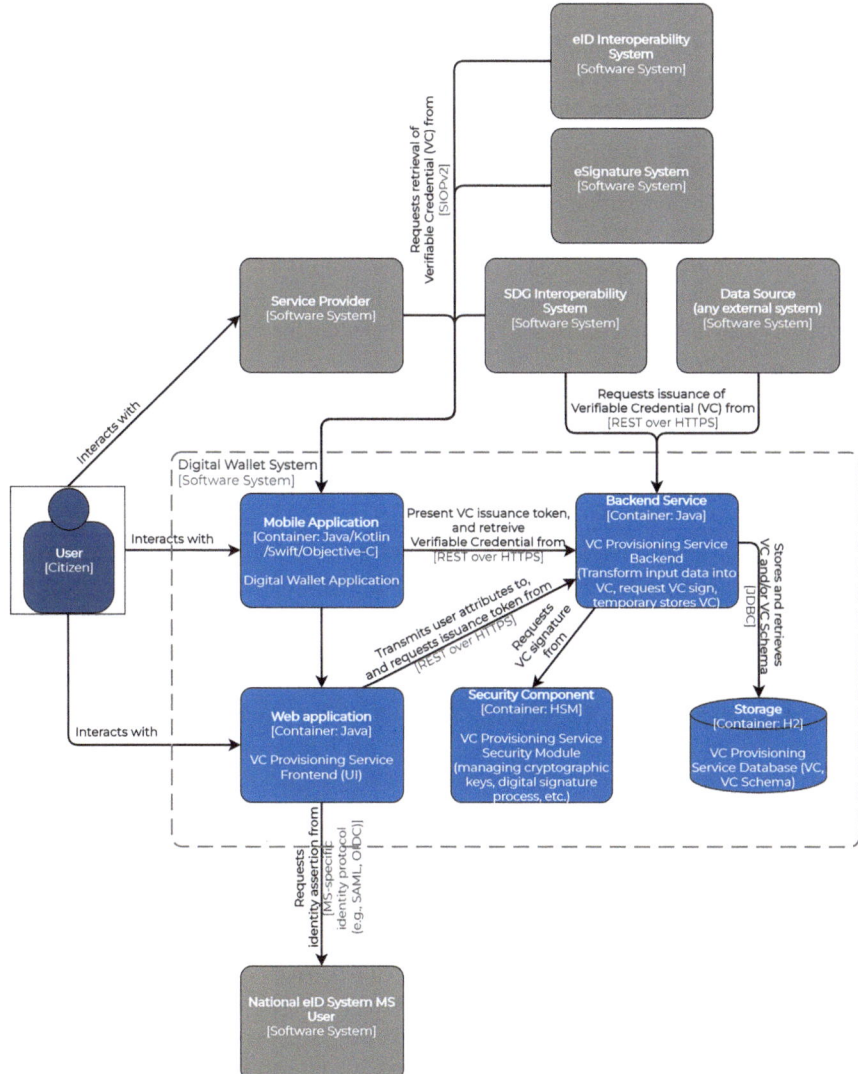

Fig. 5 Technical architecture of mGov4EU Digital Wallet System (C4 component diagram)

VCs through the Mobile Wallet Application. The presentation of these credentials occurs only with the Holder's (user's) consent.

The provisioning process involves storing data in the Mobile Digital Wallet Application as VCs. The VC Provisioning Service converts data from any external source into VCs. The Mobile Digital Wallet Application supports VPs, which is crucial for SP Apps to process generic attributes via protocols like OpenID Self-Issued OpenID Provider v2 (SIOPv2). This setup enables user authentication with a local digital wallet and allows legacy SPs to access eIDAS attributes through the eID Interoperability System. In this system, the eIDAS App functions as an Identity Provider (IdP), translating OIDC workflows into OpenID SIOPv2 procedures. Trust is established through key and ID attestation, supported by operating systems like Android and iOS.

On the SP side, an additional trust anchor is used to verify the authenticity of locally issued authentication responses. This helps to distinguish between attributes obtained from eIDAS-Nodes and those stored in the local digital wallet App. This approach simplifies authentication processes, assuming all necessary attributes are already provisioned. It is a specific application of the broader VC concept, adaptable to various use cases, and addresses operational challenges based on real-world needs and legal requirements.

7 Architectural Design of the SDG Interoperability System

This section discusses the architectural design of the SDG Interoperability System, as per the Implementing Act of the Single Digital Gateway Regulation (SDGR) [16]. This regulation mandates that authenticated citizens are granted a preview of their evidence by the Evidence Provider (EP), after which they can decide whether to have the evidence retrieved by the Procedure Portal.

In alignment with the EU eIDAS regulation [22], which focuses on electronic user identification and trust services for electronic transactions, EU Member States (MSs) are responsible for implementing national eID Systems in compliance with the regulation. However, variations in the issuance and matching of citizen identifiers across Member States can lead to challenges in cross-border identity matching. While some Member States assign a static identifier to each citizen, usable across different SPs and countries, others issue SP and/or country-specific identifiers.

Considering scenarios where multiple individuals share the same name and birth date, the process for the EP to match the correct evidence to an SDG request can be error-prone. Hence, the SDG building block design must include a variant where authentication also occurs at the EP to retrieve the citizen identifier specific to the EP, ensuring precise matching.

Addressing digital public service innovation, the recent EU eIDAS revision process [23] necessitates the SDG building block's EP component to allow citizens to store previewed evidence in their digital wallet. A secondary requirement is enabling citizens to use this evidence in subsequent SDG operations, such as retrieving evidence from their digital wallet via the OOTS Procedure Portal instead of directly from the local/cross-border EP.

Acknowledging the SDG building block's dual roles in data exchange and preliminary EP discovery and consent management for users, its components and operations (illustrated in Fig. 6) are categorized into two planes, as defined by the

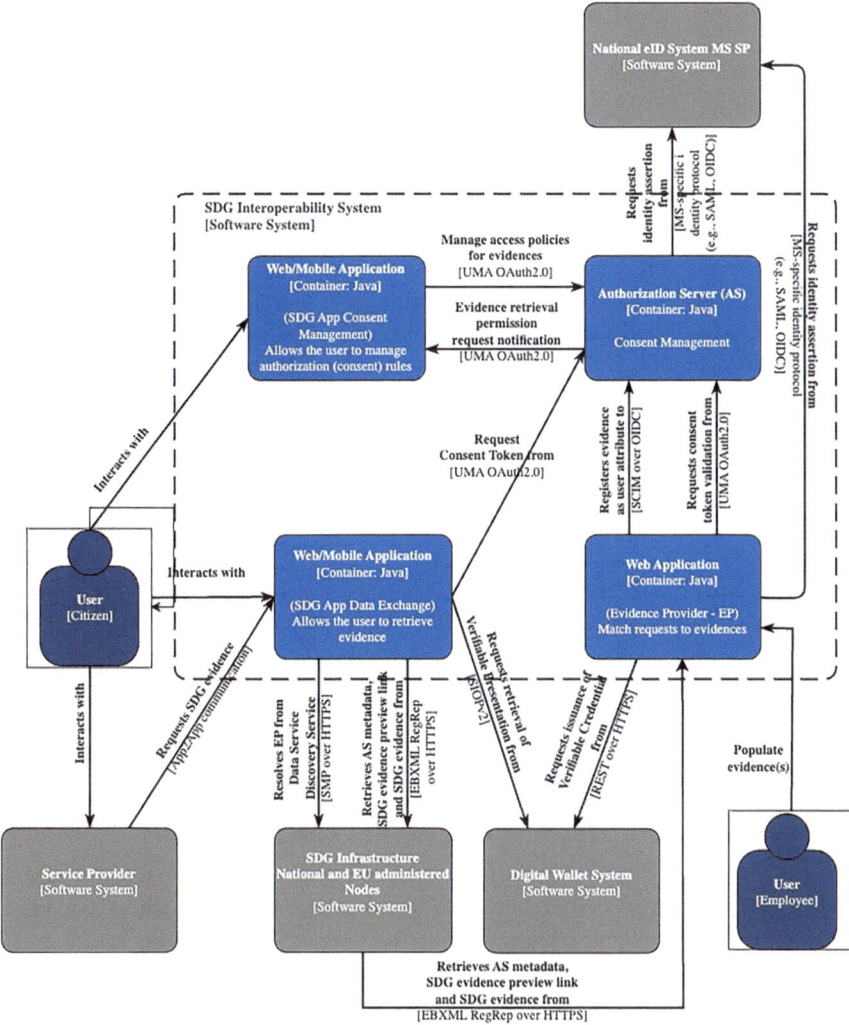

Fig. 6 Technical architecture of mGov4EU SDG Interoperability System (C4 component diagram)

International Telecommunication Union Telecommunication Standardization Sector (ITU-T) [24]:

- The **data plane**, handling evidence preview and secure data exchange, including retrieving evidence from the EP via AS4 Gateways [13], storing evidence as a VC in a digital wallet, and retrieving the evidence's VP from the digital wallet
- The **control plane**, encompassing user authentication, EP discovery, and consent management, including authorization

On the control plane, the EP registers the evidence at the Authorization Server as user attributes using evidence metadata (eIDAS identifier, family name, and given name). This registration generates a User Managed Access (UMA) [18] Personal Access Token (PAT), stored by the EP. When the SDG App Data Exchange requests an evidence preview link from the EP, the EP responds with an eBXML Not-Authorized error message and includes the PAT token and the Authorization Server API URL, assuming no valid consent token is present.

Using the PAT token, the SDG App Data Exchange interrogates the Authorization Server requesting a consent token for the evidence access. If the requesting user is the evidence owner or if the owner's policies at the Authorization Server grant access, the SDG App Data Exchange receives a consent token. Thus, the SDG App Data Exchange can subsequently request the preview link from the EP and include the consent token. The Evidence Provider validates the consent token against the Authorization Server, and if the claims include read access, the preview link will be generated and conveyed as eBXML reply to the SDG App Data Exchange.

In the data plane, the user engages with the SDG App Data Exchange to contact the EP for evidence preview. Post-preview, one can choose to either save the evidence in a digital wallet or retrieve it via the SDG infrastructure, utilizing the OASIS eBXML AS4 extension [13] for document requests and retrievals.

If the user has previously instructed the EP to store the evidence as a VC in their digital wallet, for subsequent SDG operations, they can retrieve it at the SDG App Data Exchange using the OpenID SIOPv2 protocol [25] to access the VP of the credential.

8 Architectural Design of eSignature Interoperability System

The eSignature Interoperability System has a user, which may act as Organizer to configure the signature workflow or as Signatory to authorize the creation of a signature.

As outlined in Fig. 7, the eSignature Interoperability System roughly consists of the following building blocks:

- **eSignature-Frontend**—is a mobile Web application, which has been created with JavaScript and Angular and which is available at https://Signer.eID.AS. It provides a user-friendly User Interface (UI) for the Organizer, which allows them to upload the document(s) to be signed, specify the signature placement, and invite the designated Signatories via their e-mail addresses to the signing process. Furthermore, the eSignature-Frontend also allows the different Signatories to prove their identity and authorize the signing process using their eID to start the signature generation process.
- **Mobile Application**—is an *optional* smartphone application with the same functionality as the eSignature-Frontend but with an enhanced User Experience (UX).

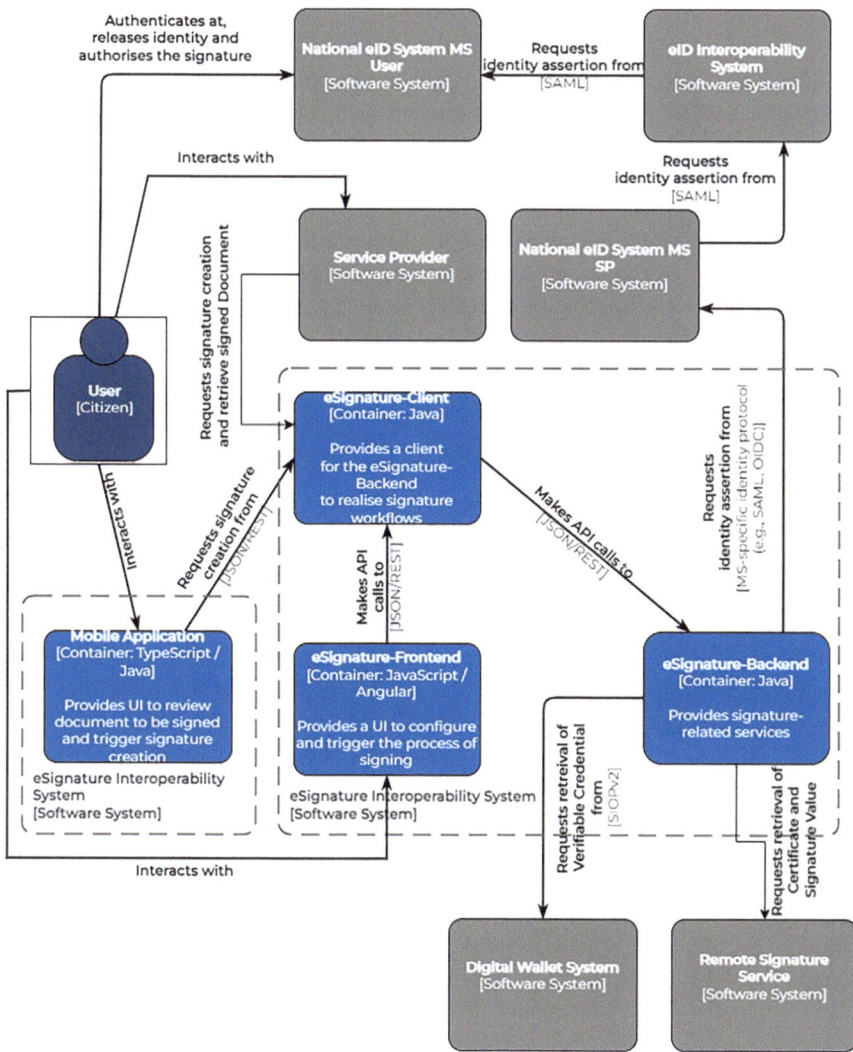

Fig. 7 Technical architecture of mGov4EU eSignature Interoperability System (C4 component diagram)

- **eSignature-Client**—is realized in Java and is called by the eSignature-Frontend, the Mobile Application, if available, or an optional SP component in order to serve as a proxy for API calls, which are forwarded to the eSignature-Backend. Note that the SP component allows the use of the signature service in different application-specific workflows in addition to the workflow induced by the eSignature-Frontend.

- **eSignature-Backend**—is also realized in Java and is called by the eSignature-Client in order to perform signature workflows. The eSignature-Backend also invokes the identification and authentication of the Signatory via the currently available eIDAS-Node infrastructure, consisting of the national eID System MS SP, the eID Interoperability System, and the national eID System MS User, or the upcoming Digital Wallet System, as soon as it is available. The eSignature-Backend also invokes suitable Remote Signature Services, which finally create the requested electronic signature or seal according to pertinent specifications for advanced electronic signatures, such as [26–29]. An important feature of the eSignature-Backend is that it is flexible enough to integrate standardized remote signature services according to [30] or arbitrary proprietary services.

9 Conclusions

This chapter has detailed the design and architecture of four foundational building blocks integral to the mGov4EU ecosystem. Three of these blocks are focused on advancing innovation in the eIDAS domain, specifically in eID, digital wallet, and e-signature technologies. The fourth block is aimed at the SDGR domain, enhancing evidence preview, secure data exchange, and consent management, including authorization. These blocks are not merely stand-alone entities; they have been meticulously crafted to work cohesively. This synergy aligns with one of the project's key goals: developing complementary, mobile-first building blocks for both the eIDAS and SDGR domains.

The technical architecture of the mGov4EU project's building blocks employs the C4 model technique and its associated tools. This strategic choice ensures alignment with the model's top tier, Level 4, particularly focusing on the code diagram aspect. Such compliance not only streamlines software implementation based on these technical architectures but also simplifies integration with external software systems. This aspect is critical in the context of the mGov4EU project's pilots, where the provided technical architecture is being validated in real use cases.

References

1. Burgstaller-Hochenwarter, L., Gagl, B., Koch, K.-M., Leitold, H., Teufl, P., Zefferer, T., Hühnlein, D., Henniger, S., Corici, A.-A., Lampoltshammer, T., Temple, L., Eibl, G., Abrahams, A., Lenz, T., Krimmer, R., Schmidt, C., Dedovic, S.: Survey of related work. In: D1.1 Mobile Cross-Border Government Services for Europe (mGov4EU) Deliverable, Project Number: 959072, Submission Date: May 11, 2022
2. Brown, S.: The C4 Model for Visualising Software Architecture. https://c4model.com/. Accessed 27 Nov 2023
3. eIDAS Interoperability Architecture, Version 1.2, 31 August 2019, eIDAS Technical Specifications. https://ec.europa.eu/digital-building-blocks/wikis/download/attachments/467109280/eIDAS%20Interoperability%20Architecture%20v.1.2%20Final.pdf

4. Federal Office for Information Security: Basics of Digital Signature Techniques and Trust Services. (BSI DSig, Version 2.0, 18th April 2023). https://www.bsi.bund.de/SharedDocs/Downloads/DE/BSI/ElekSignatur/esig_pdf.pdf
5. Lockhart, H., Campbell, B., Ragouzis, N., Hughes, J., Philpott, R., Maler, E., Madsen, P., Scavo, T.: Security Assertion Markup Language (SAML) V2.0 Technical Overview. OASIS Security Services TC, 25 March 2008. http://docs.oasis-open.org/security/saml/Post2.0/sstc-saml-tech-overview-2.0.html
6. Czerny, R., Kollmann, C., Podgorelec, B., Prunster, B., Zefferer, T.: Towards a mobile-first cross-border eID framework. In: Proceedings of the 24th Annual International Conference on Digital Government Research (DGO '23), pP. 526–535. Association for Computing Machinery, New York (2023). https://doi.org/10.1145/3598469.3598562
7. Sakimura, N., Bradley, J., Jones, M., de Medeiros, B., Mortimore, C.: OpenID Connect Core 1.0 incorporating errata set 2, Final, December 15, 2023. https://openid.net/specs/openid-connect-core-1_0.html
8. Hardt, D.: The OAuth 2.0 Authorization Framework. RFC 6749, Internet Engineering Task Force, 2012. https://datatracker.ietf.org/doc/html/rfc6749.html
9. Sporny, M., Longley, D., Chadwick, D: Verifiable Credentials Data Model v2.0. https://w3c.github.io/vc-data-model/. Accessed 30 Nov 2023
10. Podgorelec, B., Alber, L., Zefferer, T.: What is a (digital) identity wallet? A systematic literature review. In: Proceedings of the 2022 IEEE 46th Annual Computers, Software, and Applications Conference (COMPSAC), pp. 809–818. IEEE, Piscataway (2022)
11. European Union: Regulation (EU) 2018/1724 of the European Parliament and of the Council of 2 October 2018 establishing a single digital gateway to provide access to information, to procedures and to assistance and problem-solving services and amending Regulation (EU) No 1024/2012 (2018). https://eur-lex.europa.eu/eli/reg/2018/1724/oj
12. European Commission CEF Digital. eDelivery initiative: Exchange documents and data securely and reliably, CEF Digital. https://ec.europa.eu/digital-building-blocks/wikis/display/DIGITAL/eDelivery
13. OASIS: AS4 Profile of ebMS 3.0 Version 1.0 (2013). https://docs.oasis-open.org/ebxml-msg/ebms/v3.0/profiles/AS4-profile/v1.0/os/AS4-profile-v1.0-os.html
14. OASIS: eDelivery SMP specifications—1.1.0 (2018). https://ec.europa.eu/digital-building-blocks/wikis/display/DIGITAL/eDelivery
15. EU Commission. Once-Only Hub, a single environment providing reliable information and services relating to the Once-Only Technical System. https://ec.europa.eu/digital-building-blocks/wikis/display/OOTS/OOTSHUB+Home
16. European Parliament and Council of the European Union: Regulation (EU) 2016/679 of the European Parliament and of the Council of 27 April 2016 on the protection of natural persons with regard to the processing of personal data and on the free movement of such data, and repealing Directive 95/46/EC (General Data Protection Regulation). Official Journal of the European Union, L119, 1-88 (2016). http://data.europa.eu/eli/reg/2016/679/oj
17. Hardt, D.: The OAuth 2.0 Authorization Framework. IETF RFC 6749 (2012)
18. Kantara Initiative: User-Managed Access (UMA) 2.0 Grant for OAuth 2.0 Authorization (2018). https://docs.kantarainitiative.org/uma/wg/rec-oauth-uma-grant-2.0.html
19. Jones, M.B., Bradley, J, Sakimura, N.: JSON Web Token (JWT). IETF RFC 7519 (2015)
20. European Commission: The Once-Only Technical System architecture. https://ec.europa.eu/digital-building-blocks/sites/display/OOTS/Architecture
21. Czerny, R., Kollmann, C., Podgorelec, B., Prünster, B., Zefferer, T.: Smoothing the ride: providing a seamless upgrade path from established cross-border eID workflows towards eID wallet systems. In: Proceedings of the 20th International Conference on Security and Cryptography, pp. 460–468 (2023). https://www.scitepress.org/Link.aspx?doi=10.5220/0012091900003555 ISBN: 978-989-758-666-8
22. European Union: Regulation (EU) No 910/2014 of the European Parliament and of the Council on electronic identification and trust services for electronic transactions in the internal market and repealing Directive 1999/93/EC (2014). http://data.europa.eu/eli/reg/2014/910/oj

23. European Union: Proposal for a Regulation of the European Parliament and of the Council amending Regulation (EU) No 910/2014 as regards establishing a framework for a European Digital Identity (2021). https://digital-strategy.ec.europa.eu/en/library/trusted-and-secure-european-e-id-regulation
24. ITU-T: The Broadband ISDN User Part (ISUP) Signaling Protocol, ITU-T, 1995
25. OpenID Foundation: OpenID Connect Self-Issued Identity. https://openid.net/specs/openid-connect-self-issued-v2-1_0.html
26. European Telecommunications Standards Institute (ETSI): Electronic Signatures and Infrastructures (ESI); CAdES Digital Signatures; Part 1: Building Blocks and CAdES Baseline Signatures. (ETSI EN 319 122-1, Version 1.3.1,2023,6). https://www.etsi.org/deliver/etsi_en/319100_319199/31912201/01.03.01_60/en_31912201v010301p.pdf
27. European Telecommunications Standards Institute (ETSI): Electronic Signatures and Infrastructures (ESI); XAdES Digital Signatures; Part 1: Building Blocks and XAdES Baseline Signatures. (ETSI EN 319 132-1, Version 1.2.1,2022,2). https://www.etsi.org/deliver/etsi_en/319100_319199/31913201/01.02.01_60/en_31913201v010201p.pdf
28. European Telecommunications Standards Institute (ETSI): Electronic Signatures and Infrastructures (ESI); PAdES Digital Signatures; Part 1: Building Blocks and PAdES Baseline Signatures. (ETSI EN 319 142-1, Version 1.2.0,2023,10). https://www.etsi.org/deliver/etsi_en/319100_319199/31914201/01.02.00_20/en_31914201v010200a.pdf
29. European Telecommunications Standards Institute (ETSI) Electronic Signatures and Infrastructures (ESI); JAdES digital signatures; Part 1: Building blocks and JAdES baseline signatures. (ETSI TS 119 182-1, Version 1.1.1,2021,3). https://www.etsi.org/deliver/etsi_ts/119100_119199/11918201/01.01.01_60/ts_11918201v010101p.pdf
30. European Telecommunications Standards Institute (ETSI): Electronic Signatures and Infrastructures (ESI); Protocols for remote digital signature creation. (ETSI TS 119 432, Version 1.2.1,2020,10). https://www.etsi.org/deliver/etsi_ts/119400_119499/119432/01.02.01_60/ts_119432v010201p.pdf
31. W3C: Data Privacy Vocabulary (DPV). Draft Community Group Report, 0.3 (2021). https://github.com/w3c/dpv/
32. Crockford, D.: JSON - JavaScript Object Notation (2006). https://json.org
33. IANA: Media Types. https://www.iana.org/assignments/media-types/media-types.xhtml

Implementation and System Integration

Bernd Prünster (ID), Roland Czerny (ID), Andreea Ancuta Corici (ID),
and Tobias Wich (ID)

Abstract Cross-border authentication based on provisions of the European eIDAS Regulation and cross-border data exchange according to the European Single Digital Gateway Regulation (SDGR) are usually implemented using Web technologies. Consequently, the solutions currently deployed are tailored toward usage scenarios involving Web browsers on traditional end-user devices such as desktop computers or laptops. Such solutions are often difficult to apply to mobile devices like smartphones, since these devices come with different characteristics, capabilities, and limitations. Enabling cross-border authentication and cross-border data exchange on mobile devices hence requires new technical solutions and respective implementations that take into account the special requirements of current mobile devices. This chapter elaborates on the technical details of this issue. It identifies practical technical challenges in implementing eIDAS and SDG-based cross-border authentication and data exchange involving mobile end-user devices. This chapter also discusses strategies to overcome these challenges and evaluates proposed strategies by means of technical implementations relying on state-of-the-art mobile technologies. It then establishes how cross-border authentication based on the eIDAS Regulation and cross-border data exchange based on the SDG Regulation are indeed feasible on mobile devices and show directions toward suitable implementations.

B. Prünster (✉)
A-SIT Plus GmbH, Wien, Austria
e-mail: bernd.pruenster@a-sit.at

R. Czerny
Graz University of Technology (IAIK), Graz, Austria
e-mail: roland.czerny@iaik.tugraz.at

A. A. Corici
Fraunhofer FOKUS Institute, Berlin, Germany
e-mail: andreea.ancuta.corici@fokus.fraunhofer.de

T. Wich
ecsec GmbH, Michelau, Germany
e-mail: tobias.wich@ecsec.de

© The Author(s) 2025
V. Homburg et al. (eds.), *From Electronic to Mobile Government*,
https://doi.org/10.1007/978-3-031-64471-9_5

Keywords Wallet · Mobile-First Cross-Border eID · SDG · Identity Wallet · EUDIW · eIDAS-Wallet Integration · SDG-Wallet Integration

1 Vision and Requirements

Making eIDAS and *single digital gateway* (SDG) play well on mobile clients can be done in a variety of ways, and some may argue that mobile-friendly Web interfaces of existing components are enough to accomplish this goal. The mGov4EU project, however, strives to go beyond mobile-ready and instead considers a mobile-first strategy the only viable way to go. This is not only sensible from a UX perspective but also from a strategic point of view, as it aligns with increasing popularity of identity wallets [9] and the plans for an *EU Digital Identity Wallet* (EUDIW), whose regulation has been recently finalized [4]. The realization of this trend and actually deploying identity wallet systems is inherently enabled by the widespread use and the capabilities of current-generation smartphones.

This chapter first provides a technical introduction to how cross-border authentication works within the eIDAS technical framework and the challenges this introduces in a mobile context in Sect. 2. Afterward, Sect. 3 presents two distinct solutions proposed by mGov4EU for transforming the existing systems into mobile-first ones. Section 4 then outlines how further results produced by mGov4EU provide a smooth transition towards technologies building the foundation of Europe's next-generation digital identity wallet.

This technological building block has also been employed within mGov4EU itself to test its utility. Accordingly, Sect. 5 builds on these results to better provide SDG functionality in a mobile-first way, discussing integration of these technologies with other systems before Sect. 6 concludes this chapter.

2 eIDAS Cross-Border Authentication

In general, the *Regulation on electronic identification and trust services for electronic transactions in the internal market* (eIDAS Regulation) passed in 2014 defines a broad legal and technical framework, enabling secure cross-border transactions across Europe [6]. This chapter focuses on one facet of this regulation: how a user can authenticate to a *service provider* (SP) in another country using their national eID system. This in itself also encompasses legal and technical regulations, the latter of which define components, their roles, communication protocols, and security aspects. In the context of going mobile, these technical aspects are especially crucial, even though legal requirements must also remain upheld.

The following section provides a high-level overview on how eIDAS cross-border authentication works. This includes a quick recap on the actors involved when performing such an authentication procedure.[1] Section 2.2 then elaborates on challenges, which need to be overcome to make these existing components play well in the mobile context, actually transforming them toward a mobile-first system while maintaining compatibility.

2.1   Cross-Border Authentication Primer

eIDAS cross-border authentication follows a four-corner model: An SP situated in the SP *Member State* (MS) creates an authentication request, which is forwarded to the so-called *MS-specific connector*. The connector then transforms the request into an eIDAS *Security Assertion Markup Language* (SAML)[2] request, forwarding it to the SP country's eIDAS *node*, where it then leaves the SP country and is forwarded to the country used for authentication, where another transformation happens, such that the national eID system can be used for authentication. The response then travels back the same route.

Figure 1 presents a sequence diagram illustrating this process in more detail. This representation is aligned with the *eIDAS-Node integration package*.[3] In particular, Part 1 of Fig. 1 shows how an authentication request is issued in the SP country: First, the SP creates an authentication request. The SP relays the authentication request to the eIDAS node of the SP country. The eIDAS node then generates an eIDAS SAML `AuthnRequest`, which is included in a redirect to the eIDAS node of the MS housing the eID system the user wishes to authenticate with. In Part 2, the authentication request is handled in an MS-specific way by the Member State's eID implementation. Regardless of the technical details of the MS specific eID system, the user's MS eIDAS node creates an authentication response in the form of a SAML assertion and posts it to the eIDAS node of the SP country. This is depicted in Part 3 of Fig. 1. In a last step, the SP receives the authentication response to handle the authentication information.

As also shown in Fig. 1, the communication is HTTPS based and uses either redirects or auto-POST forms. All communication is handled by the browser of the user. The driving force behind this eIDAS workflow are the eIDAS nodes of each Member State. The nodes are responsible for connecting Member States with each other through a defined interface. However, some details like country selection are not standardized and are thus implemented in an MS-specific way.

---

[1] The actors themselves and all relevant terminology have already been defined in the chapter on *Design and Architecture of Mobile Cross-Border Services Building Blocks* and are not reproduced here for the sake of clarity.

[2] https://www.oasis-open.org/standard/saml/

[3] https://ec.europa.eu/digital-building-blocks/wikis/display/DIGITAL/eIDAS-Node+Integration+Package

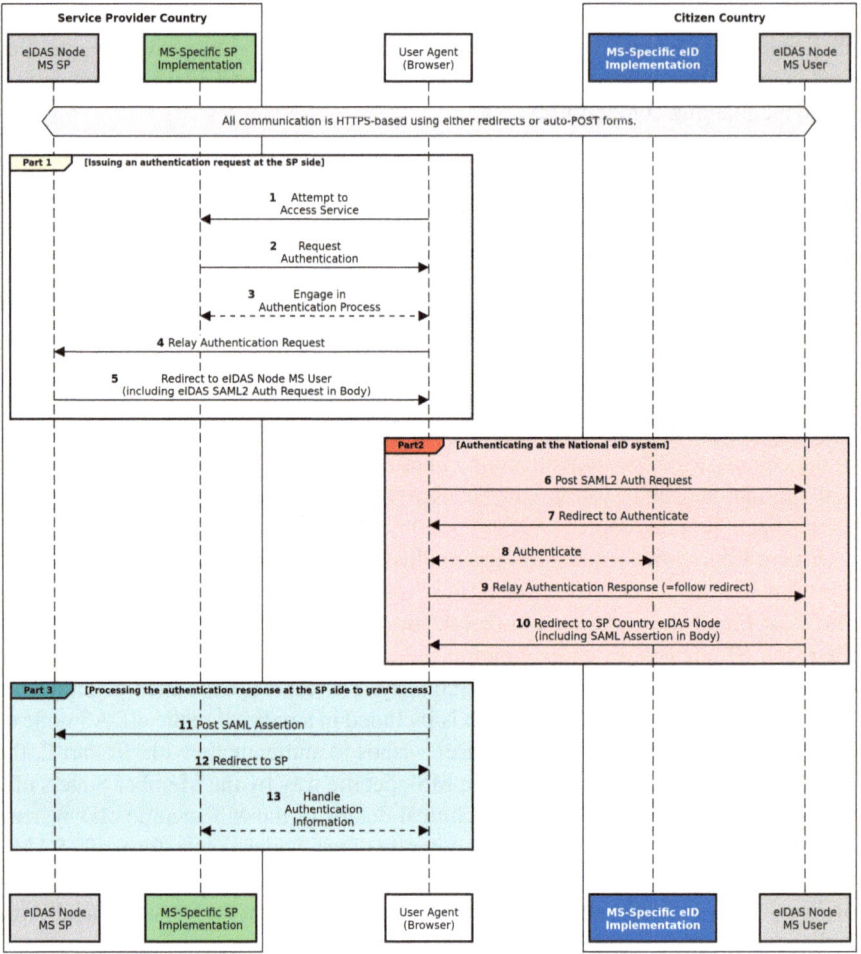

Fig. 1 eIDAS cross-border authentication sequence

Although this concept works perfectly fine when a browser is used as client, it does not integrate well in a mobile-first context. The following section elaborates on why and which additional steps are required to overcome this deficiency.

2.2 Challenges Going Mobile-First

On a technical level, eIDAS cross-border authentication relies on exchanging messages in the XML-based SAML v2 [18] format. As mentioned, the target client for eIDAS authentication flows is a Web browser, as it plays a crucial role, interpreting auto-POST forms and following redirects. Before smartphones became ubiquitous (when the technical specification of the eIDAS framework was conceived), this made perfect sense. After all, the browser as a unified client application ensured broad accessibility and compatibility with any operating system. Nowadays, however, this browser-centric design increasingly shows problematic properties, when trying to engage native mobile client apps on smartphones. Most prominently, a dedicated service app relying on a dedicated eID app for obtaining user identification information will not work in a cross-border setting as-is. The primary reason for this is that even though an application could parse HTML auto-post forms to forward SAML messages between eIDAS nodes, eID, and service apps, app-to-app communication is inherently bound to HTTP GET requests when striving for a solution that caters to apps and browsers. Since this is a constraint imposed by mobile operating systems, work-arounds do not exist. Combined with how large SAML messages can get due to the verbosity of XML, switching from POST binding to GET binding, while technically possible, is often infeasible in practice, if compatibility with browsers should be upheld. In reality, this compatibility desire is more than a mere nice-to-have, as the use of smartphones may not be enforced in all circumstances. Even though smartphones are ubiquitous, it cannot be assumed that users will always try to access services via their smartphone or that every component will have a native mobile app, for example.

This compatibility aspect becomes even more pronounced when considering the issue of country selection: The eIDAS technical framework provides no well-defined means for a user to select their home country for authentication. Instead, service providers follow different ways, depending on how eIDAS is integrated into national eID systems. In browser-based settings, this is perfectly fine, since the same client application is interfacing with every component involved along the way. When targeting native smartphone apps, however, this becomes problematic and a standardized way for choosing a country to identify with becomes necessary.

The popularity of the *OpenID Connect* (OIDC) protocol [14] on mobile devices demonstrates the importance of integrating well into the mobile ecosystem, as OIDC has become the de facto standard. Of course, re-imagining the eIDAS cross-border authentication flows for mobile devices on a protocol level won't be any good in practice, since compatibility with the existing federated system needs to be upheld. Luckily, a thorough analysis of all the technical intricacies inherent to the eIDAS technical framework shows that no such re-imagining is necessary, as long as a strict separation of concerns is upheld. The key observation here is that a single app or component can orchestrate all eIDAS-node-related communication, which hands off message processing to other apps as soon as national eID systems or services consuming identity tokens are involved.

mGov4EU introduces two distinct approaches to fulfil this promise. On the one hand, a dedicated *eIDAS app* is presented in the following section. Its primary objective is precisely this: handling communication between eIDAS nodes while natively providing state-of-the-art app-to-app communication toward eID apps and applications consuming ID tokens. Section 3.2, on the other hand, introduces a *mobile app SDK*, providing an even higher level of abstraction at the expense of requiring deeper integration. Depending on the requirements, one or the other approach is more fitting as both come with their own benefits and caveats and no single one is superior.

3 A Solution for Mobile-First eIDAS Cross-Border Authentication

Considering the challenges identified in the previous section and the observations made, the browser-based flows can be re-imagined for an app-based scenario, regardless of whether a dedicated eIDAS app is being used or an SDK is being directly integrated into SP apps. Reasoning about the technical details, however, is only possible on a per-scenario basis, which is why this section splits up the discussion on a transition to a mobile-first system, starting with the purely app-based approach below.

3.1 App-Based Approach

Relying on a dedicated eIDAS app closely resembles the browser-based approach, even though it introduces a clear separation of concerns, as depicted in Fig. 2. This approach splits responsibilities between three apps: Initially, the SP app tries to access a service and at some point sends an eIDAS authentication request. This causes the eIDAS app to launch and subsequently to display a country selection to the user. This step is especially critical in an app-based setting since a standardized API has to be used for this procedure, to uphold a strict separation of concerns between individual apps. The eIDAS app then forwards the request to the third app involved: the eID provider app of the user's selected home country. After a successful authentication, the response is delivered back to the service provider app via the eIDAS app. In a successful authentication process, app boundaries between the three involved apps are therefore crossed four times. (Note that the concept introduced in this section was previously presented by the authors of this chapter at the *24th Annual International Conference on Digital Government Research* [2].)

The transition from a browser-based eIDAS flow to an app-based approach requires careful consideration. After all, the browser-based user flow needs to remain fully functional, as apps cannot be mandated in every step. Some service providers, for example, may not provide native apps but mobile Web apps. This means that a change of protocols in order to have a fully integrated but mobile-only solution is not an option.

Luckily, both the Android and iOS operating systems provide means that allow for communication between apps while also supporting browser fallback. This

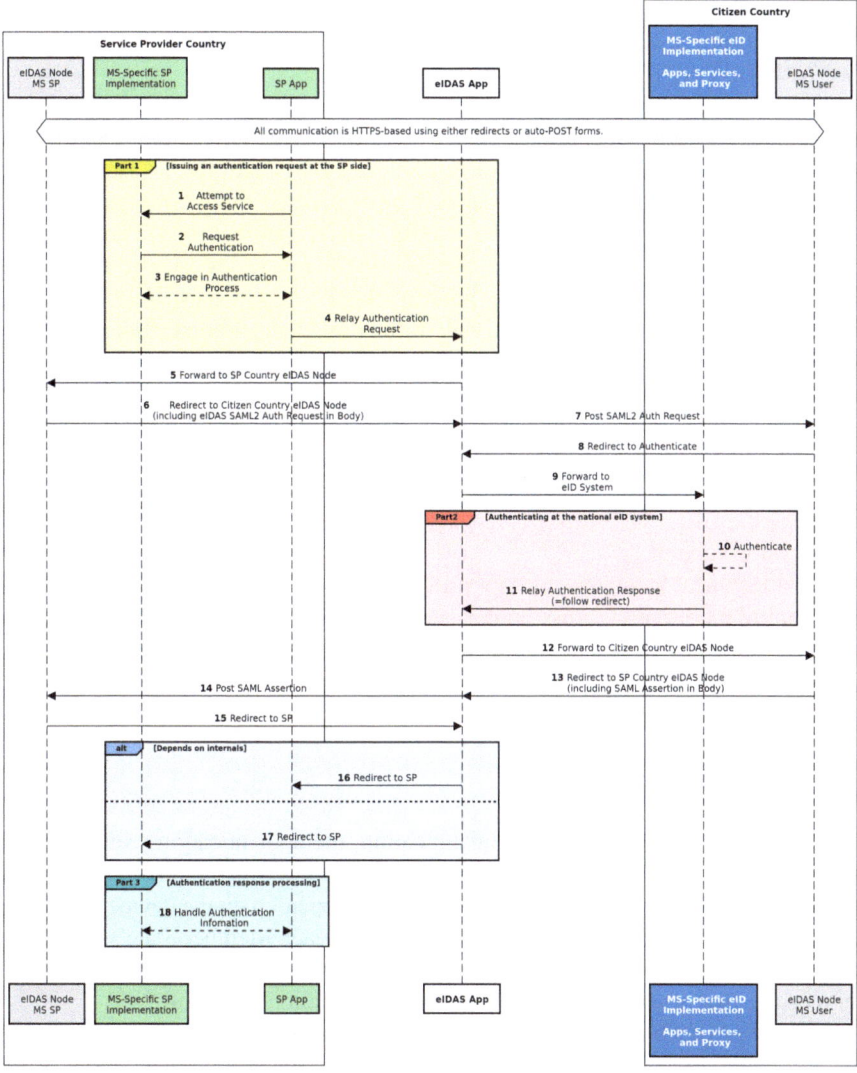

Fig. 2 Sequence diagram of a purely app-based eIDAS cross-border authentication process

enables seamlessly mixing and matching Web apps and native mobile apps along the way. Details on this matter are provided in the following section.

3.1.1 App-to-App Communication

Both the Android operating system and iOS support various means of exchanging information between applications. Only a single one, however, works on both mobile platforms while maintaining browser compatibility. The key concept to achieve this are so-called *claimed URLs* as recommended by the *Internet Engineering Task Force* (IETF) [3]

Any app can *claim* a URL. This means that, at installation time, the app informs the operating system about its capabilities to handle one or more URLs. The Android operating system will then look for a so-called *assetlinks* file at each supplied URL's domain. This *assetlinks* file needs to be hosted at a well-known path location of the domain (e.g., `https://domain.name/.well-known/assetlinks.json`). The Android operating system then checks if the file provides cryptographic proof that the app is eligible to handle links to the URL. On iOS, this mechanism works along the same principle and only differs in details. For example, the Apple developer documentation calls this concept *associated domains* and the file to be hosted needing to be called `apple-app-site-association`.

Whenever an app, including the browser, sends an HTTP GET request to a *claimed* URL, the operating system will either open the app or, in case more than one app *claims* the same URL, ask the user to select an app. In the absence of an app claiming the URL, the browser is invoked to handle the request, providing fallback and desktop support.

On a technical level, this concept provides all the required means to implement and deploy mobile-first, cross-border authentication in accordance with Fig. 2. In the case of the eIDAS app (which serves a central role), however, this approach falls short without further augmentation, as elaborated on in the following section.

3.1.2 Relay Service

In an eIDAS-based cross-border authentication, the authentication request from a service provider app is sent to the eIDAS Node Connector within the same Member State. At this point, the eIDAS app is supposed to open up on the device. In a naive approach, the eIDAS app would claim the URL of each Member State's connector, and everything would work fine. In reality, however, this is infeasible for a variety of reasons, two of which are touched here for illustration purposes.

First of all, each Member State would need to host the *assetlinks* file described in Sect. 3.1.1 to allow the eIDAS app to trigger. Yet, a far bigger issue is the consequence this federated approach would entail. Each change in deployment in a single Member State would require an update to the eIDAS app. Simply put, this is infeasible in practice, which is why mGov4EU follows another approach to provide a dedicated eIDAS app.

The solution developed within mGov4EU works as follows: Instead of sending the authentication request to the eIDAS Node Connector, the request is encoded in a query parameter to a so-called *relay service*. This relay service's only purpose is to decode the query parameter and redirect the user to the encoded link. The service itself is a static Web site, and its functionality is implemented as a purely client-side script. To authorize the eIDAS app to handle requests to the service, the relay service also hosts an *assetlinks* file.

Using this solution, the eIDAS app only needs to claim the URL of the relay service instead of each eIDAS node connector from every Member State. Moreover, the eIDAS app does *not* need to send the request to the service. Instead, the query parameter containing the original request is decoded on the user's device. The eIDAS app just needs to retrieve a whitelist containing allowed redirect locations. This could, for example, happen in periodic intervals.

One of the disadvantages of this solution is that the relay service needs to be hosted at a trusted, central location. This naturally raises observability concerns. However, the relay service is actually only involved in the browser fallback case. While this remains problematic, legal tools can be employed to prohibit actually observing users, while on a technical level, the mobile-first scenario is respected as well.

The last remaining open issue for making a dedicated eIDAS app work well in practice is country selection. As mentioned, in Sect. 2.2, no standardized way for a user to select a country to identify at exists. Given that this must also be handled by the eIDAS app for a consistent user experience, an app-consumable API needs to be put in place for this purpose.

3.1.3 Country Selection

In the browser-based approach, lack of a well-defined country selection is not an issue. In fact, the various member-state-specific implementations providing such a functionality integrated well within the various member-state-specific parts of the authentication workflow. However, the eIDAS app needs a well-defined interface to retrieve a list of supported countries from Member State-specific eIDAS node connectors. Moreover, a clean handoff from service provider app to eIDAS app must be possible. Otherwise, it would not be feasible for the the eIDAS app to display a list of countries to the user, regardless of Member State. Standardizing this part of the authentication process also enables the eIDAS app to store a user's preference and/or remember the previously selected country. In most cases, this eliminates manual country selection after it has been done once, streamlining the user experience even further.

The difficulty of this task becomes apparent when more closely examining Part 1 of Fig. 2, as made more explicit by Fig. 3. As can be seen, various aspects need to be considered in order to create a standardized API for country selection. To begin with, country selection must remain optional. This is rooted in the fact that the country might already be selected at the SP or at the eIDAS node connector. Next, country selection must not break existing systems. Hence, means of retaining session information like cookies must be present in the country selection process. Additionally, country selection must work in both the browser-based and the app-based scenario. With these constraints in mind, a solution was conceived within the mGov4EU project, while an existing one was integrated later on.

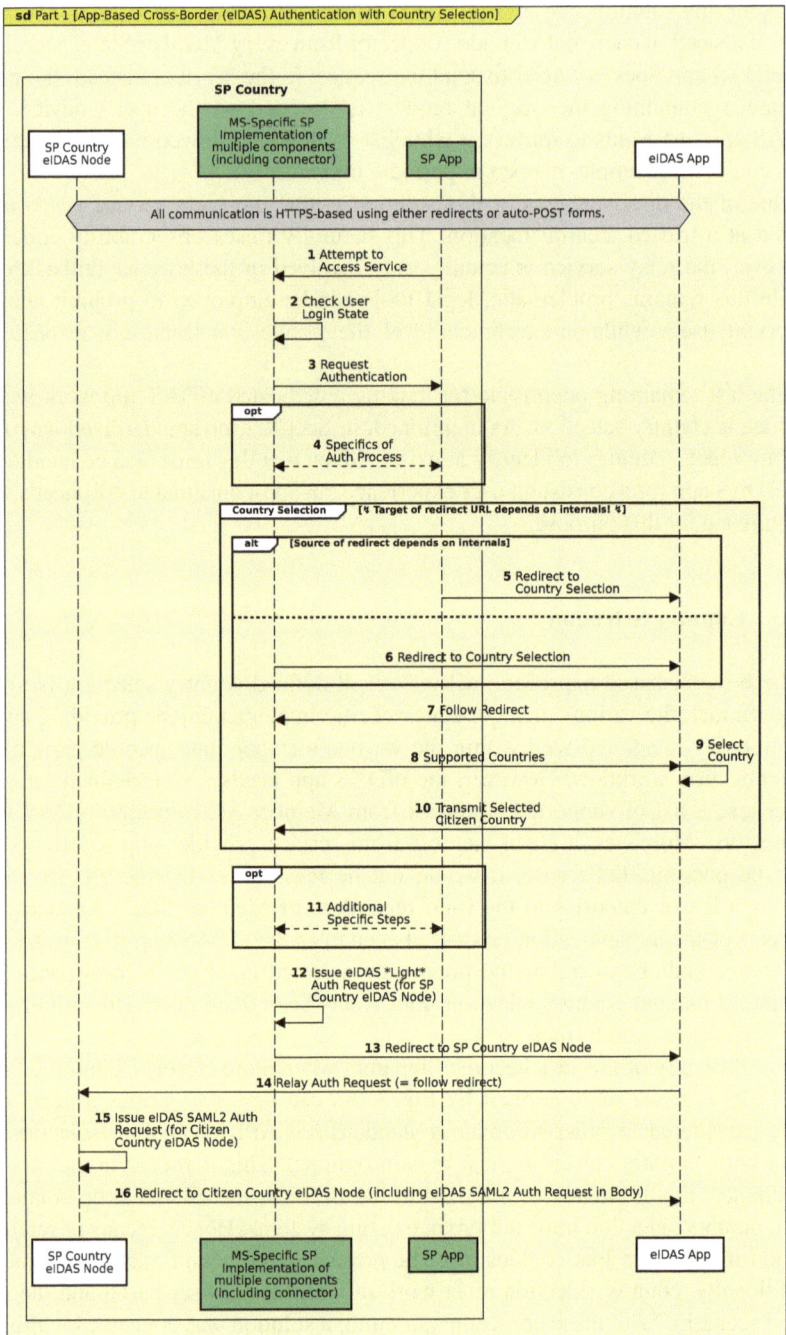

Fig. 3 Detailed view of app-to-app communication between SP app and eIDAS app. As indicated by the background color, this corresponds to Part 1 of Fig. 2

Options API

The first solution supported by the eIDAS app was developed by ecsec GmbH and is called *Options API*.[4] It consists of two API endpoints. The first endpoint is an HTTP GET endpoint and provides the requester with a list of countries. If the request includes the `Accept: application/json` header, the list of countries is sent in a JSON file. This is important in the mobile scenario, since the eIDAS app requires a machine-readable format to provide a consistent user experience across different MS specific node implementations. A country list with just one entry looks as follows:

```
1   {
2   "profile":"GetOptions",
3   "display_options":
4   [
5     {
6       "display_type":"option",
7       "display_data":
8       {
9         "en":
10        {
11          "country":["AT"],
12          "loa":null,
13          "name":"AT",
14          "description":"Austria",
15          "logos":
16          [
17            {
18              "type":"pixel",
19              "url":"data:image/png;base64,iVBORw0KGgoAA ...",
20              "mimetype":"image/png",
21              "width":30,
22              "height":40
23            }
24          ]
25        }
26      },
27      "option_id":"AT"
28    },
29  ],
30  "options":
31  [
32    {
```

[4] https://git.ecsec.de/mike.prechtl/options-api

```
33      "id":"AT",
34      "activation_type":"Browser",
35      "type":"EID",
36      "protocol":"eIDAS",
37      "issuers":[]
38    },
39  ]
40 }
```

For each item in the country list, the *Options API* specification defines a URL field for the image representing the option—usually an image of the country's flag. For the mGov4EU project, this field is used to directly encode the image of the flag in the form of a data-url.[5] The use of data-urls has the benefit of being completely self-contained, meaning no further requests to retrieve the images are needed. This decision was made to reduce requests and minimize network traffic and latency.

If the Accept: application/json header is not set, the endpoint returns a HTML site displaying the list of countries in the browser. This is important if the eIDAS app is not installed, as it supports browser-based fallback. To piggyback state information through the country selection process, a session parameter can be appended in a query parameter. This is important to retain compatibility with existing deployments. The overall selection procedure is the same for both the app-based and the browser-based approach.

The second API endpoint is a HTTP POST endpoint. This endpoint expects the user's choice of country (possibly including piggybacked state information). This so-called select request, conveying the user's choice, may look as follows:

```
1 {
2    "session": "c2NvcGU9b3BlbmlkJmNsYWlt ...",
3    "selected_option": "AT"
4 }
```

While this approach provides maximum flexibility, even though it remains simple on a conceptual level, it does require implementation effort at the backend and the implementation of a custom API on the mobile client.

An alternative approach used to convey a list of possible countries to authenticate with in an API-friendly manner predates mGov4EU and is already used in production in Estonia. In essence, this approach, as introduced below, sacrifices flexibility for sheer simplicity, requiring very little implementation effort at the backend and on mobile clients.

---

[5] https://developer.mozilla.org/en-US/docs/web/http/basics_of_http/data_urls

OIDC Scopes

The mGov4EU team collaborated with RIA[6] (who are in charge of the Estonia eIDAS node) when preparing one of mGov4EU's pilots. During this engagement, ideas regarding mobile-first cross-border authentication were exchanged, since both RIA and the mGov4EU team faced similar challenges. One conclusion of this collaboration was RIA sharing their approach toward country selection and mGov4EU supporting it in addition to the Options API. After all, simplicity can be a virtue in itself, especially for security-critical aspects, and RIA's approach is of a simple elegance, which cannot be denied, given that it builds upon OpenID Connect, which is already employed.

OIDC defines a mechanism for an OIDC *identity provider* (IdP) to publish its metadata. This metadata can be found at a well-known URL location, like https://entity.tld/endpoint/.well-known/openid-configuration, and contains machine-readable description of the IdP and its capabilities. One of the properties found in this metadata file is the `scopes_supported` property. As the name suggests, it defines the *scopes*, which a service provider can request. Like the node hosted by RIA, the eIDAS node connector building block used within mGov4EU adds a list of supported countries to the `scopes_supported` parameter as follows:

```
 1  "scopes_supported":
 2  [
 3      "openid",
 4      "profile",
 5      "eidas:country:at",
 6      "eidas:country:be",
 7      "eidas:country:de",
 8      "eidas:country:ee",
 9      "eidas:country:es",
10      "eidas:country:fr",
11      "eidas:country:it"
12  ]
```

A service provider using this eIDAS node connector for authentication may either include a pre-selected country in the `scope` parameter of the authentication request or leave the decision to the eIDAS node connector. This fulfills the requirement that country selection must be optional. Since the selected country is just an additional value contained in the original request, no session information is lost. This also means that no further considerations regarding browser fallback are required.

The eIDAS app retrieves the configuration file from the SP MS's node connector metadata file. The disadvantage compared to the Options API described before is a general lack of flexibility. As a concrete example, country flags are not included in the published information, and complex, structured information is cumbersome

---

[6] https://ria.ee/

to encode. However, images of country flags can either be included in the app, or emoji country flags can be used. The eIDAS app follows the latter approach.

Integration is straightforward from the eIDAS app's perspective. After the user selects a country to identify with, the scope is added to the request to the eIDAS node connector, and the eIDAS authentication can proceed.

As mentioned in the beginning of Sect. 3, an alternative approach to using discrete apps was also evaluated as part of mGov4EU. The following section presents this second strategy, aiming at a higher integration.

3.2 SDK-Based Approach

While the app-based solution introduced in Sect. 3.1 requires no additional integration effort on the side of the SP, it also imposes some constraints on the eIDAS node of the user's Member State or the service provider (like assuming OIDC). The SDK-based approach follows an entirely different strategy and directly targets service provider apps.

At the same time, the SDK-based approach is not radically different to the app-based approach on a protocol level. In fact, it is compatible with respect to the interfaces of the server-side components introduced in Sect. 3.1. It should therefore be seen as an extension of the app-based model, adding further details of the architecture of the components that make up the app. From the user's perspective, the SDK-based approach can convey a stronger sense of overall integration, as fewer apps are involved.

From a process point of view, the flow shown in Fig. 4 is very similar to the flow of the app-based approach shown in the diagrams in Sect. 3.1. As it is not necessary to repeat the identical aspects, this figure only shows the part after obtaining the selection from the user and how the app containing the SDK is called again after the authentication at the eIDAS node has been completed.

Right after the selection of one of the authentication options, which has been received before from the *Options API* (see Sect. 3.1.3), the authentication module matching the `type` and `protocol` is obtained (see Steps 1 and 2). The purpose of the authentication module is to provide a clear separation between the SAML process of the user's eIDAS node and the actual authentication with the user's credential. That means in general there are two cases to consider here: (1) Federation to the eIDAS node of another Member State, (2) Authentication with a credential in the eIDAS node currently in scope.

Following the diagram in Fig. 4, it is made explicit that a browser-based authentication module is used. This kind of module is required for the first case, federating to another eIDAS node, as it is undefined how another eIDAS node will answer the SAML authentication request. Most probably, it will be a Web page driving the authentication process for the user, or it will start another authentication app with the typical mechanisms, which have been described in Sect. 3.1.1. In both cases, a browser is needed, hence the name `BrowserAuthModule`. The difference

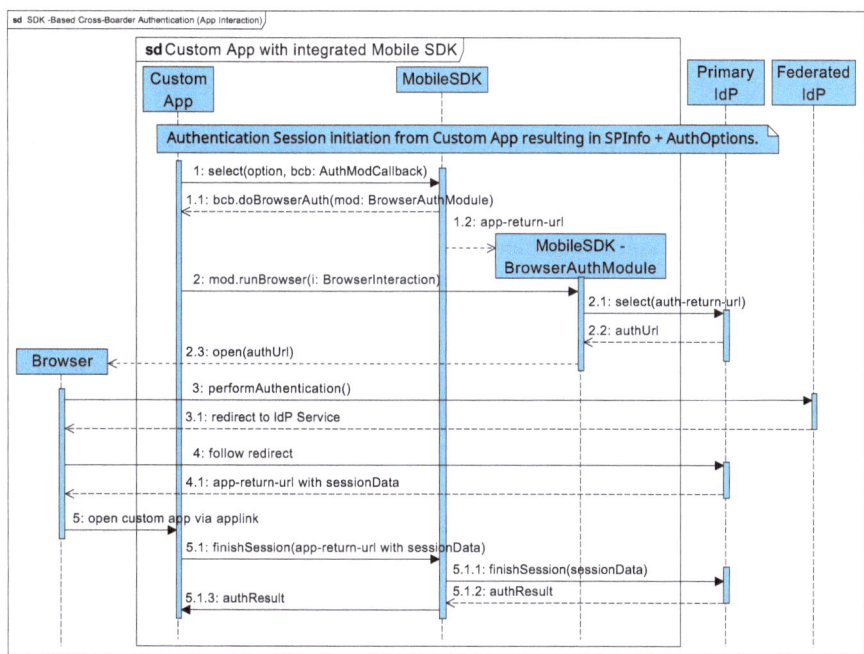

Fig. 4 Detailed view of SDK-based process flow

between the various types of modules lies in the invocation in Step 3, where module-specific interaction components have to be provided by the app. These interaction components look very different when, for example, a smart-card-based authentication should be performed instead of a browser being opened.

When the process is invoked with the obtained authentication modules (3), the selection (together with the URL of the Custom App is passed on to the server (3.1), and the URL of the current eIDAS node creating the SAML Authentication Request (AuthNReq) of the federated eIDAS node) is returned (3.2). The URL is an important difference to the process described in the preceding section, as it allows defining an arbitrary app to be used instead of being limited to one app dictated by the eIDAS node. In order to prevent malicious apps from hijacking the process, further security measures such as a URL whitelist may be necessary. Afterward, the eIDAS node URL is opened in the system browser or an embedded system browser in the app (3.3). In this step, the sub-process can be bound to the browser by issuing a respective cookie, which has to be shown when returning with the SAML Authentication Response (AuthNRes) from the federated eIDAS node in Step 5. Finally, the Custom App is started again (5.1, 6) with the URL provided earlier in Step 3.1, and the sub-process of authenticating with a federated eIDAS node is completed with the context being again in the Custom App. The further steps (6.1, ...) continue the process with the originally requested eIDAS node in order to conclude the overall authentication process.

So while the process model of the SDK-based variant is not substantially different and the client-server interface is designed to be mostly compatible, subtle points, such as the binding of the federated eIDAS node to the browser or the explicit selection of the return-URL of the Custom App, need to be considered in the final system. The major addition of the SDK-based approach beyond the general flow topics is the definition of a software framework containing components common to all apps and IdPs and components, namely, the authentication modules that can be implemented for all kinds of authentication systems. This design can therefore serve as the foundation for Member State specific apps.

While the additional choice of integrating an SDK provides more flexibility and caters better to some scenarios, it remains a traditional cross-border authentication flow. mGov4EU's goals, however, were set higher, and possibilities beyond established concepts were explored, as laid out in the following section.

4 Bridging the Gap Toward the EU Digital Identity Wallet

An important complementing pillar for mGov4EU's eID building block is the identity wallet building block. Instead of relying on the national eID system for every authentication process, identity information is stored locally on the citizen's device. Apart from the obvious privacy improvements, the wallet solution also enhances reliability, as it will also work when the national eID system is not available.

Initially, it was planned to closely follow the standards and developments of the EU Digital Identity Wallet (EUDIW), as it will succeed the current iteration of the eIDAS Regulation technical framework. However, the timeline for mGov4EU was not aligned with the developments of the EUDIW. Therefore, the wallet solution developed within mGov4EU represents a bridge from the current to the upcoming eIDAS Regulation iteration, which also focuses on identity wallets.

mGov4EU's stop-gap solution requires no effort on the service provider side to support this next generation eID system. In fact, wallet-based authentication is indistinguishable from a classical eIDAS-based authentication from the perspective of the SP. This was achieved with the help of the eIDAS app, which translates between SIOPv2 (the protocol used for wallet-based authentication; see below) and traditional OIDC authentication flows.

4.1 SIOPv2 to OIDC

To start a traditional eIDAS authentication, the SP sends an OIDC request to the eIDAS node connector housed in the same Member State. As a result of a successful authentication, the SP expects a OIDC response containing an authorization code. This authorization code can then be used by the SP's backend to retrieve the

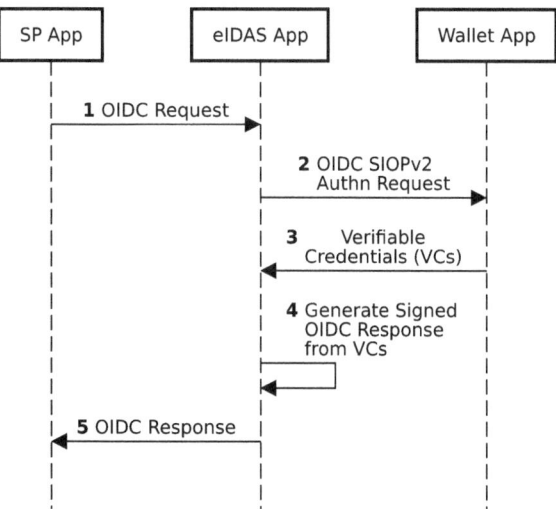

Fig. 5 eIDAS app translates SIOPv2 to OIDC

identity information from an endpoint on the eIDAS node connector. This means that everything after issuing a request up to the generation of a response happens without any involvement of the SP.

To support wallet-based authentication without changing anything on the SP side, an intermediate component is required. This requirement boils down to the fact that native wallet apps use different communication interfaces and incompatible protocols, which are currently not directly supported by SP apps. Thus, translation from one format to the other is required. Here, the eIDAS app comes into play. The wallet used for mGov4EU supports the retrieval of *Verifiable Credentials* (VCs), which it then presents in the form of a *Verifiable Presentation* (VP) during an authentication process. The protocol transporting VPs is called OpenID Connect *Self-Issued OpenID Provider v2* (SIOPv2) [21]. The eIDAS app's role is to map the credentials contained in the VP to an OIDC response.

The core library supporting VC and VP, as well as credential issuing, has been published by A-SIT Plus GmbH as free and open-source software.[7] The underlying data model used for all these procedures has been defined by the *Internet Engineering Task Force* (W3C) [19]. A high-level overview of this process is depicted in Fig. 5.

This idea is simple in principle and also implementation-wise, since a bijective mapping between SIOPv2 VP and OIDC exists for the eIDAS minimum dataset. The eIDAS app's responsibility for signing the OIDC token, however, raises a crucial question: How can the service provider establish trust in this signature?

---

[7] https://github.com/a-sit-plus/kmm-vc-library/

4.2   Trust in eIDAS App

Recalling that mGov4EU's eID solutions cater toward existing deployments, it becomes clear that legacy compatibility is considered imperative. Such constraints make tackling this challenge of trusting an OIDC response created by the eIDAS app difficult—especially considering that making alterations to the SP, including its trust mechanisms, is not an option. Yet, leveraging the established trust relationship between the SP and the eIDAS node connector offers a potential solution.

From a high-level perspective, the transfer of trust works as follows: The eIDAS node connector verifies the integrity of both the eIDAS app and the device it runs on to prevent tampering. Once this has been accomplished, the connector issues a certificate to the eIDAS app, signed by its own certificate. When the eIDAS app then signs an OIDC response using this certificate, the very same trust anchor already present at the SP can be used, since this certificate chain will also terminate there.

Obviously, this proposal raises a follow-up question: How can the integrity of the eIDAS app be verified? mGov4EU provides an answer to this question in the form of a free and open-source remote attestation library published by A-SIT Plus GmbH, which lets a backend remotely establish trust in Android and iOS clients.[8] This library itself unifies platform specifics, embedding a pre-existing library catering toward iOS[9] and a newly created one supporting Android.[10]

The concepts implemented have been widely discussed in literature and naturally require support by the mobile platform. Since the required mechanisms are accessible on both Android[11] and iOS[12] platforms in a comparable manner, this is not an issue. The process itself is rather straightforward as depicted in Fig. 6 and discussed by a peer-reviewed scientific paper published on this matter as part of mGov4EU [1].

In essence, the eIDAS connector issues a certificate (as mentioned before) upon successful authentication, based on a *X.509 certificate signing request* (CSR) for a key accessible only by the eIDAS app. This key must be stored in the hardware-backed keystore of the mobile device. Once this certificate has been issued, the eIDAS app then uses this key to sign the OIDC identity token as described before, and the SP can then verify the signature, since the root of the trust chain is the already trusted eIDAS node connector.

---

[8] https://github.com/a-sit-plus/attestation-service

[9] https://github.com/veehaitch/devicecheck-appattest

[10] https://github.com/a-sit-plus/android-attestation

[11] https://source.android.com/docs/security/features/keystore/attestation

[12] https://developer.apple.com/documentation/devicecheck

Fig. 6 Issuing a trusted
certificate to the eIDAS app

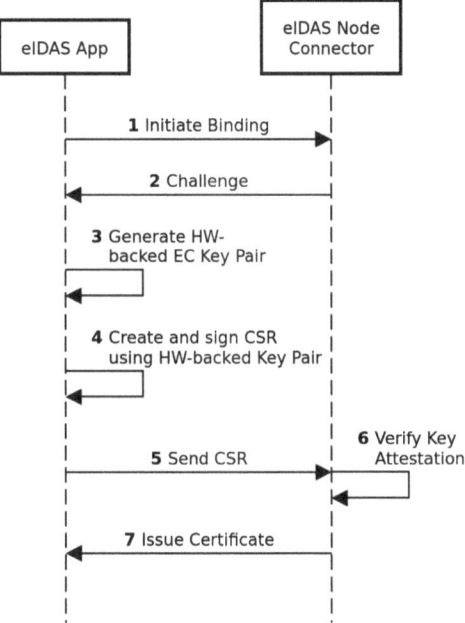

4.3 OIDC Authorization Code in Wallet Scenario

OpenID Connect provides different means to convey identity information, called *flows*. Most of the time, the Authorization Code Flow[13] is employed, where identity information is provided to the client by the IdP via a back-channel. Since the eIDAS app takes over the role of the IdP in the wallet case, this presents an issue. It is not possible for an app to provide an API endpoint to supply the identity information like an IdP does in a traditional scenario. mGov4EU's Wallet building blocks overcome this issue, by incorporating the eIDAS node connector even more in this translation between SIOPv2 and OIDC.

When the eIDAS app is finished with the creation of the OIDC identity token, the token is sent to a dedicated endpoint, which was added specifically for this purpose at the eIDAS node connector. The connector responds with an authorization code, which can later be used by the service provider backend to retrieve this identity token. The eIDAS app simply sends the response with the authorization code to the SP app, as it would in a traditional OIDC authentication flow. In both a traditional eIDAS authentication and in the wallet scenario, the SP simply uses the received authorization code to retrieve the requested identity information from the eIDAS node connector. In summary, compatibility is maintained, while wallet-based authentication is made available to existing SPs. Figure 7 depicts this whole authentication flow as a sequence diagram.

---

[13] https://datatracker.ietf.org/doc/html/rfc6749#section-4.1

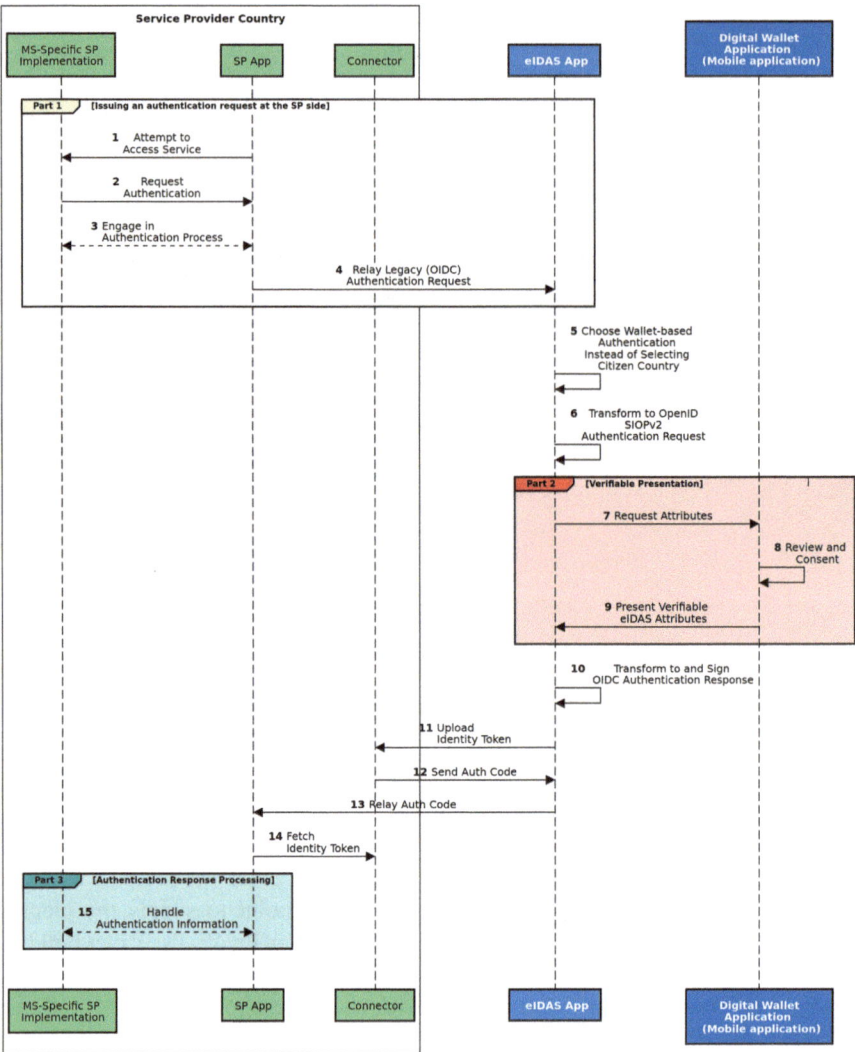

Fig. 7 Sequence diagram illustrating all involved actors when using the eIDAS app as a compatibility layer between legacy SPs and wallet-based authentication

5 Interoperable Digital Public Service Evidence Retrieval

Starting from the *Single Digital Gateway Regulation* (SDGR) [7] and the Once-Only Principle, the EU Commission introduced the *Once Only Technical System* (OOTS) [5]. The specification of the OOTS requires official data and documents (referenced as *evidences* by the EU regulation) to be stored once only but retrieved and reused as many times as needed based on user/citizen interaction. In the context of the mGov4EU project, the design of the *single digital gateway* (SDG) building block (providing this functionality and targeting the interoperable data exchange) can be found in the chapter describing the architecture and design of this book. This section, on the other hand, deals with technical challenges encountered along the way of actually implementing such a system and presents the solutions conceived.

5.1 Cross-Border Evidence Retrieval: Challenges and Solutions

A simplified sequence diagram of the cross-border interaction of the SDG components, the service provider (e.g., iVoting portal) and the digital wallet in the case of a cross-border evidence retrieval, is depicted in Fig. 8. When observing which actors are involved, one detail is of particular interest: Evidences are stored in a wallet. Hence the term *digital wallet* is used in the SDG context, as the wallet building block has been extended to support storing arbitrary evidences in addition to identity attributes (and not *digital identity wallet* as it is referred to within the EU Digital Identity Wallet legal framework).

Evidence retrieval works as follows: The service provider application (e.g., the iVoting portal, as piloted within mGov4EU) triggers the SDG evidence requester to retrieve evidence of a specific type. After discovering a suitable *evidence provider* (EP) through the *Service Metadata Protocol* (SMP) [17], the *evidence requester* (ER) can contact the EP and requests the evidence via a standard *Electronic Business XML* (eBXML) [16] request for data including the user family and given name. Up to this stage, the message flow is state of the art. However, consent management is required in this context, which is why a new component, the *Authorization Server* (AS), had to be introduced in the architecture, implementing this feature though the *User-Managed Access* (UMA) protocol [13].

According to UMA protocol, the AS stores access rules set by the owner of the evidence. The user's client acting as requesting party will first retrieve a consent token from the AS and then include the consent token in the request to retrieve the evidence.

Following this concept, the evidence provider is the decision point for allowing access to the evidence. The evidence provider checks if the requesting user is the owner of the evidence; otherwise, it will check for the consent token grants. This UMA-based interaction can be used for enabling also third-party users to get access to data (e.g., employees from digital public services, employers).

While the discussion so far is indeed rather technical, the implementation actions carried out revealed gaps, which are important to address. In fact, an issue was discovered, which boiled down to changing the message flow in such a way that the exchange of messages between the evidence requester and the evidence provider stays compatible with the eBXML standard and thus interoperable with other systems supporting this standard. After all, this is crucial in a cross-border scenario.

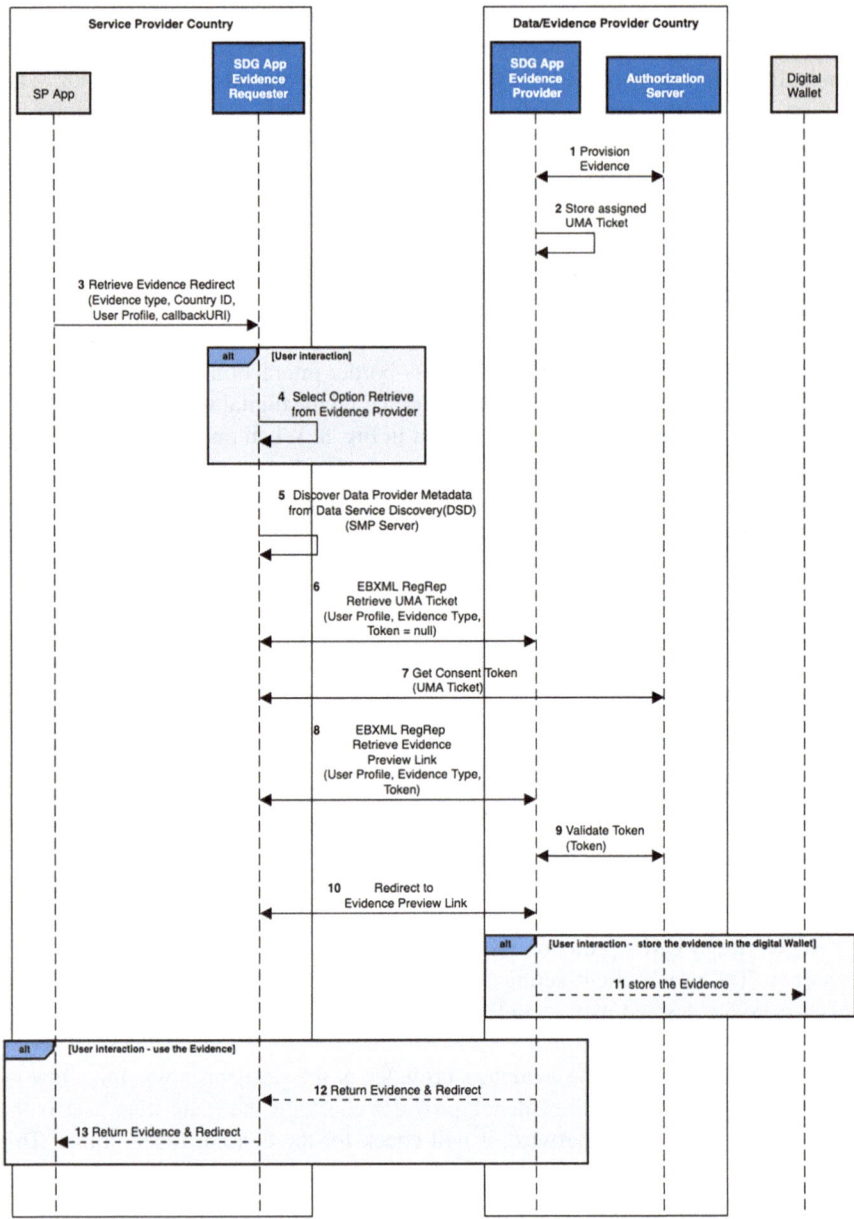

Fig. 8 Message flow for retrieving an evidence from the Evidence Provider. The term app includes Web apps and mobile apps

And at the same time, discovering the Authorization Server was also shown to be challenging when putting theory into practice.

To remain compatible, the evidence provider responds to requests having no valid consent token with an *Unauthorized* error. This response bears the metadata regarding the Authorization Server exposed interface for consent token interrogations. This way, the evidence requester is informed of the Authorization Server's location and can contact it to retrieve this consent token. Afterward, a second request toward the evidence provider will contain the token, which can then be evaluated by the evidence provider, and a corresponding reply containing the preview link will be sent to the evidence requester.

Additional challenges arose, since the official Single Digital Gateway Regulation was published only during the second year of the mGov4EU project. It then became clear that evidence preview has to take place at the evidence provider in order to avoid exchanging any evidence in case the user is not accepting for digital public service usage. The implementation of the evidence provider had to be extended to not only respond on eBXML-based requests with evidence but to provide a dynamic Web view.

At this point, *user experience* (UX) concerns are also crucial, while integration aspects also need to be considered for a sustainable solution beyond the mGov4EU's lifetime. While very technical in nature, choice of programming language and frameworks are indeed relevant, as these aspects have a profound impact on acceptance. This concerns both users and implementers. For this reason, the evidence provider was implemented using *Vaadin*,[14] as it fits well into established frameworks used at the backend and also integrates well with Kotlin—a crucial aspect to eliminate technical interoperability issues. In addition, the frontend parts have a keen focus on UX, making it play well on mobile clients (e.g., automatically adjusting the user interface accordingly).

On the message exchange level, the evidence provider communication engine was modified to reply with a link to the preview of the evidence instead of the evidence itself. In order to support multiple sessions in parallel, the link was generated based on the newly created session id at the evidence provider. This URL-based communication between actors also caters toward the mobile context, as it already fulfils the baseline requirement for app-to-app communication as described in Sect. 3.1.1. In general, this requires callback URLs to be processed on the client side, as any native apps claiming URLs need to be called.

The issue just described becomes clearer with respect to wallet integration: After the user selects and approves usage of an SDG credential from the digital wallet, they are redirected to the Web browser based on a callback previously set by the evidence requester.

Although insightful on a technical level for implementers and protocol designers, the topics discussed so far do no paint a clear picture of how the single digital gateway-related components work from the user's point of view. The following

---

[14] https://vaadin.com/

section provides this perspective, illustrating the user journey when interacting with this system comprising multiple building blocks.

```
% beforeEnterEvent.getUI().getPage()
%      .executeJs("return window.location.hash")
%          .then(fragment -> {
%              processFragment(fragment.asString());
%          });
% }
```

5.2 Resulting User Journey

The SDG building block components were integrated with the eID and the digital wallet building blocks from the mGov4EU project. The user journey's paths resulting from interacting with this integrated system are shown in Fig. 9. This graph also visualizes the complexity of the process as a whole, highlighting many intricacies that can cause issues in practice, when not being considered during the implementation phase.

This apparent complexity, however, brings immediate benefits to the user. For example, apart from checking the family name and given name of the requesting party, an improved matching at the EP is enabled by also checking the identifier from the user profile retrieved from the eID building block. Furthermore, while previewing the evidence at the evidence provider, the user can directly opt for storing the evidence into their digital wallet as an SDG credential (which is a particular format of a Verifiable Credential). This SDG credential contains (among others) the following attributes, relevant in the single digital gateway context, which can be stored in the digital wallet:

- name: name of the evidence
- issuer: issuer of the evidence
- timestamp: timestamp of the evidence
- evidence: the evidence itself, encoded as a string of bytes without further inherent semantics[15]

This information is stored in the digital wallet in an encrypted format by leveraging the according functionality of the mobile operating system. When in need of the evidence, the user can retrieve it directly from the digital wallet, without contacting the EP, thus reducing the SDG infrastructure load. This avoids congestion and reduces the required time for accessing the evidence as well, thus improving user experience.

---

[15] This deliberate lack of semantics applies only to the transport layer, not to the application layer, where the meaning of data is well defined.

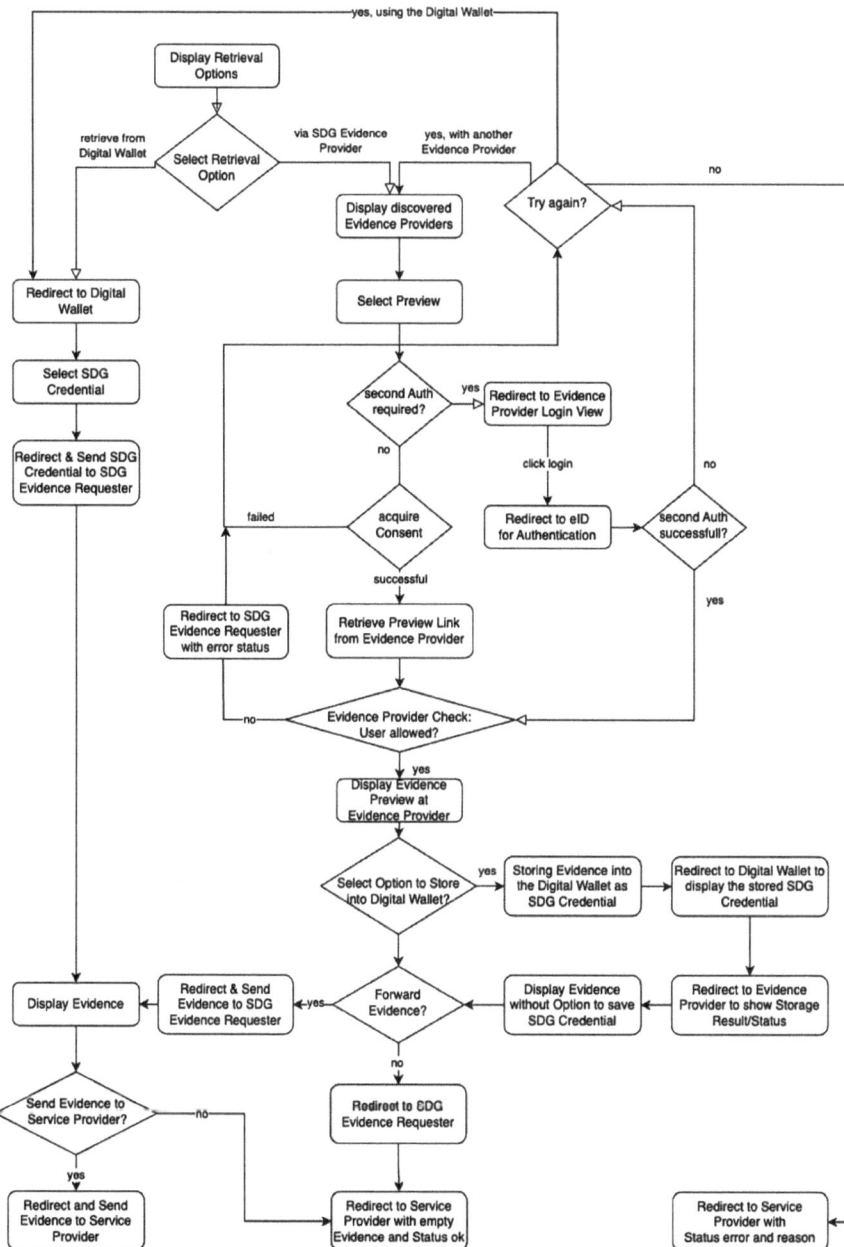

Fig. 9 User journey paths while retrieving the evidence

Retrieving the evidence as SDG credential using a Verifiable Presentation process relies on the SIOPv2 protocol at the evidence requester side, just as presenting identity attributes does when using the wallet building block as a digital identity wallet.

5.3   Employed Technological Elements

As touched before, choice of technologies is crucial, as broad acceptance among implementers is a fundamental requirement for sustainable technical results. After all, even a solution of highest technological finesse is destined to remain trapped in academia and fade into oblivion, if it requires niche expertise and the knowledge of esoteric programming languages and cryptic frameworks. Hence, established technologies and pre-existing components were re-used where possible.

The SDG evidence requester and EP implementation started from the open-source software components of Data Consumer and Data Provider that resulted from *The Once Only Project* (TOOP) [20].

For a fast integration with the digital wallet, the wallet building block developed within mGov4EU was adapted to also handle single digital gateway evidences. Hence, functionality for issuing, storing, and verifying Verifiable Credentials was already available, and integrating it with the SDG building block benefited all involved components. For the evidence requester acting as the software client of the user, the initial TOOP Data Consumer component was implemented using the Vaadin Web application framework.

The Vaadin framework works especially well in enterprise deployments while also enabling rapid prototyping. It allows Web applications to be developed directly in Java and works well with Spring Boot or Jetty as underlying Web engines— both of which are staples in the field. Hence, it is a sustainable choice. Moreover, it is designed from a rather traditional technical point of view, making it easy to understand for any programmer with knowledge in object-oriented programming. As for the rapid prototyping capabilities, Vaadin also includes a fast UI prototyping from *Figma* design kit [8] but also directly supports accessibility features like screen readers.

Implementing the *data provider* (DP) component that was used for implementing the mGov4EU project evidence provider has produced entirely different results. Here, an alternative technical solution was explored, based on the *Javalin.io* Web application framework [12]. Although compatible with both Java and Kotlin programming languages and established frameworks, the Javalin.io framework was proven quite limited in UX regards. Most commonly, difficulties in creating dynamic views based on a user's current Web session information within the context of the overall system. This, again, highlights how something seemingly mundane as a choice of framework can have a profound impact on the actually obtained results after implementing a design.

Another challenge arises, which is often disregarded as part of research projects, but which is equally crucial when trying to move to production: licensing issues. For example, the Authorization Server component and the *OAuth2.0 authorization framework* (OAuth 2.0) [11] libraries to interact with the eID building block and implement the consent management were adopted from the Gluu federation [10]. Although some of the binaries are released with MIT license [15], the license for the production system has changed over time. While this change in license was unforeseen and can happen to any project consuming an existing library, it still highlights how research projects and production deployment differ.

In the end, this whole experience shows how seemingly minor details can have a substantial impact. Moreover, it also outlines how sustainability, dissemination, and exploitation efforts may be hindered by aspects irrelevant in a research project, if these are not considered from the get-go. This is especially crucial when integrating a large number of components from different sources as it is the case for the single digital gateway system developed within mGov4EU.

6 Conclusions

This chapter presented details on mGov4EUs eID, wallet, and SDG building blocks, as well as their integration with each other. Compared to high-level architectural discussions on these matters, actually implementing concepts and deploying system revealed some rather intricate issues—after all, the devil really is in the details. This is all the more true when seeking to transform inherently browser-centric flows to a mobile-first setting. As illustrated, for example, by challenges intro-duced when deploying a standardized country selection and providing app-to-app communication, profound insights are gained by carrying out such implementation tasks. These findings are especially crucial when looking beyond the scope of established cross-border authentication procedures. Conceiving and implementing a digital identity wallet in the spirit of the upcoming EU Digital Identity Wallet as part of mGov4EU not only provided opportunities to explore how smooth upgrade paths can be established. These implementation actions also benefited applications providing single digital gateway functionality, as the wallet solution developed within mGov4EU enabled storing of evidences, i.e., retrieving them once only and providing them to service providers whenever requested afterward.

The results obtained through implementing and integrating eID, wallet, and SDG building blocks clearly show the potential of mobile-first solutions in the larger eGovernment context. In summary, the exploratory approach followed by mGov4EU, providing multiple solutions to the same problem, paid off. It showed that multiple paths lead to a common goal and both subtle and significant differences in their characteristics can be crucial enablers or blockers depending on the context and deployment specifics. Hence, all developed solutions contributed to the project's success and far fewer findings could have been obtained, had the project followed a singular strategy.

References

1. Czerny, R., Kollmann, C., Podgorelec, B., Prunster, B., Zefferer, T.: Towards a mobile-first cross-border eID framework. In: Proceedings of the 24th Annual International Conference on Digital Government Research. DGO '23, pp. 526–535. Association for Computing Machinery, New York (2023). https://doi.org/10.1145/3598469.3598562
2. Czerny, R., Kollmann, C., Podgorelec, B., Prünster, B., Zefferer, T.: Smoothing the ride: providing a seamless upgrade path from established cross-border eID workflows towards eID wallet systems. In: 20th International Conference on Security and Cryptography, pp. 460–468 (2023). https://doi.org/10.5220/0012091900003555
3. Denniss, W., Bradley, J.: OAuth 2.0 for native apps. 4566 8252, 21 pp. Internet Engineering Task Force (2017). https://datatracker.ietf.org/doc/rfc8252 (visited on 11/30/2023)
4. European Commission: Final Agreement on EU Digital Identity Wallet. https://ec.europa.eu/commission/presscorner/detail/en/ip_23_5651 (visited on 11/30/2023)
5. European Commission: Once-Only Hub, a single environment providing reliable information and services relating to the Once-Only Technical System. https://ec.europa.eu/digital-building-blocks/wikis/display/OOTS/OOTSHUB$+$Home
6. European Parliament and the Council of the European Union: Regulation (EU) No 910/2014 of the European Parliament and of the Council of 23 July 2014 on Electronic Identification and Trust Services for Electronic Transactions in the Internal Market and Repealing Directive 1999/93/EC, (2014). 10. https://doi.org/5040/9781509909568. https://eur-lex.europa.eu/legal-content/EN/TXT/PDF/?uri=CELEX:32014R0910 (visited on 05/06/2021)
7. European Union: Regulation (EU) 2018/1724 of the European Parliament and of the Council of 2 October 2018 establishing a single digital gateway to provide access to information, to procedures and to assistance and problem-solving services and amending Regulation (EU) No 1024/2012 (2018). https://eur-lex.europa.eu/eli/reg/2018/1724/oj
8. Figma Team: Figma design kit (2023). https://www.figma.com (visited on 12/14/2023)
9. Gaehtgens, F.: Hype Cycle for Digital Identity, 2022. Tech. rep. ID G00770428, Gartner (2022). https://www.gartner.com/document/4016895
10. Gluu Federation: Gluu Federation GitHub repository of the oxAuth library (2023). https://github.com/GluuFederation/oxAuth (visited on 12/14/2023)
11. Hardt, D.: The OAuth 2.0 Authorization Framework. RFC 6749, Internet Engineering Task Force (2012). https://datatracker.ietf.org/doc/html/rfc6749.html
12. Javalin Team: Javalin web application framework (2023). https://javalin.io (visited on 12/14/2023)
13. Kantara Initiative: User-Managed Access (UMA) 2.0 Grant for OAuth 2.0 Authorization (2018). https://docs.kantarainitiative.org/uma/wg/rec-oauth-uma-grant-2.0.html (visited on 12/14/2023)
14. Okta, Inc.: OpenID Connect Protocol, Auth0 Docs. https://auth0.com/docs/ (visited on 11/30/2023)
15. Open Source Initiative: The MIT License (2023). https://opensource.org/licenses/MIT (visited on 12/14/2023)
16. Organization for the Advancement of Structured Information Standards (OASIS): AS4 Profile of ebXML Messaging Services (ebMS) 3.0 Version 1.0 (2013). https://docs.oasis-open.org/ebxml-msg/ebms/v3.0/profiles/AS4-profile/v1.0/os/AS4-profile-v1.0-os.html (visited on 04/11/2023)
17. Organization for the Advancement of Structured Information Standards (OASIS): eDelivery SMP specifications - 1.1.0 (2018). https://ec.europa.eu/digital-building-blocks/wikis/display/DIGITAL/eDelivery (visited on 12/14/2023)
18. Organization for the Advancement of Structured Information Standards (OASIS): Profiles for the OASIS Security Assertion Markup Language (SAML) V2.0 – Errata Composite. Working Draft 07 (2015). https://www.oasis-open.org/committees/download.php/56782/sstc-saml-profiles-errata-2.0-wd-07.pdf (visited on 06/29/2021)

19. Sporny, M., Longley, D., Chadwick, D.: Verifiable Credentials Data Model v2.0. https://w3c.github.io/vc-data-model/ (visited on 11/30/2023)
20. TOOP4EU: Toop4EU GitHub page (2023). https://github.com/TOOP4EU (visited on 12/14/2023)
21. Yasuda, K., Jones, M., Lodderstedt, T.: Self-Issued OpenID Provider v2 (2023). https://openid.net/specs/openid-connect-self-issued-v2-1_0.html (visited on 03/14/2023)

An i-Voting Pilot in the eIDAS and SDG Context

Jordi Cucurull ⓘ, Polina Toropova, Andreea-Ancuta Corici ⓘ,
Bernd Prünster ⓘ, Thomas Zefferer ⓘ, and Blaž Podgorelec ⓘ

Abstract This chapter describes the design, implementation, and execution of the i-voting pilot of the mGov4EU project. The pilot has integrated some of the main building blocks of the project into an i-voting software and has demonstrated their functionality applied to a real use case. The chapter also describes the experience and lessons learned while passing from a laboratory proof of concept to the deployments to be used by real users both at the University of Tartu in a first stage and at the University of Stuttgart in a second stage. During the first stage, the identification with eIDAS has been tested, and during the second stage, validation of documents retrieved via single digital gateway (SDG) components and authorizing users to vote in the election have been tested. Also, some insights obtained from the final users of the pilots have been presented.

Keywords Online voting · eIDAS · SDG · Piloting · Identity · Authorization

J. Cucurull (✉) · P. Toropova
Scytl Election Technologies S.L.U, Barcelona, Spain
e-mail: jordi.cucurull@scytl.com; polina.toropova@scytl.com

A.-A. Corici
Critical Infrastructures Department (ESPRI) - Fraunhofer FOKUS Institute, Berlin, Germany
e-mail: andreea.ancuta.corici@fokus.fraunhofer.de

B. Prünster · T. Zefferer
A-SIT Plus GmbH, Graz, Germany
e-mail: bernd.pruenster@a-sit.at; thomas.zefferer@a-sit.at

B. Podgorelec
Institute of Applied Information Processing and Communications – Graz University of Technology, Graz, Germany
e-mail: blaz.podgorelec@iaik.tugraz.at

© The Author(s) 2025   93
V. Homburg et al. (eds.), *From Electronic to Mobile Government*,
https://doi.org/10.1007/978-3-031-64471-9_6

1 Online Voting, Authentication, and Authorization

Online voting offers the possibility to citizens to remotely participate in elections and democratic processes and cast their votes using their own devices via Internet. Online voting can be combined with traditional paper voting when required, and in the long term, it might completely replace it due to the advantages it offers. For example, in online voting, it is possible to implement accessibility features that facilitate the voting to disabled voters [1], there is no need to travel to the polling stations, and, as a consequence, this type of voting is more environmentally sustainable [2]. In addition, it is also possible to implement several languages, thus opening voting for a larger amount of voters.

However, in order to guarantee the security of the voting process, several security requirements must be implemented [3]. Developing authentication and authorization security measures was the main focus of the mGov4EU project. The authentication of the voter enables the system to ascertain that the person voting behind the computer or smartphone screen is who they claim to be. And the authorization of the voter enables the system to ensure voter eligibility, i.e., that only votes from eligible voters in a certain election are accepted.

Voter authentication can be achieved in different manners, but it is common to be based on something you know (knowledge), something you have (ownership), and/or something you are (biometrics) [4]. Typically, the usage of credentials based on login/passwords (something you know) has been the more popular authentication mechanism. However, during the last years, governments have started to provide electronic identities (eID) for their citizens, which typically rely on multi-factor authentication, e.g., by combining ownership and biometric elements. These electronic identities can also be leveraged for authenticating the voters in online voting elections when they are linked to the corresponding governmental identity provider (IdP). These governmental IdPs were defined and limited in the context of their own national country. That is why, in order to enable cross-country interoperability of electronic identities and digital signature mechanisms, the eIDAS regulation has been created. eIDAS enables citizens to authenticate with an electronic identity of one European Member State into the system of another European Member State that is compliant with it. In this context, the i-voting pilot described in this chapter has been based on the technical approach to the implementation of eIDAS regulation. The building blocks of the project facilitate the cross-country authentication on a mobile-only based scenario. That is why authentication is conducted via mobile phone apps (see Sect. 2 for a thorough description of it).

Voter authorization is usually achieved by ensuring that the eID and its related unique identifier of the authenticated voter is present in the electoral roll setup in the online voting system by the election administrators. In the i-voting pilot, we have dealt with two challenges related to authorization. On one hand, we had to face the lack of a single unique identifier at the European level. Despite eIDAS attempts to overcome the issues created by the diversity of electronic identifiers in different Member States, it does not impose a unique identifier that can be used out of the box in all Member States. Instead, in most cases, received eIDAS identifiers from other Member States need to be matched to the respective national eID system and the identifiers used therein. This complicates the authorization of voters from different Member States. On the other hand, a different approach instead of the traditional static electoral roll list that is configured at the beginning of the election was meant to be explored. Thus, a dynamic electoral roll based on the issuance of individual voter authorizations that entitled a given voter to cast a vote in a certain election was implemented. In this manner, a number of different entities could authorize their voters in a certain election before the election and when it is already running. Voter authorizations have been provided to each voter using the SDG components of mGov4EU. After the voter retrieved the appropriate voter authorization, he was redirected to the online voting system that would validate it and allow the voter to cast a vote.

Hence, the rest of the chapter explains how the pilot has integrated some of the main building blocks of the project into the i-voting software. The chapter also describes the experience and lessons learnt while passing from a laboratory proof of concept to the deployments used both at the University of Tartu in a first stage and at the Fraunhofer Institute in Stuttgart in a second stage. Also, some insights obtained from the final users of the pilots are presented.

2   eIDAS App Integration for Authentication (and Authorization)

The i-voting pilot integrates several building blocks of the mGov4EU. In the first phase, we integrated the eID and Wallet authentication building blocks. Both of them enable a voter to authenticate, using an eID or a credential stored in the mGov4EU wallet.

2.1   eID Authentication

The eID authentication building block enables voters to authenticate themselves using their electronic identity issued by their home Member State, which can be different to the one operating the service provider (in this case, the i-voting system) and the national IdP (eID system) serving this service provider. This authentication is done via eIDAS [5] using only mobile apps and a notified eID scheme. The standard procedure to authenticate with eIDAS is browser-based; thus, the user is asked to select their country of origin and is then redirected to the IdP (eID system) of the user's home country. Instead, with the eID building block developed in mGov4EU, an app called eIDAS App (see Fig. 1) appears just when the authentication process starts and allows the user to select their country of origin. Then the eIDAS App appropriately redirects the user to its user's home country IdP (eID system). At that point, if the identity provider has an app, it also appears

Fig. 1 eIDAS App

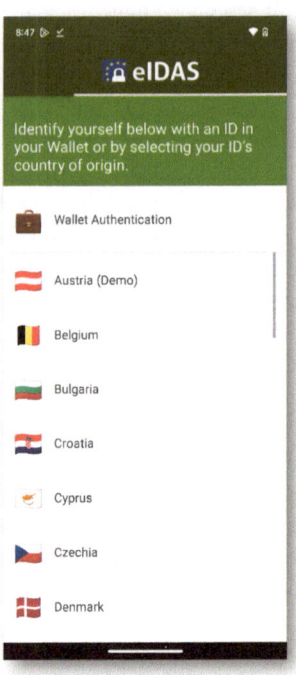

seamlessly for the user (see Fig. 2). Then, the user authenticates with their eID, and if the authentication is successful, there is a redirection to the service provider's IdP, which gets a confirmation of the successful authentication via eIDAS procedures.

The online voting system is composed of two main modules (see Fig. 3), the i-voting Voter Portal and the i-voting Admin Portal, where the voter votes and elections are set up and managed, respectively. In addition to these two modules, there is another one, the i-voting Voter Manager, that contains several submodules needed for the integration. For the case of delegated authentications, i.e., authentications conducted using an external identity provider, as in this project, there are two sub-modules called Service Provider and Certificate Issuer. The Service Provider is connected to its local Identity Provider (IdP), represented by the National eID System Member S Service Provider in Fig. 3, and it is the one in charge of handling the authentication process with the IdP. The Certificate Issuer, after a successful authentication, certifies a pair of keys dynamically generated by the Voter Portal frontend as the pair of keys that the authenticated voter will use to sign the vote. In Fig. 3, we can also see the remote IdP (National eID System Member State User), that is, the one of the home country of the voter, and the eID Interoperability System, that is, the eID authentication building block.

The Service provider sub-module is connected to the local IdP using the OpenID Connect[1] authentication protocol. During the first steps of the integration, this sub-

---

[1] https://openid.net/developers/specs/

Fig. 2 User's home country
IdP App

module has been adapted to support the OAuth2 Implicit Flow grant type.[2] Later, in order to maximize compatibility and security, Authorization Code grant type support has been added to the eID authentication building block, and the Service Provider sub-module has been adapted to use it.

The integration did not only imply the development and adjustment of components but also to define how to uniquely identify the voters. In order to know if a voter is eligible to vote, it is needed to generate an electoral roll that contains the authorized identifiers of the eligible voters. This electoral roll is part of the election configuration, and when a voter is authenticated, the system checks the voter is within the electoral roll. As mentioned before, there is no single unique identifier at the European level. Because of this, and despite the fact that eIDAS defines a unique identifier as mandatory, the identifier that is retrieved when the citizen is authenticated cannot be easily predicted to pre-fill an electoral roll given that we know some personal data of the citizens, such as their fiscal number or another local unique identifier (see eIDAS specification Sect. 2.2.3[3]). The consequence of that is the electoral roll cannot be based on the eIDAS citizen's unique identifier without

---

[2] https://datatracker.ietf.org/doc/html/rfc6749#section-1.3.2

[3] https://ec.europa.eu/digital-building-blocks/sites/display/DIGITAL/eIDAS+eID+Profile?
preview=/467109280/704841743/eIDAS%20SAML%20Attribute%20Profile%20v1.4_final.pdf

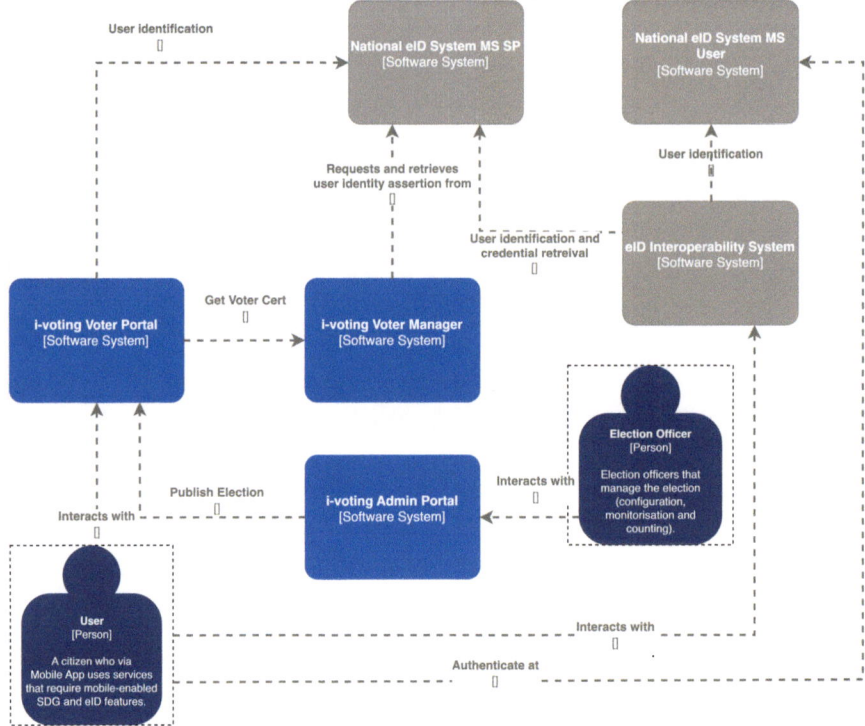

Fig. 3 Online voting system modules integrated with eID building block

a preliminary registration phase used to gather this identifier. In order to overcome this issue, we used a different approach to uniquely identify the citizens. We used the Name, Family Name, and Date of Birth attributes, which are information always provided by eIDAS. Thus, our unique identifier for the citizens was a concatenation of these three attributes. This, of course, has some disadvantages, such as the possibility of collisions, which at the European level may occur. Another possible issue that may occur is that the known name of the person might not totally match the one returned by eIDAS, e.g., due to compound names or tildes.

2.2 Wallet Authentication

The wallet building block enables the voter to store several pieces of data, such as credentials, inside a virtual wallet implemented as a mobile app (see Fig. 4). The wallet complements the eID authentication building block; thus, the user's identity information (identity attributes) can be stored in advance within the wallet (see Fig. 5). In this case, the user can directly authenticate without the need to be redirected to the IdP (eID system) of the user's home country. In this case, when this building block is used and the voter starts the authentication process, the eIDAS App (see Fig.

Fig. 4 Wallet app

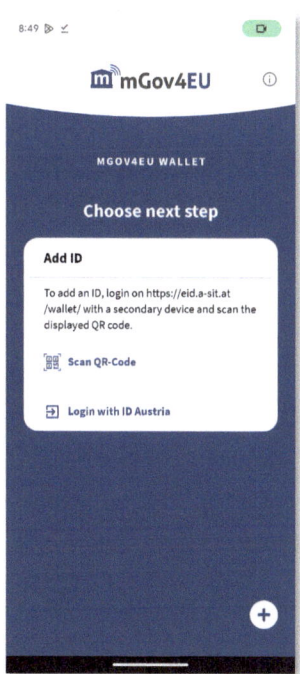

1) appears as in the previous case, but the user selects Wallet Authentication. Then, the Wallet App appears seamlessly for the user (see Fig. 6). Then, the user just has to accept to disclose their identity information in the form of verifiable credentials, and there is a redirection to the local IdP, which checks whether the credential is valid.

In the case of the wallet, no additional modules had to be integrated from the i-voting software point of view. However, it required some adjustments to make it work and some additional testing. For example, one of the elements that required attention was the format of the dates. Since the birth date of the voter was used as part of the unique identifier selected for the electoral roll, it was highly important to be consistent with the format of it. At the beginning we had some discrepancies between the format used in the eID building block and the wallet. This had to be corrected on the building blocks to ensure both eID and wallet users were seamlessly authenticated and authorized to vote. It is also worth mentioning that the Wallet App required several secure hardware capabilities on the smartphones to be used, which implied only real hardware could be used for testing (as opposed to emulators that simulate real phones such as the one included in the Android Studio SDK[4]).

---

[4] https://developer.android.com/studio

Fig. 5 Wallet credential

3 SDG Integration for Authorization

In the second phase of the i-voting pilot, the i-voting system was integrated with the single digital gateway (SDG) building block. SDG enables cross-country exchange of data among public administrations, e.g., birth certificates or residence certificates. For the i-voting pilot, the use case used SDG as a mechanism to exchange voting authorizations, i.e., a document that entitles a particular voter to vote in a given election. During the pilot, voters participated in an environment having the test election organized by as if it were organized by a university. The voters would require further authorization to vote with documents (e.g., certificate of enrolment) obtained via SDG from the University Portal.

After the voters authenticated their identity with either the Wallet or an eID, they needed to complete one more step to retrieve further student information from SDG, i.e., voter authorization. The voter was redirected to the SDG Requester (see Fig. 7) to start the process to retrieve voter authorization. The SDG Requester redirected again the voter to a SDG Data Provider, which is an entity that holds data and that could be in a different Member State. At the voter's request, the SDG Data Provider Web portal and a preview of the possible voter authorization were displayed to the voter (see Fig. 8). At this point, the voter had the option to accept and retrieve the data back to the SDG Requester. Finally, the voter has the possibility to accept to use the voter authorization retrieved and continue to the voting client to vote (Fig. 9).

Fig. 6 Wallet credential use

The integration of the SDG building block did not only imply modifications to enable the voters to retrieve the voter authorizations via SDG. It also implied the creation of a whole ecosystem to replace the regular electoral roll list for authorizing the voters by voter authorizations. An updated systems' diagram for this second phase is shown in Fig. 10, which includes the SDG elements that are provided as part of the SDG building blocks and the new interactions created. As a part of the new ecosystem, two new components were implemented, called Voter Authorization Manager and Voter Authorization Service; this last part of the i-voting Voter Manager software system is depicted in Fig. 10.

In this stage, the authorization of voters works in the following manner. The entity issuing voter authorizations has access to the Voter Authorization Manager and, from that service, has the possibility to issue voter authorizations for particular voters and elections. In order to do so, it is just needed to set up the identifier of the election and, later, introduce the unique identifier of the voter, which, as in the previous stage, is based on the name, family name, and date of birth of the voter. Authorizations have to be exported to be uploaded into the SDG Data Provider. The functionality to export them within a file is implemented in the component and a procedure based on scripts to upload them in the SDG Data Provider created. However, in a final production system, there should be a complete integration between the Voter Authorization Manager and the SDG Data Provider. After creating and importing voter authorizations in the SDG Data Provider (operation that can be conducted at any time, even during the election), the

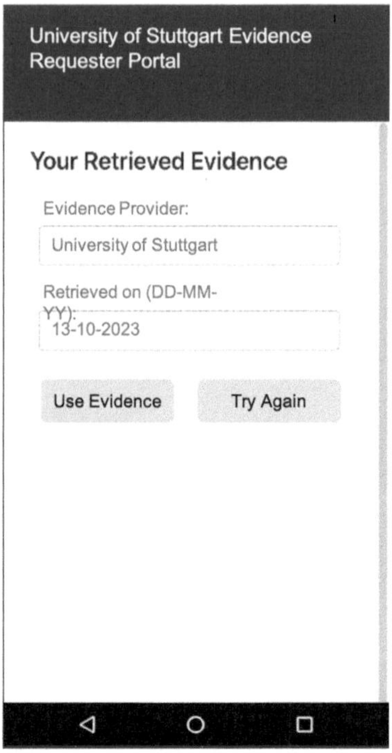

Fig. 7 SDG Requester (first)

voters for which a voter authorization is issued, can log into the system, retrieve the voter authorization via SDG and cast a vote. The procedure to retrieve the voter authorization is orchestrated by the Service Provider component described in Sect. 2.1. This component takes care after the authentication of redirecting the voter to the SDG Interoperability System (a.k.a. SDG Requester) to retrieve it. Once the voter authorization is retrieved, the Voter Authorization Service is used to validate it and keep it into a register of authorized voters, i.e., a list equivalent to the classical electoral roll. After that, each time it is necessary to check if a voter is authorized, from the i-voting Voter Portal or the i-voting Admin Portal, the Voter Authorization Service can be used. The service validates the digital signature of the voter authorization and that the name, family name, and date of birth match the ones of the voter. The public key used to validate voter authorization is generated by the Voter Authorization Manager and can only be installed by and administrator into the Voter Authorization Service.

4 Pilot Events

Two pilots were conducted for the mGov4EU project, one in the University of Tartu and the other in the Fraunhofer Institute in Stuttgart. In the first pilot, the

Fig. 8 SDG Data Provider

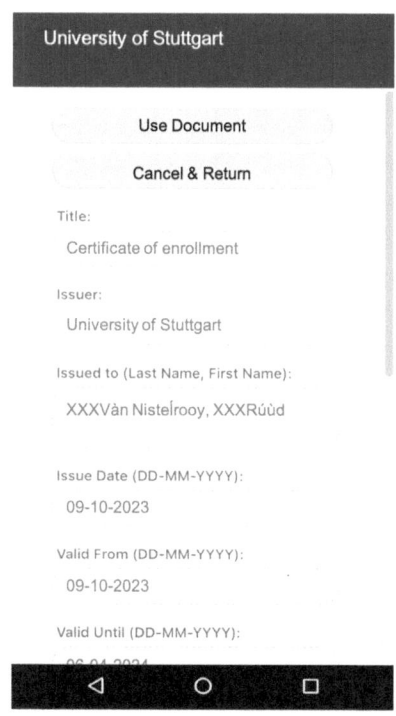

authentication with eID and Wallet has been tested, and in the second pilot, in addition to the authentication, we have also tested the authorization retrieved via SDG.

4.1 Pilot Event #1: University of Tartu

The first pilot took place in June 2023 in the University of Tartu, where eight persons participated during a shared session with their own smartphones in most of the cases. Some of the users were requested to enrol and authenticate with the eID and some with the Wallet. Although the enrolment process was not part of the pilot, it was necessary to configure the personal phone of each participant. The pilot consisted of the following steps:

1. **Training to prepare the smartphones:** The first part of the session consisted of a presentation explaining to the users how they could install and use all the applications needed to conduct the pilot: Biometrics app, eIDAS app, eID app, and Wallet app. The first application was used to conduct a compatibility test to see if the phone supported certain characteristics required for the eID and Wallet apps. The other applications are the ones described in Sect. 2, except the eID App, which is an application that allowed using test eIDs of Austria.

Fig. 9 SDG Requester
(back)

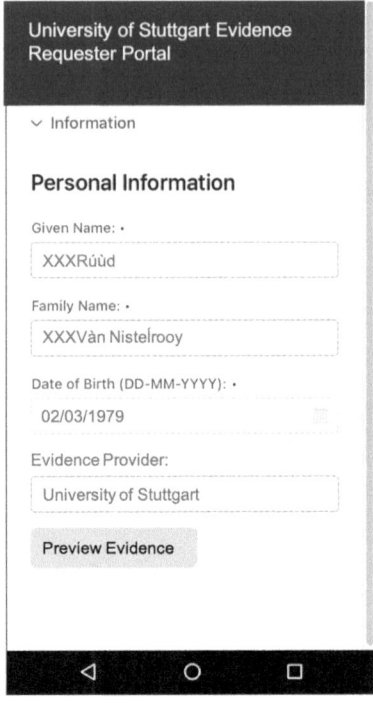

2. **Enrolment of voters**: After the training, we performed the process of enrolment with the users. We created a user for each pilot participant that was linked to the eID app in their smartphone or loaded as user credential in the Wallet app. In both cases, the process required the user to scan a QR code provided by us to do the enrolment.
3. **Authentication and voting session:** After the process of enrolment was completed, the users were able to authenticate and vote using the eID or Wallet depending on the type of credential created during the enrolment.
4. **Survey:** After voting, the users filled out a survey about the pilot experience they had.

In this pilot, all the participants successfully voted with a smartphone. The pilot proved to be valuable in uncovering aspects that were not initially anticipated. For instance, there were reservations among some individuals about using their fingerprints, fearing possible misuse elsewhere, even though their fingerprints were managed by the operating system of their respective phones. As the users were given the responsibility of installing and configuring the prototype apps and the eWallet handles cutting-edge technology not known before to the users, a lot of support and a personalized attention had to be provided to some of the users in order to enable them to successfully use the system.

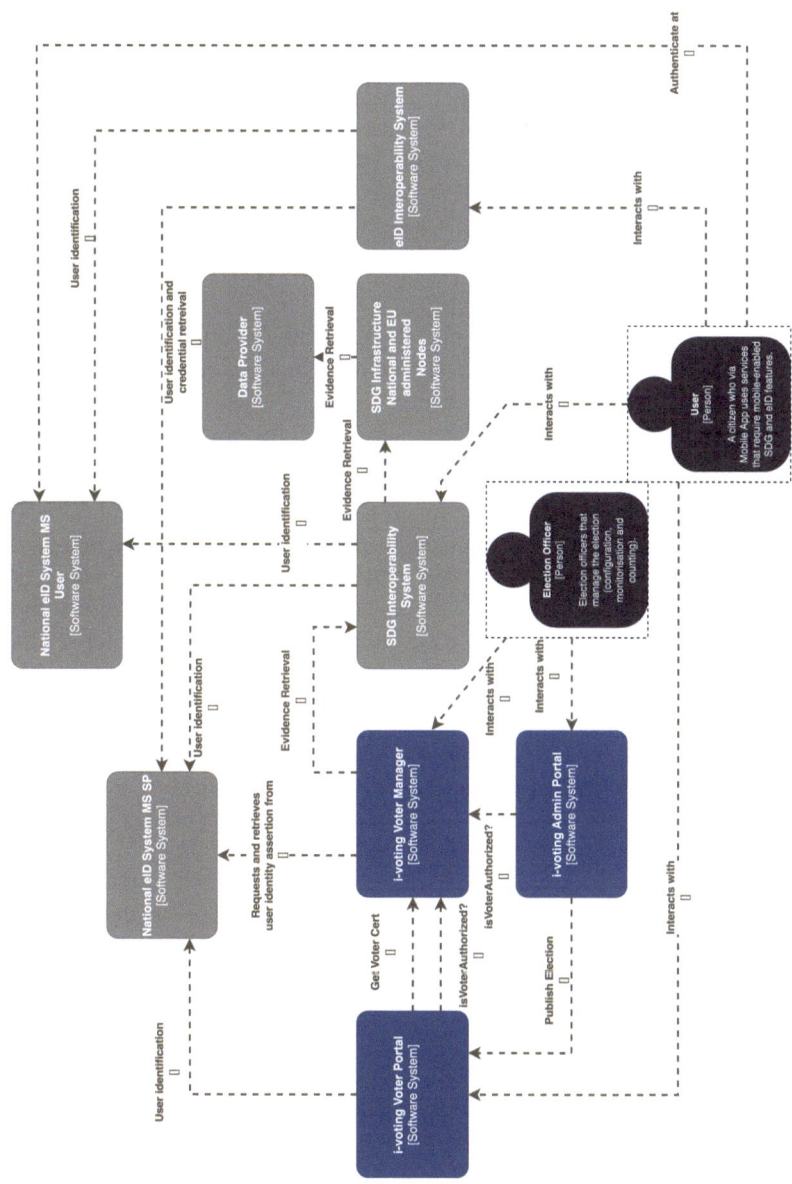

Fig. 10 Online voting system modules integrated with eID and SDG building blocks

4.2   Pilot Event #2: University of Stuttgart

The second pilot took place in October 2023 at the Fraunhofer Institute in Stuttgart. This pilot was organized in a different manner compared to the first one. We collaborated with Fraunhofer IAO to define and evaluate the user experience of the participants of the pilot. Each participant was given a time slot of 1 hour during the 2 days of pilot testing. The participant went through a series of interview questions and questionnaires. Starting off, each participant received a description of a hypothetical use case where they were students and had to participate in a university election where students had the right to vote. After being introduced to the user story, they had to complete an interview alongside completing different tasks they would have going through the pilot.

These tasks were to:

1. Authenticate themselves with either the Digital Wallet or eID.
2. Retrieving documents (e.g., certificate of enrolment) needed for extra voter authorization using the SDG component.
3. Casting their vote. After this interview, the user completed a series of various usability and user experience surveys.

Eleven persons participated with test smartphones that had been previously set up and provided to them. In this manner, in comparison to the first pilot, the pilot only focused on evaluating authentication, voter authorization with SDG, and voting, not the enrolment process of the phones, which was not part of the scope of the pilot. Half of the participants used the eID and the other half the Wallet for authentication. The pilot user test consisted of the following steps:

1. **Presentation and start of interview:** Each participant was explained about the simulated use case, and the user test interview started.
2. **Authentication:** The participant tried to authenticate using the eID or the Wallet, depending on the instructions given, and was interviewed about the experience regarding the authentication part of the pilot.
3. **Retrieval of voter authorization:** Then the participant tried to retrieve voter authorization using the SDG mechanism and was interviewed about the experience regarding the SDG part of the pilot.
4. **Voting:** After that, each participant selected the desired voting option, casted the vote, and was interviewed about the experience regarding the voting part of the pilot.
5. **End of the interview:** After completing all the steps of the pilots, each participant had to answer final questions on their general perceptions of the components or steps conducted. Users reflected on the user experience and usability along with stating challenges or pain points they had or gave suggestions.
6. **Completion of usability and user experience surveys:** after completing the interview, the user was asked to reflect on the usability and user experience that they had by filling out a variety of surveys (e.g., SUS, UEQ).

In the second pilot, all the participants could vote, except one. An unforeseen technical issue occurred and did not allow the user to participate within the allocated timeslot. In contrast to the initial pilot, in the second pilot, participants were given test phones containing pre-configured fingerprints of the supporting staff. This approach eliminated the need for users to manage configurations or engage with biometrics directly. Hence, we incorporated lessons learned from the initial pilot and modified our approach in the second pilot to concentrate solely on gathering feedback regarding the usability of the components developed within the project.

5 Lessons Learned and Conclusions

After finishing the two pilots of mGov4EU, we have gathered several valuable insights and lessons learnt. This section will outline them, bringing this chapter to a conclusion.

- **Lack of unique citizen identifier at the European level:** The lack of this unique identifier is troublesome because it implies that the same user in two different Member States might have associated two different profiles. In practice, this means that the same physical person might be seen as two different persons. This is very important in the context of elections. If this person has two different eIDs, one from the home country and another from the residence country, it might end up, for example, voting twice in the European elections. This emphasizes the relevance of appropriate identity-matching mechanisms that ensure that identity information obtained through eIDAS-based authentication processes can be successfully match to existing identity-data records even if unique identifiers differ. Because of this, for our pilots, we decided to use a combination of the name, family name, and date of birth. This approach prevents the same person to vote twice, but it requires consistency of these parameters among the different Member States, so small differences such as abbreviations or similar can lead to two profiles for the same person. Also, there is a risk that two persons in the same origin and residence country share the same name, family name, and date of birth. If that would be the case, then only one of them could vote.
- **Lack of awareness of common biometric functionalities included in present smartphones:** In the first pilot, we had several cases of participants who did not know how the fingerprint mechanism of their personal phones operated. In these cases, they do not even had it configured, and we had to help them do it. People participating in the first stage of the pilot were significantly older than those who participated in the second pilot. Probably, young people are more used to these kinds of mechanisms that are included in our current smartphones. This is a factor to take into account because by including applications that necessitate cutting-edge technologies, certain groups of citizens may find themselves unable to use them.

- **Reluctancy of participants to use biometrics:** During the first pilot, one participant did not want to use biometrics due to the sensitivity of this type of data. Despite receiving the explanation that this data would only be managed by the operating system of their personal smartphone and would be stored within secure hardware, the person did not agree to use it. As in the previous point, we might have some groups of citizens that do not want to use biometrics, and if it is a requirement for the application, these citizens will be reluctant to use it.
- **Thorough user interface design is highly important to guarantee a seamless user experience:** In the second pilot, we have analyzed the user experience, and it has become clear that the user interface is a very important factor in the usability of a system. If the user interface is well designed, all the elements of the application are self-explanatory, and it is not needed to do complex trainings to the users in order to use the system.

The pilot has proven to be an enriching experience, allowing us to test the project's building blocks with real users. We could analyze and detect aspects that we did not foresee during the design, e.g., the unawareness of some users about the usage of biometrics in current smartphones. Additionally, we had the opportunity to test emerging technologies like SDG in the context of online voting.

References

1. Fuglerud, K., Halbach, T.: An evaluation of Web-based voting usability and accessibility. Univ. Access Inf. Soc. (2011)
2. Willemson, J., Krips, K.: Estimating carbon footprint of paper and internet voting. In: Volkamer, M., et al. (eds.) Electronic voting. E-Vote-ID 2023. Lecture Notes in Computer Science, vol. 14230. Springer, Cham (2023)
3. Neumann, S., Volkamer, M., Budurushi, J., et al.: SecIVo: a quantitative security evaluation framework for internet voting schemes. Ann. Telecommun. **71**, 337–352 (2016)
4. Volkamer, M.: Evaluation of electronic voting: requirements and evaluation procedures to support responsible election authorities. Springer, Berlin, Heidelberg (2009)
5. Regulation (EU) No 910/2014 of 23 July 2014 on electronic identification and trust services for electronic transactions in the internal market and repealing Directive 1999/93/EC

Ethical and Data Protection Considerations in Mobile Government: An EU Perspective

Hans Graux ⓘ

Abstract The European legal and policy framework in the last few years has increasingly focused on ways to empower citizens in taking control over their data. With respect to mobile eGovernment, this can be seen both in data protection law, in legislation concerning once-only information exchanges, and in the current proposals surrounding mobile identity wallets. This chapter will examine how these rules interact, what the legal and ethical implications are, and what the limitations and points of conflict might be. We will also examine how a project like mGov4EU is impacted by these rules and where the project can and has innovated or expanded on the general legal and ethical principles within the confines of the law.

Keywords Fundamental rights · Ethics · Data protection · GDPR · eIDAS · Mobile wallets

1 Fundamental Rights and Data Protection in the EU and in eGovernment

1.1 General Background

In recent years, data protection and privacy protection have become increasingly prominent in our information society, and public services are no exception to this rule. As citizens, we know—and sometimes appreciate—that our various public administrations rely on fairly extensive and high-quality data collection and exchanges in relation to us and our activities to organise the performance of public tasks effectively. Taxation, education, health care, social services, law enforcement, and any other essential tasks of government either require such data to function or can be made much more effective because of it.

H. Graux (✉)
Timelex Law Offices, Brussels, Belgium
e-mail: hans.graux@timelex.eu

109

V. Homburg et al. (eds.), *From Electronic to Mobile Government*,
https://doi.org/10.1007/978-3-031-64471-9_7

Nonetheless, this does not imply that there are no limitations to the collection and exchange of personal data in an eGovernment context. The mere fact of acting in the public interest doesn't justify excessive or otherwise unjustifiable intrusions into our private life. A balanced and equitable assessment is always required, through which public authorities—like any other stakeholder—must determine and justify whether any intended collection and use of personal data is in line with the European fundamental rights framework and with their mandate as defined under national law.

Data protection and privacy play an important role in this balancing act. These are two separate fundamental rights, which can be found, among other sources, in the *Charter of Fundamental Rights of the European Union* [1], where they are enshrined in Articles 7 and 8, respectively. Although these two rights look and feel similar and have many points in common in practice, they are nonetheless distinct. Privacy protection relates in general to respect for one's private life, family life, home, and communications. Data protection requires that one's personal data—i.e. data that can somehow be linked to an individual, such as their name, address, e-mail, photos, evaluations, or identification numbers—is handled in a proper and careful manner.

The difference is not without importance, and an unjustified equating of privacy and data protection regularly causes misunderstandings. It is perfectly possible (and common) to handle someone's personal data carelessly—and thus infringe on the right to data protection—without violating their privacy. A typical example is the making of decisions based on incorrect personal data or accidentally deleting someone's data: these are clear violations of the right to data protection, but it does not necessarily have an impact on privacy.

Public administrations are not exempted from these considerations: the fact that they act in the general interest, and have a legal mandate to do so, does not override the need for them to respect the rights to privacy and data protection. The aforementioned charter also contains a fundamental right to good administration (Article 41), but this right focuses on the citizen's rights in relation to EU bodies, rather than granting administrations any particular privileges on this point. As a result, public administrations must also be able to justify why they are allowed to collect and use certain personal data, how it falls within their legal mandate, and how they respect the fundamental principles of EU data protection law.

The main legal source in Europe with respect to personal data protection is, of course, the well-known General Data Protection Regulation (GDPR) [2]. The GDPR is a European regulation, and as such, it is directly applicable in all Member States of the European Union. It establishes a set of general rules and principles, which apply in the absence of a more specific framework for a particular sector. For most public service activities, the GDPR is the main source of data protection law.

The GDPR sets out a set of basic principles that must be respected in any processing of personal data—i.e. whenever personal data is collected, exchanged, analysed, or modified, including by public sector bodies. These are neatly listed in Article 5 of the GDPR. Very briefly summarised:

- Any processing activity must be *lawful and transparent*. Lawfulness requires that one must be able to justify why the collection or use of the personal data is permissible, for example, because one had the consent of the data subject, because there is a legal obligation to conduct the data processing activity, or because the processing is necessary for the performance of a task carried out in the public interest.
  The latter possibility is of course most commonly applicable to eGovernment services, where the task be defined under national or EU law (i.e. it is not possible for a public administration to merely declare that it is acting in the public interest—it must be able to point to a specific mandate that allows it to perform this task).
- Any processing must be limited to *specified, explicit, and legitimate purposes*. Even public administrations therefore have to indicate what they intend to do with the data and respect that constraint. Thus, the fact that personal data were lawfully collected does not imply that they may subsequently be used for any purpose.
- All processing must be *minimal*: no more data may be collected than necessary for the intended purposes.
- All processing must be as *accurate* as possible: all reasonable measures must be taken to collect accurate data and to correct it when it is no longer correct.
- Any processing must be *limited in time*: data may be kept for as long as necessary for the intended purpose, and then it must be erased or anonymised.
- All processing must be *secure*: taking into account the context, the sensitivity of the data, and the available technology, measures must be taken to avoid unauthorised processing (including loss, damage, and unauthorised access).
- And finally, each data controller is responsible for compliance with all these principles, with an obligation to be able to demonstrate compliance (so-called accountability).

With respect to the notion of a data controller, the approach of European data protection law has always been that a party (or a group of parties) must be designated as a "controller" for every act of processing of personal data. According to the GDPR, this controller determines the purpose and means of the processing and must ensure that the GDPR is demonstrably complied with. By way of example, a public sector body providing an eGovernment service will generally be considered the data controller for any data processing activities that it conducts in the context of that service.

These notions also apply in the context of mobile eGovernment services. When using a mobile device to interact with a public administration, that public administration will generally be the data controller for the processing activities that it undertakes following its receipt of the personal data. For that reason, it will have to adhere to all of the aforementioned principles: it must be able to identify its legal basis (general the legal mandate that it was given), to conduct the processing activities, request minimal data only, and process that data only for the purposes that it communicated specifically to the citizen.

1.2   mGov4EU: At the Intersection of Identification, Once-Only, and Reliable Information Exchanges

As an EU-funded research project, mGov4EU explores the intersection between various eGovernment functions. Specifically, the project assesses how mobile applications can be used to identify oneself towards public and private sector service providers, to create legally binding electronic signatures, and to organise trustworthy information exchanges. Beyond the GDPR that was briefly discussed above, there are two other legal frameworks that strongly affect legal and ethical challenges in the project: the Single Digital Gateway Regulation (SDGR) [3] and the eIDAS Regulation [4].

The SDGR is a regulation that essentially aims to facilitate eGovernment information exchanges in relation to certain common life events: birth, moving residences, retiring, and so forth. These life events are set out in the SDGR itself. For the purposes of the mGov4EU project, the salient element of the SDGR is that it requires Member States to establish, by the end of 2023, a technical system that satisfies EU-level compliance requirements and which can be used to reliably exchange information between trusted public administrations.

One of the objectives of the European Single Digital Gateway, as supported by the technical system, is to enable once-only information exchanges between public administrations in different Member States. For the purposes of this contribution, the once-only principle implies that governments should not ask a citizen (or a company, but this contribution focuses on citizens) to provide information that they could also get from another administration. Instead, they should request it directly from the administration that already holds it. The citizen, therefore, provides the information "once-only" to the first administration, and thereafter all other administrations must request it from the first recipient. This reduces the administrative burden for the citizen, increases efficiency and effectiveness of eGovernment, and improves the quality of public administration.

The data protection and ethical challenges in relation to the once-only principle have already been extensively discussed elsewhere [5]. Briefly summarised, especially in a cross-border context, the European legislator found it necessary to allocate a central controlling role as a gatekeeper for information exchanges to the citizen itself. Exchanges of information, including personal data, cannot be exchanged via the technical system under the SDGR, except with the prior explicit request of the citizen, and after giving them the opportunity to review the information to be exchanged. While there are certain limited exceptions to this rule, citizens are therefore in charge of the application of the once-only principle at the EU level: public administrations in different Member States will not be able to request or exchange information without the prior knowledge and approval of the citizen. This has been considered an important data protection and ethics safeguard for EU data protection authorities [6].

The SDGR is important for the mGov4EU project, since the mobile applications that are designed within the project are intended to be capable of interacting with the SDGR technical system. The services piloted in mGov4EU are not, as such, services falling within the scope of the SDGR—they are not among the "life events" listed in the regulation—but they do aim to pilot features (identification, pseudonymisation, data minimisations, signing) that are crucial for the operation of the Single Digital Gateway.

For that reason, the mGov4EU app must also be able to sustain the requirements of the SDGR, such as the prior request and preview functionalities. This is especially important since mobile services are not directly referenced in the SGDR, nor in the specifications of the technical system [7]: while no part of these frameworks prohibits mobile identification and authentication apps, they do not explain how they should function in a once-only context either. This is one of the areas in which mGov4EU was required to advance upon the state of the art.

Second, next to the SDGR, the mGov4EU project also had to take into account the provisions of the eIDAS Regulation [4]. This regulation mainly focuses on two different topics, both of which are important to the project:

- **Electronic identification** in a cross-border eGovernment context. Essentially, the eIDAS Regulation allows Member States to inform each other and the European Commission of electronic identification schemes that are used in national eGovernment services. Following a successful peer review, these schemes are placed in a publicly accessible list, and thereafter other Member States are required to accept the notified means of identification in their own eGovernment applications. The Regulation foresees the establishment and maintenance of a network of so-called eIDAS nodes, which ensure that the notified identification means are also supported in practice. The eIDAS Regulation formally only targets public sector services; the private sector is not required to support notified schemes.
- **Trust services, including electronic signatures.** The Regulation allows citizens to use several types of electronic signatures, with varying levels of legal scrutiny and legal authority behind them. The category of electronic signatures with the highest compliance threshold, so-called qualified signatures, are legally considered equivalent to handwritten signatures. Where electronic identification is essentially under government control, trust services are a market service that can be freely provided by private companies across the EU.

Within the mGov4EU project, the objective was to establish a mobile solution that allowed electronic identification and electronic signing, including at the qualified electronic signature level. Compliance with the eIDAS Regulation was therefore essential. It is worth noting that the Regulation as it stands today is mute on the use of mobile solutions: they are neither explicitly endorsed nor explicitly forbidden. In practice, for both identification and signatures, there already are mobile-driven solutions in the EU market. mGov4EU's mission was to seek a solution that could satisfy both the requirements of the SDGR and the eIDAS Regulation, including by piloting minimal disclosure solutions (which are in practice not supported by the eIDAS Regulation). In this way, mGov4EU could improve the data protection and ethical safeguards of eIDAS compliant solutions, including towards eGovernment services.

When considering these elements, it is also important to note that mGov4EU is not, in fact, restricted to a purely public sector context. The ambition is to support a broader ecosystem of stakeholders, including in the private sector. This applies to all three pilots: the eSigning pilot can be used towards any public or private sector entity; the iVoting pilot could also be used for voting in a private company; and the mobility pilot uses the mobile application to interact with private mobility services providers, such as taxi companies. None are inherently limited to public sector use cases.

Through this perspective, mGov4EU extends the legal and ethical safeguards that are built into the SDGR and eIDAS context to a broader range of stakeholders.

However, it is also important to recognise the influence of an initiative that emerged after the mGov4EU proposal was submitted: the amendment of the eIDAS Regulation and notably the introduction of EU Digital Identity Wallets. This topic will be discussed in detail in the next section of this chapter.

2   The eIDAS 2 Amendment and the EU Digital Identity Wallet Model: Concept and Key Fundamental Rights Choices

2.1   General Concept of the Wallets

The eIDAS Regulation can be credited with introducing the first cross-cutting (non-sector specific) legal framework for eID interoperability in Europe. It was, however, not without flaws. One of the choices of the Regulation was to remain as agnostic as possible on the underlying technologies used by citizens to identify themselves or to sign documents. This created flexibility but also resulted in doubts on the ability of mobile solutions to satisfy the requirements of the legal framework. It is not unreasonable to say that the eIDAS Regulation was "mobile-tolerant", rather than "mobile-aware".

In June 2021, the Commission therefore proposed an amendment to the eIDAS Regulation [8], which is occasionally referenced as eIDAS 2, eIDAS 2.0, or the EUDIR (EU Digital Identity Regulation); the present chapter will refer to it as eIDAS 2. Following extensive negotiations, a provisional agreement on the proposal was reached between the Council and the European Parliament [9], although the full legislative procedure is still to be concluded at the time of drafting of this chapter (December 2023), as the formal adoption by the Parliament and the Council is still pending.

The eIDAS 2 amendment brings many innovations to the table. From the perspective of mGov4EU, the most significant ones are undoubtedly the introduction of EU Digital Identity Wallets (EUDIWs or simply Wallets in this chapter) and the creation of a legal framework for electronic attribute attestation.

EU Digital Identity Wallets represent a fundamental shift in the European landscape for electronic identification, on many grounds. Firstly of course, there is the simple fact that they represent a clear technological choice: Wallets are inherently a mobile solution, thus abandoning the relatively technology agnostic approach of the original eIDAS Regulation. While Member States are free to create their own national variant(s) of the Wallet, all Wallets must support key functionalities and follow the same basic architecture to ensure interoperability.

Perhaps even more importantly, all Member States are obliged to offer Wallets to their citizens, free of charge. This is a significant departure from the eIDAS model, where the impacts of electronic identification were to some extent an "opt-in" choice for the Member States: they were not required to notify any electronic identification scheme. While they would still need to accept notified eIDs from other Member States, this could significantly limit the practical benefits of the Regulation in Member States that chose not to sign up to the logic of the European legislator.

Finally, the original eIDAS Regulation focused only on electronic identification towards public sector services—not towards the private sector. This too is abandoned under eIDAS 2: the Wallets can be used towards a broad range of relying parties, without any inherent limitation to the public sector.

Next to the Wallet, a second innovation that eIDAS 2 brings to the table is the notion of electronic attribute attestations. Essentially, such attestations are digital statements that specify one or more characteristics in relation to a specific person. Examples could be a statement of their nationality, whether they are adults, whether they have a specific degree, and so forth. The attestations are signed by their issuer, allowing their reliability to be verified by relying parties (provided of course that those parties can determine their trust in the issuer).

Attribute attestations are significant from a data protection perspective, since they allow information to be shared pseudonymously: information about a person can be released to a third party without necessarily and automatically also disclosing their identity. In this way, applications can much more easily respect the data minimisation principle, since they only receive the information they require, instead of also receiving irrelevant information that they then are technically required to immediately delete.

Moreover, attribute attestations offer an extensible model for increasing the information that can be stored in a Wallet in a standardised and transparent manner: in addition to a set of basic identity information that was supported under the original eIDAS (name, address, nationality, date of birth, and so forth), the concept of attribute attestations allows citizens to determine which information they wish to carry with them—diplomas, driving licences, passports, customer cards, etc. The options are unlimited.

In that sense, the Wallet is a significant tool for empowering citizens to take charge of their own data.

2.2 Ethical and Data Protection Perspectives in Relation to the Wallets

Based on that assessment, the beneficial potential of Wallets is clear. There are however also some implicit and explicit ethical and data protection choices that were made to establish the Wallet concept as described above. These are worth discussing briefly, since they are relevant for mGov4EU as a project and also because they create potential tensions for the future.

A first question that always arises whenever a digital technology is enabled, promoted, or mandated is the question of accessibility and non-discrimination and the digital divide. Using a Wallet effectively requires literal and digital literacy. While awareness raising and training campaigns can improve the status quo, a December 2023 study [10] showed that approximately 32% of Europeans still lack basic digital skills. These citizens are likely to struggle when using a Wallet, or they may not be able to use it at all.

The eIDAS 2 amendment contains no obligation for citizens to request or use a Wallet, and it imposes accessibility requirements to ensure usability for persons with disabilities, but nonetheless, persons with strong digital skills may de facto be able to access and use digital services more easily via their Wallets. This is an ethically risky premise, since the Wallets are emphatically also used for eGovernment services— i.e. services that public administrations should make available for all citizens, irrespective of digital skills. In practical terms, this will likely be managed by ensuring the availability of non-digital alternatives, but nonetheless, the digitally less capable will suffer a disadvantage.

There may also be challenges related to economic discrimination. While the eIDAS 2 draft text makes no explicit references to the choices that need to be made, it is not rationally feasible to create Wallets that will support literally every phone and every operating system that has ever been available in Europe. Reasonable choices will need to be made, as with any other app, to support mobile devices and mobile operating systems that are reasonably up to date, secure, and sufficiently common. But even when applying these criteria in the most careful and well-considered manner, inevitably some small amount of users will find themselves in a situation where they will not be able to interact with their government in the same manner as their neighbour, for the sole reason that their phone is too old or too much of a niche model. The choice is ethically inevitable and partially inherent to every eGovernment service (whether mobile or not), but an assumption that every

EU citizen has access to a sufficiently recent and secure smartphone would be overly optimistic. The acceptance of this limitation is also an implicit ethical choice.

Secondly, it should be recognised that eIDAS 2 is quite explicit and clear about the Wallet's capability to identify specific citizens: under the newly minted article 11a, Member States have to ensure unique identification of the citizen whenever a Wallet is used for authentication. Each Wallet must contain a predefined minimum set of person identification data, which must contain "a unique and persistent identifier in conformity with Union law, to identify the user upon their request in those cases where identification of the user is required by law". Pseudonymity is permissible; anonymity is not. This is not an unreasonable choice, given that the Wallet aims to support and enable trustworthy identification of citizens, but it is not ethically neutral. Traceability of user behaviour—albeit only with the cooperation of the relevant government entities—is a key characteristic of the Wallet.

A third and much more overt ethical choice that eIDAS 2 makes in relation to the Wallet is the statement that "the user shall be in full control of the European Digital Identity Wallet. The issuer of the European Digital Identity Wallet shall not collect information about the use of the wallet which are not necessary for the provision of the wallet services, nor shall it combine person identification data and any other personal data stored or relating to the use of the European Digital Identity Wallet with personal data from any other services offered by this issuer or from third-party services which are not necessary for the provision of the wallet services, unless the user has expressly requested it" (article 6a.7 of the amended eIDAS Regulation).

In simpler terms: the organisation (which can be a public or private sector body) that issues Wallets to citizens) is not allowed to monitor, track, or evaluate the use of the Wallet or to combine information in or via the Wallet to increase their knowledge of the user. This is an important ethical and data protection safeguard, since the issuer of the Wallet could otherwise introduce functionalities (transparently or covertly) that allow them to build a profile of the citizens and subject them to risks and penalties. This type of behaviour is explicitly banned under eIDAS 2.

This approach has broader data protection implications as well, which are worth briefly addressing. As was highlighted in the introductory sections of this chapter, EU data protection law is based on the principle that personal data processing activities fall under the responsibility of a so-called data controller, i.e. the party that determines the purposes and means of the data-processing activity. With respect to Wallets and the personal data that they contain, multiple types of processing activities can occur, each of which can have different data controllers. By way of examples:

- The *issuance and onboarding of a Wallet* will imply personal data processing activities, since each Wallet instance must be linked to a specific holder and authentication credentials must be issued. This is a data processing for which the Wallet issuer will be the data controller.
- When *creating personal identity documents or issuing attribute attestations to a Wallet,* that too is a transfer of personal data and thus a data-processing activity, for which the data provider will generally be the data controller.

- Whenever *providing data from the Wallet to a relying party*, that relying party will process the personal data for whichever business purposes that it may have defined. This too is a personal data-processing activity, for which the relying party will be the data controller.

All of the above are relatively self-evident examples. But what about the data that's being stored and managed in the Wallet by the user themselves? Is this also a data-processing activity that's subject to the GDPR? And if so, who is the data controller?

The answer cannot be found in the text of eIDAS 2 itself, which mainly points out that the GDPR should be fully adhered to in relation to the Wallet. However, logically, only one answer seems realistic: the management of the Wallet by the user itself should be considered (in the phrasing of the GDPR, recital (18) and article 2.2 c) an act of "processing of personal data by a natural person in the course of a purely personal or household activity and thus with no connection to a professional or commercial activity. Personal or household activities could include correspondence and the holding of addresses, or social networking and online activity undertaken within the context of such activities". Under this so-called "household exemption", the GDPR does not apply.

This outcome is desirable and has no readily apparent alternatives. If the management of one's own Wallet would not be considered a purely personal or household activity, the citizen would be qualified as a data controller in their own right and need to adhere to the obligations of the GDPR (e.g. by publishing transparency notices, keeping records of its processing activities, creating a data protection impact assessment, negotiating appropriate data processing agreements prior to every use of the Wallet, etc.). This would clearly not be reasonable or feasible.

If, on the other hand, an existing entity—such as a public administration or the Wallet issuer—would be considered to be a data controller for the mere management of the Wallet, that would imply that that entity would need to be able to document the purposes for which the Wallet is used and who the data is shared with and again negotiate appropriate agreements with every relying party. It would grant that entity precisely the central monitoring role that the eIDAS 2 proposal aims to resolve. Thus, this approach is neither desirable nor logical in the context of the Wallet.

This leads to the situation where citizens are indeed free to manage their own personal data, including by choosing to whom they would disclose it, precisely as envisaged by eIDAS 2. The ethical and data protection choice that eIDAS 2 makes is to grant the user control over their data. This, however, also comes with complex risks, as will be explored below.

2.3   Reliable Interactions with eGovernment Services and with Third Parties

In principle, citizens are thus free to choose whether they wish to own a Wallet, whether they use it, which information (in the form of the attribute attestations) they store on it, and to whom they make it available. Citizen empowerment seems ethically unproblematic—and at any rate, the concept of an electronic Wallet thus remains intuitively close to that of a physical wallet: usage decisions are generally under the sole control of the holder.

However, this freedom also comes with some risks, which are not (yet) conclusively addressed in eIDAS 2. The Regulation foresees that relying parties—entities that wish to rely on information received from the Wallet—must first register themselves in the Member State where they are established. This registration includes their identification and a description of their intended use case, including their data needs. They are required to respect the terms of this registration.

However, the registration and the limitations set out therein are not enforced by the Wallet. A relying party must identify itself to the user of the Wallet, and Member States must provide a common mechanism for allowing the identification and authentication of relying parties (article 6b of the amended eIDAS Regulation). But it is not required for a Wallet to block the disclosure of attribute attestations if the relying party cannot be authenticated as being registered for a use case that requires access to the attributes. In simple terms: when the Wallet cannot determine whether a requesting party is allowed to receive information, the user makes the decision.

This places a significant risk management duty with the users, since they will decide whether, e.g. their birth certificate or medical data can be entrusted to a relying party; there are no safeguards to protect them against unwise decisions. Given the aforementioned claimed digital illiteracy rate, this is an ethically risky proposition, as has also been examined elsewhere [11].

The approach is also a significant step away from the exchanges of information in the context of the Single Digital Gateway described above. In the SDG's technical system, claimed competent authorities have to be registered at the national level, and an inability to determine their identity and competences will result in information exchanges being halted—the citizen cannot override the architectural protections. From a data protected by design perspective, this approach is clearly superior—albeit with the caveat that it is also inherently somewhat condescending and patronising, since it assumes that citizens must be protected against themselves.

For completeness, it should be recognised that the final text of eIDAS 2 is still undergoing cleanup, and it is not impossible that the implementation of the text (i.e. the standardised architecture and technical specifications of the Wallet) is stricter than what is outlined above. It would, e.g. be feasible to allow citizens to make decisions freely in proximity scenarios (where they are physically close to a desiring party that wishes to access the data, e.g. in the context of a traffic stop) while imposing more rigid authentications for fully remote processes (e.g. when a citizen wants to use their Wallet to start a company in a new Member State). In this way, an equitable balance between empowerment and protection could be struck.

3   An mGov4EU Perspective

The mGov4EU project encountered the ethical and data protection challenges above, albeit with the caveat that it was not formally subjected to either the SDGR nor to the eIDAS 2 amendment: the SDGR does not enter fully into force until the end of 2023, and at any rate, the pilot services did not fall within the scope of the SDGR, and the eIDAS 2 amendment is not yet even definitively adopted at the time of closing of this chapter. For that reason, neither of their requirements technically applied (and indeed, the eIDAS 2 ambitions with respect to Wallets were not even clearly understood or articulated yet when the mGov4EU proposal was prepared). Nonetheless, the project has endeavoured to explore some of the ethical and data protection challenges and can therefore provide some lessons learned and some insights.

A first and somewhat predictable insight was that, in the absence of any clear legal framework other than the GDPR and the original eIDAS Regulation, it was challenging to set up appropriate contractual frameworks that satisfied the requirements of the GDPR (i.e. data processing agreements). This was not due to their unusual complexity but mainly due to delays in finalising piloting preparations and due to administrative slowdowns. This issue might be mitigated to some extent in cases where the services would also fall under the SDGR and information exchanges are thus based on a legally defined duty, rather than on a pilot project; but nonetheless, legal formalities must not be overlooked.

A second insight was the importance of user-friendliness and ease of use. In order to realistically test potential compliance with the GDPR, SDGR, and eIDAS, it is necessary not only to follow specific steps (initiating a request, identification of the user, disclosing the parties involved, showing information to be exchanged, and obtaining consents) but also to show these steps to the pilot participants. While this is undoubtedly transparent and ethically sound, it also resulted in a suboptimal user experience, with users commonly indicating that they had to take many more steps than they had anticipated. It should not be forgotten that the intuitive benchmark for users are modern apps on their phone, not traditional paper procedures.

Finally, it should also be recognised that the mGov4EU project was not a good test case to determine, e.g. risks in relation to unresponsible disclosure to unknown and untrusted relying parties. The pilots were all conducted in tightly controlled conditions, where the service providers were known to be trustworthy and authenticated as such, where this could be clearly communicated to the pilot participants and where there were at any rate no real-life risks involved. On that critical ethical question—are users capable of protecting themselves in the absence of conclusive technological safeguards—the mGov4EU project cannot offer an answer.

4   Perspectives for the Future

As the sections above have hopefully demonstrated, the legal framework surrounding mobile eGovernment in the EU is strongly in flux at this moment, with both the SDGR being under implementation and the eIDAS 2 amendment in its finalisation stages before adoption. While this flux was not entirely foreseen when the mGov4EU proposal was being prepared, this has created an interesting dynamic for the project, allowing it to spearhead the identification of potential ethical and data protection challenges and to test potential solutions.

Generally, piloting outcomes have been positive for the most parts, and the legal and ethical constraints could be appropriately managed. Principally, the GDPR and SDGR were admittedly found to be administratively demanding during piloting, but not problematic as such.

Nonetheless, it is also important to recognise that several problems were not in scope of mGov4EU and will still need a structural solution in the future:

- As described above, the question of *verification of relying parties* towards whom data will be shared from a Wallet is important. Both the empowerment model ("citizen decides, no protections needed") and the protective model ("only registered and known relying parties can be interacted with") have their ethical and data protection merits, but the choice made by the eIDAS 2 amendment is still fairly vague. Solutions to effectively protect less digitally literate users should be explored.
- Interactions with specific legal frameworks, such as the *SDGR,* are not clearly understood yet. Wallets can be used to identify a user in an SDGR process, but what freedoms and liberties does a user then have? Specifically, if a user receives information in the context of an SDGR procedure, can they choose to store that information in their Wallet? If so, this opens the door to potential misuse, since it allows SDGR procedures to be initiated in order to get access to evidentiary documents that are not easily available elsewhere, to cancel the procedure before it completes, and to retain the documents on one's own Wallet. In effect, it allows the SDGR framework—with its tightly controlled scope and safeguards—to be used for other purposes, such as generic data access rights requests, which have an entirely different purpose and procedure.
- Thirdly, *user interaction* should be optimised. The approach of being possibly too transparent on individual steps was not well received, since the overload of information caused doubts and uncertainty in the users, rather than assuring them of the legitimacy of the interaction.
- Fourthly and finally, it is important to recognise that a paradigm that focuses exclusively on *citizen control is not universally an optimal approach.* The challenge of digital illiteracy was already mentioned above; moreover relying on the actions of citizens does not always result in ethically and socially desirable outcomes. Persons who are vulnerable and less privileged are less likely to be able to create a Wallet and to find the appropriate channels through which they can express their wishes. For example, in the context of once-only

exchanges, it can be more beneficial to automatically exchange information in situations where this creates benefits (e.g. financial or other support) for vulnerable users that are entitled to them, rather than relying on them to file an appropriate request, via a Wallet or otherwise. This is not an issue that emerged (or could emerge) in mGov4EU, since piloting focused on volunteer users with acceptable digital skills who were guided through the process of the pilot applications. This is however not a representative sample of all eGovernment situations.

All of the above should not be taken as a criticism of the notion of Wallets, let alone of mobile eGovernment in general. It is clear, and mGov4EU has been able to demonstrate this, that there are massive benefits for the vast majority of EU citizens in using mobile eGovernment solutions. It is also obvious that the maturity of the European legal framework is increasing by leaps and bounds and that Wallets are a significant step forward in European identification and trust services. It is however also important to acknowledge that Wallets are only one solution, rather than the only solution, and that continuous expansion and optimisation of other eGovernment services are required to achieve a social optimum.

References

1. Charter of Fundamental Rights of the European Union. OJ C 326, 26.10.2012, p. 391–407; see http://data.europa.eu/eli/treaty/char_2012/oj
2. Regulation (EU) 2016/679 of the European Parliament and of the Council of 27 April 2016 on the protection of natural persons with regard to the processing of personal data and on the free movement of such data, and repealing Directive 95/46/EC (General Data Protection Regulation), OJ L 119, 4.5.2016; see http://data.europa.eu/eli/reg/2016/679/oj
3. Regulation (EU) 2018/1724 of the European Parliament and of the Council of 2 October 2018 establishing a single digital gateway to provide access to information, to procedures and to assistance and problem-solving services and amending Regulation (EU) No 1024/2012, OJ L 295, 21.11.2018; see http://data.europa.eu/eli/reg/2018/1724/oj
4. Regulation (EU) No 910/2014 of the European Parliament and of the Council of 23 July 2014 on electronic identification and trust services for electronic transactions in the internal market and repealing Directive 1999/93/EC, OJ L 257, 28.8.2014, http://data.europa.eu/eli/reg/2014/910/oj
5. Krimmer, R., Prentza, A., Mamrot, S. (Eds.): The once-only principle - the TOOP project. Springer (2021); see https://link.springer.com/book/10.1007/978-3-030-79851-2
6. Opinion 8/2017 of the EDPS on the proposal for a Regulation establishing a single digital gateway and the 'once-only' principle; see https://edps.europa.eu/sites/edp/files/publication/17-08-01_sdg_opinion_en.pdf
7. Commission Implementing Regulation (EU) 2022/1463 of 5 August 2022 setting out technical and operational specifications of the technical system for the cross-border automated exchange of evidence and application of the 'once-only' principle in accordance with Regulation (EU) 2018/1724 of the European Parliament and of the Council, OJ L 231, 6.9.2022, p. 1–21; see http://data.europa.eu/eli/reg_impl/2022/1463/oj
8. Proposal for a Regulation of the European Parliament and of the Council amending Regulation (EU) No 910/2014 as regards establishing a framework for a European

Digital Identity, COM/2021/281 final; see https://eur-lex.europa.eu/legal-content/EN/TXT/?uri=COM%3A2021%3A281%3AFIN

9. "European digital identity: Council and Parliament reach a provisional agreement on eID", Press release from the Council of the EU, 8 November 2023; see https://www.consilium.europa.eu/en/press/press-releases/2023/11/08/european-digital-identity-council-and-parliament-reach-a-provisional-agreement-on-eid/
10. Digital literacy in the EU: A roadmap; see https://data.europa.eu/en/publications/datastories/digital-literacy-eu-roadmap
11. Graux, H. (2023). Whose data is it anyway? Diverging perspectives in EU policy on the current and future role of the citizen in digital government. DGO '23: Proceedings of the 24th annual international conference on digital government research, July 2023, pp. 508–513. doi:https://doi.org/10.1145/3598469.3598526

Evaluating Digital Government Projects: Emphasizing Process and Relevance Through Transdisciplinary Research

Lucy Temple ⓘ and Gregor Eibl ⓘ

Abstract Government organizations worldwide focus on digital solutions to improve public services and enhance citizen experience. These initiatives continue to receive significant resource allocation. There exists the need for a thorough evaluation to ensure that these projects deliver the intended benefits and address citizen needs. Currently, the absence of a single suitable evaluation method poses a challenge. The complexity of these projects demands a dynamic evaluation environment to understand societal impact and relevance. Relevance implies assessing to what extent a project aligns with the stakeholders' goals, needs, and desires, mainly government organizations and citizens or businesses. This chapter explores the importance of relevance in evaluating such projects and highlights the reasons for adopting a transdisciplinary research approach. Unlike traditional disciplinary-focused approaches, transdisciplinary research focuses on real-world context and interdisciplinarity, goes beyond just science, and promotes interaction and integration among involved parties to produce high relevance. By focusing on project outcomes and processes, this research aims to propose relevant metrics for evaluating digital government projects and their relevance in a real-world context. To do so, a series of European research and development projects focusing on digital government will be analyzed using the proposed transdisciplinary evaluation framework to understand if outcomes and processes promote project relevance. This research will help enhance current evaluation approaches for digital government projects. The findings of this study will contribute to the widening of evaluation frameworks for digital government initiatives.

Keywords Transdisciplinary research · Digital government projects · Evaluation framework

L. Temple (✉) · G. Eibl
University for Continuing Education Krems, Krems an der Donau, Austria
e-mail: lucy.temple@donau-uni.ac.at; gregor.eibl@donau-uni.ac.at

© The Author(s) 2025
V. Homburg et al. (eds.), *From Electronic to Mobile Government*,
https://doi.org/10.1007/978-3-031-64471-9_8

1 Introduction

Digital transformation has become part of the European Union's (EU) agenda throughout the recent years due to the growing impact of digital technologies on economy, society, and governance. Moreover, the number of projects focused on digital transition and digital government research has increased. New legislative and regulatory frameworks are being introduced, and governments continue to explore new tools and opportunities that digitalization offers [1]. The problems that digital government seek to address require a variety of disciplines to work hand in hand to offer a solution. These disciplines range from science to practice and require collaborative engagements and expertise to address the existing problems. In order for all these disciplines to work together, a transdisciplinary approach is required to create spaces where science, policy, and industry can work together to solve the problems.

Transdisciplinary research seeks to address complex real-world problems through collaboration and teamwork [2, 3]. It focuses on finding solutions to complex problems that can't be solved from a single discipline, overcoming a fragmented view and the hyper-specialization of science with dialogue and integration [2]. Transdisciplinarity allows for mutual learning processes to occur with the integration of knowledge and perspectives from different disciplines and stakeholders, to create a more comprehensive understanding [4, 5]. This specific type of research seeks to contribute to scientific and societal progress, creating a bridge between them, by involving actors from both these areas and generating solution-oriented knowledge [4].

Digital government projects are by nature transdisciplinary or have transdisciplinary elements [6]. These are beneficial for complex undertakings, where the main goal is to support governance or technological change. They combine knowledge and experiences from a variety of domains ranging from public administration, computer science, law, and citizen science (2). Digital government requires bringing together different kinds of expertise, and the design of artifacts often requires complex negotiations and compromises between differing views, interests, strategies, regulations, and values. Therefore, transdisciplinary projects including digital government projects need to be evaluated and monitored against expected impact and planned objectives.

Evaluation is a key element of transdisciplinary projects and processes, for quality control, and as a base for continuous improvement. Due to the complexity of transdisciplinary projects, overarching methods of evaluation should be applied. Also, evaluation will help transdisciplinary research in improving its practice [3]. Within digital government, evaluation is still one of the most challenging areas, to assess if the project results produce the desired impact [7]. It becomes challenging to provide well-rounded evaluations when a variety of disciplines are included [8]. Many evaluation frameworks exist that seek to measure the impact of transdisciplinary projects [9, 10], yet there seem to be no clear way to include all stakeholder views, the mix between research and practice into the evaluation of transdisciplinary projects [5, 9]. Therefore, a custom approach needs to be designed, based on project particularities, developed by stakeholders, and considering the desired impact.

In this book chapter, we seek to provide researchers and practitioners with a transdisciplinary evaluation framework for digital government projects. We firstly present the different aspects of the evaluation framework and a few examples of indicators that could be measured within each of the pillars of transdisciplinarity. Due to the high complexity present in these processes, we also present some recurring challenges associated with transdisciplinarity. As an example, we apply the framework to the ongoing Horizon 2020 project Mobile Cross-Border Government Services for Europe (mGov4EU). To finalize, we explore a series of Horizon 2020 projects to see if they contain any transdisciplinary evaluation elements.

2 Mobile Government Evaluation Framework

In this section, the mobile government evaluation framework developed withing the mGov4EU project will be presented: the main attributes involved, how and why they are important to consider when carrying out a transdisciplinary project, and the methodology that has been used to create this framework. The six main pillars of the transdisciplinary evaluation framework are (1) real-world context, (2) interdisciplinarity, (3) beyond science, (4) interaction, (5) integration, and lastly (6) relevance [11]. This section is divided into five parts: Firstly, the method used to derive this framework will be described, and then the six pillars will be introduced, followed by an overview of the importance of indicators identified in the literature and through the workshops grouped accordingly to each pillar. Transdisciplinary evaluations do not occur as frequently as expected; the challenges associated with such evaluations will also be presented, as one should understand the challenges to be able to address them where possible. Then finally, the last subsection will focus on how the six pillars of transdisciplinarity were applied or involved in the mGov4EU project, alongside some of their corresponding indicators.

3 Method

Within the mGov4EU project, a thorough literature review was conducted on transdisciplinary evaluation, selecting the most recent and relevant academic publications. Transdisciplinarity is an interdisciplinary field of study; therefore, the search for publications was conducted in two of the most relevant peer-reviewed literature databases: Scopus and Web of Science. Following the PRISMA method, the search string used was as follows:

TITLE-ABS-KEY ((transdisciplin* AND (framework OR model) AND (evaluation OR benchmark* OR assessment))).

The search resulted in 806 results in Scopus and 631 in Web of Science. After duplicates and papers not available in English were removed, the search revealed 1006 papers. To narrow down the number of publications, a deep review of the title and abstract of the list of publications was conducted, removing those following the following criteria: undetected duplicates; publications that were too specific, for example, belonging to the field of medicine, veterinary, or ecology; and those publications that did not focus on transdisciplinary evaluation and lacked indicators or relative sources of information for the research at hand. This resulted in a list of 185 publications that, through a conjoint examination discussing those articles, brought down the final sample to 75, with a final total of 73 being available for download.

In order to conduct the analysis of the relevant papers, MAXQDA[1] was selected as a suitable software for qualitative coding. An inductive approach was done where the coding schema was defined after a sample of the literature was reviewed: the same five papers were coded by three different researchers. A hybrid workshop with the academic researchers was set up to discuss the codes and sub-codes, and a final set of codes was agreed upon in this workshop. A total of 1375 segments were extracted from the text using the selected codes.

When defining this evaluation framework, the goal was to have not only a sound theoretical background but also a practical foundation. Therefore, a series of workshops were designed to complement the literature review findings. These allowed to tailor the evaluation framework and to meet and set realistic expectations, objectives for the project pilots, requirements, indicators, and ways of measuring them.

An initial alignment workshop took place in an online environment, involving scientific partners of various disciplines and an industry partner in the field of digital services and electronic voting. Here, a better understanding of the roles of partners and the first draft of the expectations were determined.

After the initial alignment workshop and literature review, a series of pilot-focused workshops were conducted. These workshops had a series of phases. The first two phases were developed in a hybrid setting, with 16 in situ participants and 10 participants online. Firstly, the partners sought to answer the "5 Ws" (32), referring to (i) what the pilots are about, (ii) why the pilots are necessary, (iii) when and (iv) where they are going to happen, and (v) who is going to be involved. Following this activity, the pilot leaders were asked to elaborate on potential, pilot-specific indicators, which could either be provided by the indicators identified in the literature review or derived by the pilot development. These indicators were then divided into those related to the design process of the pilots and its implementation, and in case of a high number of indicators, the partners were requested to prioritize the indicators. Finally, participants were asked to reflect on how they would be measuring each indicator and where the information for the assessment could be found and also to identify those indicators that were relevant for the project as

---

[1] https://www.maxqda.com/es

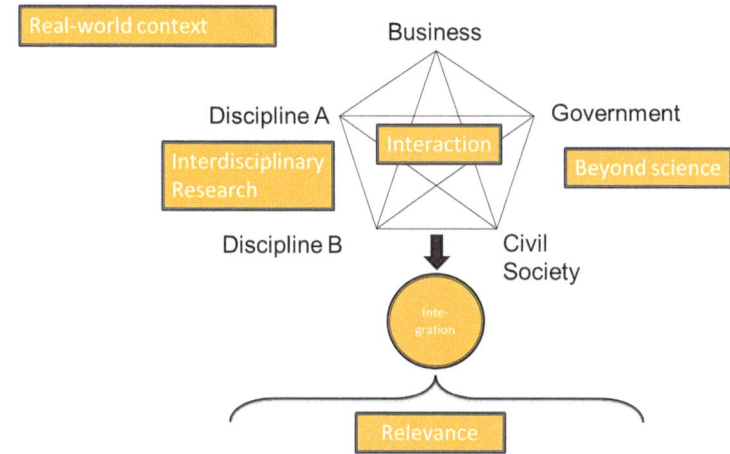

Fig. 1 Transdisciplinary evaluation framework. Retrieved from Eibl et al. [12]

a whole and those that were pilot-specific. This method helped design the final transdisciplinary evaluation framework depicted in Fig. 1 [11].

After applying the framework to the mGov4EU project, we decided to see if other research projects followed a similar transdisciplinary approach. Therefore, we conducted an analysis of other Horizon 2020 projects. The official portal for European data data.europe.eu hosts a comprehensive dataset on projects and their results funded by the European Union under the Horizon 2020 framework program for research and innovation from 2014 to 2020. The dataset contains H2020 project deliverables with metadata and links to the deliverables since May 2019. The downloaded files were consolidated and filtered for titles containing the words "final evaluation" using a small R script, which gave us links to 20 publicly available final evaluation reports.

Next, the 20 downloaded files were manually checked by using a checklist to see if the documents contained evaluation results along the six pillars of transdisciplinarity.

Figure 1 depicts the final transdisciplinary evaluation framework and the corresponding pillars of transdisciplinarity. In the following subsections, the pillars will be described in detail.

3.1 Real-World Context

The first pillar of the transdisciplinary evaluation framework centers around the real-world context. At the start of any transdisciplinary research, there is the need to identify a real-life problem that demands a solution [3]. For practitioners, it is important that these solutions address everyday life issues. These everyday life challenges are analyzed to shape tangible processes while also considering the legal frameworks and potential courses of action within their specific context [3]. In essence, transdisciplinary research is intricately tied to resolving authentic problems and queries, with the overarching objective of generating knowledge that is inherently solution-oriented toward issues of societal relevance [2, 5]. This viewpoint is shared by other scholars as well, emphasizing the central role of this problem-solution approach in transdisciplinary research [4]. The knowledge emerging from transdisciplinary research is deeply rooted in the specific application context and is fundamentally driven by societal problems, which serve as catalysts for framing scientific research questions [13]. As depicted in Fig. 1, the real-world context is symbolized by the encompassing grey rectangle, serving as the point of origin and the bedrock of the entire transdisciplinary process. Within the literature, several indicators associated with the real-world context suggest that research must translate into tangible practice and align with policy interests [14].

3.2 Interdisciplinarity

Another fundamental pillar of the evaluation framework is interdisciplinarity. Transdisciplinary research encompasses both interdisciplinary and transdisciplinary research, with the latter serving as the overarching term. The primary objective of transdisciplinary research is to seek solutions to complex issues or problems that defy resolution using the knowledge and techniques confined within a single discipline [2]. In essence, it frees itself from the constraints of disciplinary boundaries, enabling the framing and resolution of problems independently of disciplinary constraints. This is an approach to ensure that problems are not approached through a one-dimensional lens, limited to a solely specialized or disciplinary perspective [13]. Interdisciplinary research entails taking into consideration the context of multiple disciplines and the inherent knowledge they bring within the same environment, transcending and transgressing disciplinary boundaries [2]. It involves incorporating perspectives from various disciplines [5]. Achieving this necessitates researchers from diverse fields to collaborate and work together [3], and this can be assessed by identifying the amount of fields and disciplines engaged in a project and the diversity of qualifications among the project members [2]. In Fig. 1, interdisciplinarity is symbolized by the diversity of disciplines represented.

3.3 Beyond Science

An additional point in transdisciplinary evaluation is its key role of bridging science and practice, effectively transcending the boundaries that separate scientific disciplines from societal actors. It highlights the need for a project to extend its reach beyond the confines of pure science [4, 13]. A fundamental part of transdisciplinary research projects is the active involvement of a diverse array of non-academic stakeholders [3]. These stakeholders can range from business and government entities to civil society organizations and from industrial players to societal entities, all with a shared aim of applying the research outcomes to practical challenges [2]. To foster a successful transdisciplinary approach, it's imperative to establish a connection between societal issues and scientific challenges [15], enabling researchers to collaboratively engage with practitioners [3]. This collaboration is based on a principle of equality [5] and needs the incorporation of both scientific and non-scientific knowledge and practices [16]. Aligning the needs and aspirations of all partners ensures that the process remains relevant to all stakeholders [17], contributes to advancements in both societal and scientific domains, takes into account the rich diversity of perspectives [13], and can foster a culture of accountability [2]. It is essential for stakeholders to feel heard, adequately represented, and to trust that researchers will consider their input [5, 18–20]. Project leaders play a pivotal role in facilitating this collaboration process [21], a task that requires thoughtful consideration of which stakeholders should be involved in the design phase, the number of stakeholders required, who has the authority to determine the goals of a design initiative, and the basis and legitimacy of such decisions [22]. As illustrated in Fig. 1, the "beyond science" pillar is symbolized by the interactions between various parties and scientific disciplines, such as businesses, government bodies, and civil society. A pertinent indicator of the success of this pillar is the extent of interaction between academia, the productive sector, and society, as well as the active participation of professionals beyond the academic sphere [2].

3.4 Interaction

Interaction plays a key role as the third pillar of transdisciplinarity. It involves the collaboration of diverse individuals from various disciplines and extends beyond the realms of conventional scientific inquiry within a transdisciplinary project. Multiple definitions and descriptions of transdisciplinary research highlight the significance of this interaction. Central to this concept is the idea of "co-production," which stands as a fundamental tenet of transdisciplinary research, signifying the importance of meaningful engagement between stakeholders [2]. Others focus on the idea of research collaboration [5, 13] or the convergence of different methodologies and approaches [16]. The overarching objective is to unite expertise and knowledge through collective effort and collaborative networks [2]. This entails cooperative learning, problem-solving [16], active involvement of all stakeholders [3], and the engagement of participants in reflective, deliberative, and negotiation processes [23]. In the visual representation of this framework, interaction is illustrated in Fig. 1 through lines connecting the various stakeholders, disciplines, and representatives from both the private and public sectors. A possible measure of this interaction is the extent and frequency of participatory events and networks established and/or expanded during the project's development [23].

3.5 Integration

The previously presented pillar of interaction serves a vital purpose in transdisciplinary research, encompassing terms such as integration, synthesis, and transition.
Transdisciplinary research seeks to go beyond the fragmented nature of scientific
knowledge and the tendency toward hyper-specialization by promoting dialogue
and the incorporation of diverse forms of knowledge [2]. Integration is presented
as the fifth pillar of transdisciplinary evaluation. It can be understood as the
cognitive process of establishing connections among the various epistemic, socio-
organizational, and communicative components that constitute the given problem
context [13]. Through this process, it produces fresh insights by harmonizing
scientific and non-scientific discoveries, creating new knowledge [15], a concept
that is often referred to as the synthesis of individual findings [5]. In Fig. 1,
integration is depicted as the cumulative outcome of stakeholder interaction, the
results obtained, and the learning that occurs throughout this process. Key indicators
associated with this pillar encompass shifts in participants' attitudes, the acquisition
of new insights and learning experiences, as well as the generation of fresh scientific
knowledge [5, 24].

3.6 Relevance

The last pillar of the transdisciplinary evaluation framework is the concept of
relevance. This can be somehow divided into the relevance for internal stakeholders,
within the project, and those external stakeholders. Within the project boundaries,
mutual learning should be facilitated [5] between users and researchers. The
partnerships should also allow for mutual accountability, ownership, and leadership
[23]. When focusing on the outside of the project boundaries, the transdisciplinary
research should contribute to scientific and societal progress [13, 15]. This is clearly
related to the fact that transdisciplinary projects must go beyond just science and
address a real-world problem, as mentioned previously. Moreover, some authors
highlight the importance of practical benefits for society [23] and to secure the
promised benefits [5]. In Fig. 1, relevance is depicted as the final overarching
outcome. Some of the indicators related to relevance can be changes in practice,
new institutional frameworks created, and decisions made [5].

4 Indicators

In this section, we will present some of the indicators found in the literature
and specific indicators agreed upon within the project consortium through the
workshops conducted both online, in person, and hybrid. Indicators help aggregate

Table 1 Example indicators for each pillar of transdisciplinary evaluation

Pillar of transdisciplinarity	Indicators
Real-world context	Does the project development meet current policy interests? How likely would it be to use the applications outside of the project context?
Interdisciplinary research	Do the project results/products combine knowledge from different fields? How many fields are being integrated?
Beyond Science	Is there participation of extra-academic professionals? Are there representatives from all important stakeholder groups involved?
Interaction	Did a diversity of participatory activities exist? Was the work carried out iteratively to ensure collaborative inputs were taken into account and to improve transparency?
Integration	Has the knowledge and information created been made accessible? Are there any mutual learning processes established throughout the project to promote a knowledge exchange between science and practice?
Relevance	Has the project had any impact on policy changes/improvements? Was the project socially relevant and solutions oriented?

information, allowing for the analysis of complex issues and adding value to help decision-makers [3]. The indicators were first extracted from the literature on transdisciplinary evaluation. These focused on whether a project or research was socially relevant, rigorous, and scientifically robust [25]. Moreover, evaluators, especially internal evaluators, should attempt to question and analyze their actions and thoughts on how things were done [13]. This was an activity that was conducted several times throughout the project, finding ways to improve and recommendations for the future. Table 1 presents some of the main indicators found in the literature. These were used for designing the checklist for evaluating the H2020 projects with the transdisciplinary evaluation framework.

5   Challenges of Transdisciplinary Evaluations

A key characteristic of transdisciplinary projects is the inclusion of a variety of disciplines working together. Many disciplines, professions, and fields are usually involved [9]. The literature on transdisciplinary evaluation has highlighted several potential challenges that can arise in transdisciplinary processes. Most of these challenges are related to the complex nature of a transdisciplinary process and range from privacy and ethical considerations, time and project size, stakeholder involvement, and working with a variety of disciplines [26–28]. Taking into consideration and understanding the existing challenges associated with the transdisciplinary process and evaluation may help implementors design processes according to their needs and building upon their strengths to find ways to mitigate the challenges. In this section, a few of the main challenges and possible ways of avoiding them are presented. These are (1) differences between different disciplines, (2) time for processes to have an impact, (3) the need for adequate competences of the involved partners, (4) relevant and motivated stakeholders, and (5) the role of the evaluators.

The nature of transdisciplinary research includes a variety of disciplines, both from science and practice. The first of the challenges identified is that there exist differences between the organizational and institutional variances of disciplines [26]. When conducting transdisciplinary research, the specific context of all involved parties needs to coexist [29]. It is important for project members to identity suitable methods for collaborating, knowledge integration, and ways to evaluate the advances that address all involved disciplines [30]. The authors mention that a way to address this is by using a broader conceptual framework especially for evaluation, as traditional ways are insufficient [25, 31]. Analyzing the project as a whole and not a sum of parts is crucial to avoid being viewed as disjointed pieces [31].

Another important challenge mentioned in the literature is the variable of time. Firstly, the impacts of transdisciplinary processes may take a while to have a big impact, as their contribution and consequences may be long-term effects. This means a long time frame needs to be considered to evaluate this aspect, and many times, project duration does not allow for an evaluation to be conducted later [10, 25, 32]. Many times, impacts are not possible to be traced back to a particular project, and results can take a long time to materialize [33, 34]. Projects evaluated immediately may have skewed impressions from recent activities, and it may be difficult to see the long-term contributions of activities that extended through several months or years [35]. Nevertheless, some of the impacts may be visible immediately especially the temporary impacts [25]. Within the time variable, a key challenge is making sure that the timing for the project is precise and at the same time allocating the correct amount of time and money when defining objectives, key for a successful transdisciplinary endeavor [29, 36].

The third relevant challenge identified in the literature is the need for adequate competences within transdisciplinary projects. Some of the competencies required are clear communication and facilitation of knowledge, interdisciplinary coordination, and collaboration [26]. Academic and non-academic partners need to be able to collaborate and learn throughout the project duration [37]. Within transdisciplinary projects, changes may occur that range from technological, to attitudinal, to cultural, and organizational, requiring stakeholders to adapt and acquire new competences [20]. A way to address this challenge is to ensure constant continuing education of the involved partners and workshops to foster collaboration and communication techniques.

Stakeholders are key to transdisciplinary developments. When involving stakeholders from different areas, backgrounds, and disciplines, a series of challenges may arise for the projects. In many cases, identifying the right stakeholders to involve may represent a barrier for the projects; sometimes, not all relevant stakeholders are available or can take part in the process [29, 30]. Moreover, understanding the power relations and dynamics is very important [23, 29]. It is many times not easy to involve and keep the relevant stakeholders motivated for participation, and many times, developing the relationship with the stakeholders takes time and requires a lot of effort [29, 38]. Moreover, stakeholders need to feel heard and represented and trust the team and researchers to take into consideration their input, and project leaders need to facilitate the collaboration process to be able to consider stakeholder knowledge and expertise [5, 18–20]. Not articulating the different disciplines and actors may lead to disappointment of those involved [39]. Finally, it is important for project managers to address society's existing power imbalances and to select stakeholders representing those less powerful groups in society, creating a balance of views, priorities, and goals while at the same time creating a coherent whole [9, 24].

The final challenge identified in the literature review was associated with the people carrying out the evaluations of transdisciplinary project: the evaluators. Evaluators may be somehow part of the project, therefore internal or external parties or a mix of both. When external, the distance to the project may provide them with some benefits, but at the same time, they lack the comprehension on the internal dynamics developed, which represent ideal criteria to assess a project process [30]. When reviewers are internal, they need to be able to consciously review their actions and reflect on the activities carried out [25]. A way to overcome this is by having clear guidelines and peer reviews detailing how to take into consideration all the disciplinary standards, as it is not an easy task to find evaluators with cross-disciplinary experience [9, 18].

6 Applying the Transdisciplinary Evaluation Framework to the mGov4EU Project

In this subsection, we will shortly introduce how the mGov4EU project implemented a transdisciplinary approach and identify some of the main aspects of each of the previously presented pillars and indicators that are found within this Horizon 2020 project.

6.1 mGov4EU Real-World Context

In the context of our project, when applying the evaluation framework, the real-world context serves as both the backdrop and the goal for the pilot initiatives. These pilot programs are specifically designed to execute and verify improved infrastructure services for electronic voting, smart mobility, and mobile signature. The primary objective of the project and its pilot initiatives is to leverage the capabilities of Single Digital Gateway Regulation (SDGR) and eIDAS (Electronic

Identification and Trust Services for Electronic Transactions) in tandem, thereby advancing the practical application of inclusive mobile government services across Europe. Consequently, the project aligns with policy imperatives, addressing a critical concern within the EU by enabling seamless cross-border services for users.

Furthermore, a key objective of the project was to create reusable building blocks, providing Member States and other implementors with the necessary tools to enhance their cross-border services. Therefore, the decision to release the components of the Single Digital Gateway (SDG) as open source is expected to facilitate their adoption and implementation across diverse scenarios. One significant advantage lies in the project's provision of modular building blocks that can be seamlessly integrated into the systems of various Member States. This approach is deemed viable from both the eIDAS and SDG perspectives.

The introduction of wallet-based systems emerges as a potential game-changer, promising substantial improvements in citizens' lives by replacing traditional paper-based services with digital alternatives accessible via mobile phones. The application of wallets in Internet-based voting introduces another relevant real-world scenario. Enabling cross-border identification for electronic voting, particularly in European elections or specific regional/organizational elections (such as student unions at universities) conducted at the European level, extends beyond individual Member States to encompass various Member States and citizens from different nations.

6.2   mGov4EU Interdisciplinary Research

The mGov4EU consortium is comprised of a team belonging to a variety of disciplines in order to be able to address the research gap the project seeks to tackle, leveraging the use of SDG and eIDAS for mobile cross-border services. The project identified the need to go beyond disciplinary boundaries to provide solutions to the issues and the importance of sharing their knowledge and to add perspectives and collaboration for producing better outcomes. The disciplines involved throughout the project include developers, mobile developers, back-end experts, software architects, legal experts, management and coordination experts, and research and academic experts, which focus on what is happening at the EU level. The different perspectives allowed for cross-checking of ideas and outputs, mainly through collaboration and exchange. The regular exchange between the technical and scientific fields was rated as beneficial for the project. Some of the tools used to be able to exploit the interdisciplinarity of the project include co-creation workshops, academic conferences, open-source software repositories, plenary meetings, and regular bi-monthly consortium meetings.

6.3   mGov4EU Going Beyond Science

The mGov4EU project worked toward sharing the results beyond just scientific borders. Of course, a key aspect of the project dissemination was attending scientific conferences and publishing results in scientific journals. Nevertheless, the project created building blocks for the pilots that help demonstrate use cases and ways to implement EU legislation regarding cross-border services. Also, technical developments within the project helped serve as a bridge between science and practice, helping translate technical information and legislation in a way that is accessible to users and citizens. A close collaboration was established with other H2020 projects, such as ACROSS[2] and InGOV[3], to exchange knowledge acquired, to disseminate results with stakeholders, and to create synergies. In two occasions, conference publications were developed jointly between the ACROSS and the mGov4EU team. A series of webinars were conducted together. Moreover, mGov4EU partners were involved in other national-level projects related to the field of e-government eID, EIDAS, and SDG, allowing for a constant exchange of lessons learnt and creating professional business networks on similar topics.

6.4   mGov4EU Interaction

Since the start of the mGov4EU project, interaction has been key to the development and deployment of the project. To start with, regular meetings were held within consortium partners for joint work produced between the academic and industry members. Workshops to further the understanding on the work carried out were conducted on several occasions, furthering the collaboration and exchange, and to help with the needs elicitation of the pilots. When asked, the consortium rated respect to be high and having a constructive and accommodating interaction. Due to the variety of fields involved in the project, there is a high dependence on each other's knowledge. When needed, conference calls and bilateral calls were increased, and there was a push for collaboration. Many times, small groups promoted better interaction among partners.

6.5   mGov4EU Integration

Transdisciplinarity seeks to overcome the fragmented view of science and practice and go beyond individual findings. When the project started, each partner focused

---

[2] https://across-h2020.eu/

[3] https://ingov-project.eu/

on setting up their tasks and activities in a siloed way. When moving forward, there was a need for sharing knowledge and results and an integration of joint work. When establishing the requirements list for the project, a collaboration was promoted, to be able to understand both technical and non-technical aspects as a whole. To solve this, technical partners had a biweekly call where they gave an update on the tasks they were working on, even if not being involved in some, which gave a visibility on the activities of others and possibility to avoid double work as well. Some tasks done by other partners could have been recycled and reworked, which contributed to the smart ways of working. Moreover, the technical building blocks were assembled and went through a series of integration processes to create the final pilots. Sharing of knowledge is not only promoted internally within the project but also through joint publications and deliverables, where technical and scientific staff work jointly. In the last 6 months of the project, an exchange of ideas through several loops of user experience (UX) feedback and software enhancement was key to prepare the final version of the pilots. Moreover, the project continues to integrate with the outside by contacting governments, other H2020 projects, and Member States.

6.6 mGov4EU Relevance

The mGov4EU project has the goal of making an impact on policy changes and improvements. The main aim is to develop pilots tackling the issue of cross-border services within EU, by using EIDAS, SDG, and digital wallet solutions. These focus areas are key issues in the EU, seeking to offer the citizens options for being able to conduct business in foreign countries. The pilots provide options for Member States to replicate the activities developed within the project. The design of the building blocks, and using annotated methodologies and open-source software, allows for the reuse and evolution of the technical components of the project. The project also analyzed those factors affecting mobile government solution adoptions, as many efforts to design mobile government services can fail if certain aspects are not considered [12]. While the pilots have a limited and specialized focus to realize an implementation during the project runtime, the results achieved will go beyond the pilot targets themselves by producing open-source code, building blocks, and lessons learned. The building blocks may be reused and implemented for future solutions using eIDAS and wallet solutions.

7   Evaluation of Horizon 2020 Evaluation Reports on Pillars of Transdisciplinarity

The evaluation framework presented provides the opportunity to evaluate research projects along the six pillars of transdisciplinary research. In the previous section, we applied the framework to the mGov4EU project. In this section, we try to

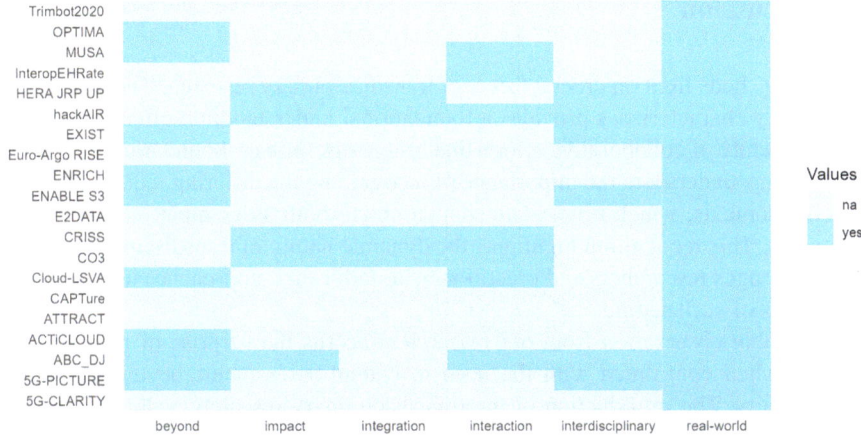

Fig. 2 Transdisciplinary Research in Horizon 2020 evaluation reports (Author's own figure)

understand whether the pillars of transdisciplinarity are somehow already present in other research projects, such as those funded by the European Union. To do so, we analyzed publicly available evaluation reports on the degree of coverage of the six pillars. The methodology used to identify these projects is presented previously in this chapter. As the evaluation framework was designed specifically for a project such as mGov4EU, we believed it would be interesting to understand if other H2020 projects had presented a similar approach to evaluation and if the aspects identified in the literature were present in a variety of similar research endeavors.

Figure 2 shows the results of the manual check of transdisciplinary elements along the six pillars: (1) the real-world context, (2) interdisciplinary research, (3) going beyond science, (4) interaction, (5) integration, and (6) relevance. NA indicates that no information was available that would fall into this category, while a "yes" indicates that information is available.

Every project report examined mentions a problem in everyday life that needs to be solved. Participation beyond science is mentioned in 9 of the 20 evaluation reports. Seven documents record interaction efforts such as co-creation events, six reports mention interdisciplinary research to build on the knowledge of different disciplines, and five report on internal benefits for project members and/or external benefits for external stakeholders such as mutual learning, which is summarized as a relevance/impact dimension of the framework. The least mentioned dimension in four reports is integration, which aims to produce new knowledge by integrating these different scientific and non-scientific findings.

8 Discussion

Our study sheds light on crucial facets of transdisciplinary research. The identification of key characteristics provides a foundational understanding, offering insights into the nature of collaborative efforts that bridge disciplinary boundaries. However, our findings underscore the importance of recognizing the differing requirements of specific contexts, which necessitate adaptations to both assessment indicators and processes. This recognition highlights the dynamic nature of transdisciplinary work and challenges researchers and practitioners to tailor their approaches to the unique intricacies of each setting.

A notable observation from our research concerns the surprise of many stakeholders when confronted with the need to extend assessments beyond technical functionality. The introduction of the transdisciplinary research evaluation framework in the context of the mGov4EU project helped researchers to think beyond the functional testing that is typical of evaluation in digital government research projects.

This insight highlights the dimensions and impacts of transdisciplinary initiatives, challenging conventional expectations and prompting a re-assessment of evaluation criteria. Broader evaluation criteria thus increase the likelihood that project results will be relevant in a real-world context. Moving beyond conventional metrics of scientific success, our study advocates a paradigm shift that emphasizes the importance of collaborative action. We argue that a shift in perspective to focus on collective outcomes and contributions to societal challenges is essential for a comprehensive understanding of transdisciplinary endeavors.

The results of the evaluation of the existing project reports are mainly in line with the expectations of the authors, who could observe a strong focus on the development of specific solutions to real-world problems, which ultimately evaluate whether all the requirements defined in the requirements phase have been adequately addressed, and less on the transdisciplinary processes, such as the integration of different disciplines with external stakeholders.

In conclusion, our study not only contributes to the theoretical understanding of transdisciplinary research but also argues for a practical realignment of evaluation frameworks. The need to move beyond a knowledge-oriented perspective to one centered on collaborative action becomes imperative in order to accurately capture the holistic impact of transdisciplinary initiatives in different contexts.

In considering opportunities for future research, several promising directions emerge. First, the model requires exploration in various government projects to assess its adaptability and effectiveness in different contexts. This empirical testing could provide valuable insights into the model's robustness and applicability in real-world scenarios. In parallel, there is a need for in-depth case study research to collect qualitative data that can shed light on the nuanced dynamics and outcomes of implementing the model in specific contexts. This qualitative approach can enrich our understanding of the model's impact on different dimensions within a given setting, as it presented insights and the need to improve collaboration within the mGov4EU project.

Another central aspect of future research is the formulation of a comprehensive set of indicators tailored to measure the success of transdisciplinary endeavors. This requires a systematic effort to identify and refine metrics that capture the multifaceted nature of transdisciplinary collaboration and can be based on the first set of indicators proposed in our research. In addition, there is a compelling opportunity to develop a process model that outlines the application of the proposed general framework. Such a model would serve as a roadmap to guide practitioners and researchers in the effective implementation of the framework in diverse settings. By bringing these elements together, our research not only offers an understanding of transdisciplinary evaluation but also argues for concerted action to move the field forward.

References

1. Ndaguba, E.A., Ijeoma, E.O.C.: Exploring the epistemology of transdisciplinarity in public policy and administration in South Africa. TDSA. **13** (2017). https://doi.org/10.4102/td.v13i1.406
2. de Oliveira, T.M., Amaral, L., Pacheco RC dos, S.: Multi/inter/transdisciplinary assessment: a systemic framework proposal to evaluate graduate courses and research teams. Res. Eval. **28**, 23–36 (2019). https://doi.org/10.1093/reseval/rvy013
3. Heilmann, A., Reinhold, S.: Evaluation of a transdisciplinary research project for a sustainable development. In: Leal Filho, W., Skanavis, C., do Paço, A., et al. (eds.) Handbook of theory and practice of sustainable development in higher education, pp. 201–214. Springer International Publishing, Cham (2017)
4. Hoffmann, S., Pohl, C., Hering, J.G.: Methods and procedures of transdisciplinary knowledge integration: empirical insights from four thematic synthesis processes. E&S. **22**, art27 (2017a). https://doi.org/10.5751/ES-08955-220127
5. Zscheischler, J., Rogga, S., Lange, A.: The success of transdisciplinary research for sustainable land use: individual perceptions and assessments. Sustain. Sci. **13**, 1061–1074 (2018). https://doi.org/10.1007/s11625-018-0556-3
6. Gil-García, J.R., Pardo, T.A.: E-government success factors: mapping practical tools to theoretical foundations. Gov. Inf. Q. **22**, 187–216 (2005). https://doi.org/10.1016/j.giq.2005.02.001
7. Esteves, J., Joseph, R.C.: A comprehensive framework for the assessment of eGovernment projects. Gov. Inf. Q. **25**, 118–132 (2008). https://doi.org/10.1016/j.giq.2007.04.009
8. Sellung, R., Roßnagel, H.: Evaluating Complex Identity Management Systems – The FutureID Approach. 7 (2015)
9. Klein, J.T.: Evaluation of interdisciplinary and transdisciplinary research. Am. J. Prev. Med. **35**, S116–S123 (2008). https://doi.org/10.1016/j.amepre.2008.05.010
10. Walter, A.I., Helgenberger, S., Wiek, A., Scholz, R.W.: Measuring societal effects of transdisciplinary research projects: design and application of an evaluation method. Eval. Program Plann. **30**, 325–338 (2007). https://doi.org/10.1016/j.evalprogplan.2007.08.002
11. Eibl, G., Temple, L., Sellung, R., et al.: Towards a transdisciplinary evaluation framework for mobile cross-border government services. In: Janssen, M., Csáki, C., Lindgren, I., et al. (eds.) Electronic Government, pp. 543–562. Springer International Publishing, Cham (2022b)
12. Eibl, G., Lampoltshammer, T., Temple, L.: Towards identifying factors influencing mobile government adoption: an exploratory literature review. JeDEM. **14**, 1–18 (2022a). https://doi.org/10.29379/jedem.v14i1.693

13. Hoffmann, S., Pohl, C., Hering, J.G.: Exploring transdisciplinary integration within a large research program: empirical lessons from four thematic synthesis processes. Res. Policy. **46**, 678–692 (2017b). https://doi.org/10.1016/j.respol.2017.01.004

14. Czúcz, B., Kalóczkai, Á., Arany, I., et al.: How to design a transdisciplinary regional ecosystem service assessment: a case study from Romania, Eastern Europe. OE. **3**, e26363 (2018). https://doi.org/10.3897/oneeco.3.e26363

15. Jahn, T., Keil, F.: An actor-specific guideline for quality assurance in transdisciplinary research. Futures. **65**, 195–208 (2015). https://doi.org/10.1016/j.futures.2014.10.015

16. Pyshkin, E.: Designing human-centric applications: transdisciplinary connections with examples. In: 2017 3rd IEEE international conference on cybernetics (CYBCONF), pp. 1–6. IEEE, Exeter (2017)

17. Eanes, F.R., Silbernagel, J.M., Hart, D.A., et al.: Participatory mobile- and web-based tools for eliciting landscape knowledge and perspectives: introducing and evaluating the Wisconsin Geotools Project. J. Coast. Conserv. **22**, 399–416 (2018). https://doi.org/10.1007/s11852-017-0589-2

18. Belcher, B.M., Rasmussen, K.E., Kemshaw, M.R., Zornes, D.A.: Defining and assessing research quality in a transdisciplinary context. Res. Eval. **25**, 1–17 (2016). https://doi.org/10.1093/reseval/rvv025

19. Hohl, S.D., Knerr, S., Thompson, B.: A framework for coordination center responsibilities and performance in a multi-site, transdisciplinary public health research initiative. Res. Eval. **28**, 279–289 (2019). https://doi.org/10.1093/reseval/rvz012

20. Pinto, L.G., Ochôa, P.: Information science's contributions towards emerging open evaluation practices. Perform. Meas. Metrics. (2018)

21. Kliskey, A., Williams, P., Griffith, D.L., et al.: Thinking big and thinking small: a conceptual framework for best practices in community and stakeholder engagement in food, energy, and water systems. Sustain. For. **13**, 2160 (2021)

22. Gidlund, K.L.: Designing for all and no one-practitioners understandings of citizen driven development of public e-services. In: Proceedings of the 12th participatory design conference: research papers, Volume 1, pp. 11–19 (2012)

23. Wiek, A., Talwar, S., O'Shea, M., Robinson, J.: Toward a methodological scheme for capturing societal effects of participatory sustainability research. Res. Eval. **23**, 117–132 (2014). https://doi.org/10.1093/reseval/rvt031

24. Holzer, J.M., Carmon, N., Orenstein, D.E.: A methodology for evaluating transdisciplinary research on coupled socio-ecological systems. Ecol. Indic. **85**, 808–819 (2018). https://doi.org/10.1016/j.ecolind.2017.10.074

25. Piggot-Irvine, E., Zornes, D.: Developing a framework for research evaluation in complex contexts such as action research. SAGE Open. **6**, 215824401666380 (2016). https://doi.org/10.1177/2158244016663800

26. Axelsson, R., Ljung, M., Blicharska, M., et al.: The challenge of transdisciplinary research: a case study of learning by evaluation for sustainable transport infrastructures. Sustain. For. **12**, 6995 (2020). https://doi.org/10.3390/su12176995

27. Chillakanti, P., Ekwaro-Osire, S., Ertas, A.: Evaluation of technology platforms for use in transdisciplinary research. Educ. Sci. **11**, 23 (2021). https://doi.org/10.3390/educsci11010023

28. Hitziger, M., Aragrande, M., Berezowski, J.A., et al.: EVOLvINC: EValuating knOwLedge INtegration Capacity in multistakeholder governance. E&S. **24**, art36 (2019). https://doi.org/10.5751/ES-10935-240236

29. Woltersdorf, L., Lang, P., Döll, P.: How to set up a transdisciplinary research project in Central Asia: description and evaluation. Sustain. Sci. **14**, 697–711 (2019). https://doi.org/10.1007/s11625-018-0625-7

30. Verwoerd, L., Klaassen, P., van Veen, S.C., et al.: Combining the roles of evaluator and facilitator: assessing societal impacts of transdisciplinary research while building capacities to improve its quality. Environ. Sci. Pol. **103**, 32–40 (2020). https://doi.org/10.1016/j.envsci.2019.10.011

31. Pregernig, M.: Transdisciplinarity viewed from afar: science-policy assessments as forums for the creation of transdisciplinary knowledge. Sci. Public Policy. **33**, 445–455 (2006)
32. Schulte, R., Heilmann, A.: Presentation and discussion of an evaluation model for transdisciplinary research projects. EJSD. **8**, 1 (2019). https://doi.org/10.14207/ejsd.2019.v8n3p1
33. Gómez-Villarino, M.T., Ruiz-Garcia, L.: Adaptive design model for the integration of urban agriculture in the sustainable development of cities. A case study in northern Spain. Sustain. Cities Soc. **65**, 102595 (2021). https://doi.org/10.1016/j.scs.2020.102595
34. Stokols, D., Fuqua, J., Gress, J., et al.: Evaluating transdisciplinary science. Nicotine Tob. Res. **5**, S21–S39 (2003)
35. Williams, S., Robinson, J.: Measuring sustainability: an evaluation framework for sustainability transition experiments. Environ. Sci. Pol. **103**, 58–66 (2020). https://doi.org/10.1016/j.envsci.2019.10.012
36. Trimble, M., Plummer, R.: Participatory evaluation for adaptive co-management of social-ecological systems: a transdisciplinary research approach. Sustain. Sci. **14**, 1091–1103 (2019). https://doi.org/10.1007/s11625-018-0602-1
37. König, B., Diehl, K., Tscherning, K., Helming, K.: A framework for structuring interdisciplinary research management. Res. Policy. **42**, 261–272 (2013). https://doi.org/10.1016/j.respol.2012.05.006
38. Hansson, S., Polk, M.: Assessing the impact of transdisciplinary research: The usefulness of relevance, credibility, and legitimacy for understanding the link between process and impact. Res. Eval. **27**, 132–144 (2018). https://doi.org/10.1093/reseval/rvy004
39. Schmidt, L., Falk, T., Siegmund-Schultze, M., Spangenberg, J.H.: The objectives of stakeholder involvement in transdisciplinary research. A conceptual framework for a reflective and reflexive practise. Ecol. Econ. **176**, 106751 (2020). https://doi.org/10.1016/j.ecolecon.2020.106751

Ensuring Security in Development-Oriented Collaborative Research Projects

Thomas Zefferer (iD), **Bernd Prünster** (iD), **Roland Czerny** (iD), and **Blaž Podgorelec** (iD)

Abstract Security is of paramount importance in collaborative research projects, particularly those focusing on software development. The security of data processed by project-developed software relies on early consideration of security aspects during the software's design and development process. Unfortunately, the unique characteristics of collaborative research projects often impede the seamless integration of security aspects, posing a risk of producing solutions with inadequate security properties. To tackle this challenge, this chapter introduces a generic method designed to seamlessly incorporate security aspects in development-oriented research projects. With an emphasis on broad applicability across diverse projects, the method maintains intentional generality. Through its application to the H2020 project mGov4EU, the chapter demonstrates the method's practical effectiveness, highlighting its adaptability and utility in a concrete project scenario. This proposed method serves as a valuable tool for researchers and practitioners aiming to seamlessly integrate security within collaborative research projects, addressing potential vulnerabilities early and ensuring the development of more secure software solutions.

Keywords Security evaluation · Security assurance · Vulnerability · Software

T. Zefferer (✉) · B. Prünster
A-SIT Plus GmbH, Wien, Austria
e-mail: thomas.zefferer@a-sit.at; bernd.pruenster@a-sit.at

R. Czerny · B. Podgorelec
Institute of Applied Information Processing and Communications (IAIK), Graz University of Technology, and Secure Information Technology Center Austria (A-SIT), Graz, Austria
e-mail: roland.czerny@iaik.tugraz.at; blaz.podgorelec@iaik.tugraz.at

© The Author(s) 2025
V. Homburg et al. (eds.), *From Electronic to Mobile Government*,
https://doi.org/10.1007/978-3-031-64471-9_9

1 Introduction

Collaborative research projects play a pivotal role in driving innovation across the *European Union* (EU). A key enabler of such research projects is the European Commission. Funding programs of the European Commission such as Horizon 2020[1] or Horizon Europe[2] bring together researchers and innovators from across the continent, fostering joint efforts in research and innovation actions. In the field of *Information Technology* (IT), collaborative research projects often center around software development, aiming for novel and innovative solutions. Consequently, the primary outcomes of these projects are frequently software building blocks, including libraries and modules. These software building blocks are typically designed and developed by the respective project as well as evaluated within the same project by means of different pilot applications.

Whenever software developed in collaborative research projects operates on critical data or is applied in security-critical application scenarios, security becomes a crucial requirement for this software. In practice, however, ensuring security for software developed in such projects often turns out to be a challenge. There are various reasons for that, one being the research character, which is inherent to this type of projects and which typically leads to rather agile development processes prioritizing the addition of new features. Another factor that complicates the appropriate consideration of security throughout the entire software development process is the often-high number of involved project partners working independently on different parts of one and the same software solution. In addition, collaborative research projects often aim for rather low *Technology Readiness Level* (TRL), which further contributes to the fact that security is often neglected. As a result, many collaborative research projects yielding software often do not consider security from the beginning as demanded by the security-by-design paradigm. For projects operating in controlled laboratory environments and on test data only, an insufficient level of security might have limited consequences. However, in many cases, core results of such projects, i.e., software building blocks, are later reused in other— potentially more critical—application scenarios. In such cases, an insufficient level of security of software building blocks can have negative consequences beyond the project's scope.

To address this issue, this chapter proposes a generic method to integrate security seamlessly into the development process of collaborative research projects, ensuring it is a core consideration from the project's inception. This method is evaluated through its application to the EU H2020 project mGov4EU,[3] focused on developing software solutions for mobile e-government processes based on concepts

---

[1] https://research-and-innovation.ec.europa.eu/funding/funding-opportunities/funding-programmes-and-open-calls/horizon-2020_en

[2] https://commission.europa.eu/funding-tenders/find-funding/eu-funding-programmes/horizon-europe_en

[3] https://www.mgov4.eu/

introduced by the EU eIDAS Regulation [1] and the EU *single digital gateway* (SDG) Regulation [2].

The rest of this chapter unfolds as follows: Sect. 2 provides a brief overview of related scientific work on the topics covered in this chapter. Section 3 further motivates the problem by elaborating on key characteristics of development-oriented collaborative research projects and discusses the challenges in achieving adequate security levels. Building on these challenges, Sect. 4 introduces a generic method to ensure the thorough consideration of security in such projects. The proposed method is then evaluated in Sect. 5 through its application to the H2020 project mGov4EU. Finally, conclusions are drawn in Sect. 6.

2 Related Work

Only a few articles discuss how security factors can be actively integrated into projects characterized by collaborative research and development activities. However, we have identified a limited number of articles that discuss the active integration of security factors into software-development processes that share characteristics with collaborative research and development projects.

For instance, Keramati et al. [3] highlight the necessity of creating secure software building blocks in systems developed using agile software methodologies, such as extreme programming, Scrum, or *Feature-Driven Development* (FDD). The authors propose a five-part method to augment the agile methodology with security actions without compromising its agile essence. Although the proposed method improves security within agile development, it does not entirely address other typical characteristics of development-oriented collaborative research projects. This distinguishes the method presented in this chapter from the work proposed by Keramati et al. [3].

In a related work, Sonia et al. [4] introduce an iterative framework named *Agile Security Framework* (ASF), which aims to incorporate security aspects at every stage of the agile software development process. While parts of this iterative framework, like threat modeling and designing, resemble elements of the method proposed in this chapter, it does not consider other typical characteristics of development-oriented collaborative research projects, such as aiming for limited TRL and complex project structures.

Similarly, ben Othmane et al. [5], employing the security reassurance method, have suggested a method for integrating security activities into the agile software development process. Furthermore, Firdaus et al. [6] have focused on FDD and have proposed a secure software development model compatible with it. Compared to the method proposed in this chapter, these two contributions and their proposed methods also primarily focus on the characteristics of agile development and do not significantly address other characteristics of development-oriented collaborative research projects discussed in Sect. 3.

In summary, the overview of related work reveals a limited number of contributions addressing the defined problem. Most of these contributions primarily focus on agile software development processes in general and do not adequately consider all the specific characteristics of collaborative research projects discussed in Sect. 3. The method proposed in this chapter fills this gap.

3 Background

This chapter introduces a method to appropriately address security considerations in collaborative research projects with a focus on software development. Before the proposed method is introduced in detail in Sect. 4, the underlying problem this method aims to solve is elaborated. For this purpose, this section follows a three-step approach. First, relevant characteristics of development-oriented collaborative research projects are identified. Then, security-related challenges emerging from these inherent characteristics are derived. As an illustrative example, this section briefly outlines the mGov4EU project, shedding light on typical characteristics and potential challenges through a concrete use case.

3.1 Characteristics of Development-Oriented Collaborative Research Projects

This section provides a summary of the common characteristics found in development-oriented collaborative research projects the authors have been involved in. Accordingly, the focus is on research projects, which aim to develop software building blocks for a defined area of application. While project characteristics may vary based on the domain, goals, consortium, and structure, collaborative research projects with a primary focus on software development share several common traits.

- **Software as main project result:** Most development-oriented collaborative research projects have in common that their main expected result is software. Of course, such projects also produce other deliverables and results. However, the projects' main emphasis is on developing new and innovative software solutions to tackle a previously defined problem.
- **Evaluation through piloting:** Most development-oriented collaborative research projects yield two types of software. First, these projects produce sustainable software building blocks, which are intended to be re-used also after the project expiration. Second, the projects also develop pilot applications, whose main purpose is to integrate and use developed building blocks and to evaluate and test them in various application scenarios.
- **Agile development:** Software development in collaborative research projects usually follows agile methods. This is a necessary consequence of the projects'

research and innovation nature, which renders classical software-development methods like the waterfall model inadequate.

- **Complex project structure:** Collaborative research projects usually come with a quite complex project and consortium structure, involving various partners and stakeholders with sometimes slightly diverging interests. This often leads to development activities being distributed over multiple work packages and tasks. This, in turn, leads to various dependencies between different work items and involved project partners.
- **Limited TRL:** Many collaborative research projects aim only for a limited TRL for developed software building blocks. This especially applies if developed building blocks are to be piloted in controlled laboratory environments and are expected to operate on test data only.

The above list of common characteristics of development-oriented collaborative research projects is non-exhaustive but focuses on those characteristics, which have an impact on the security of software building blocks developed in these projects. Security-related challenges arising from the listed characteristics are summarized in the following section.

3.2 Security-Related Challenges in Development-Oriented Collaborative Research Projects

The unique characteristics of development-oriented collaborative research projects in practice give rise to several challenges in appropriately addressing security requirements. These challenges often lead to security not being well integrated into the overall project, which ultimately leads to software solutions that fail to meet relevant security requirements. Based on the typical characteristics of development-oriented collaborative research projects, various security-related challenges frequently emerge in such projects.

- **Primary focus on functional requirements:** Due to their research-oriented nature, the projects' primary goals is typically to get things working to demonstrate that their proposed solutions are actually feasible. With the primary focus on functional requirements, security requirements are not always considered a top priority. Instead, security features are often only added at a later point on top of the already existing solution. This violates the security-by-design paradigm and leads to software solutions with insufficient security properties.
- **Limited TRL:** Another possible reason why security requirements are not always considered a top priority is the rather low TRL often targeted by collaborative research projects. If project partners know that the software developed within the project scope will never leave controlled laboratory environments and will operate on test data only, security is often implicitly assigned a lower priority. Again, this can lead to software solutions with insufficient security properties.

- **Complex project structure and agile development:** Agile approaches and complex project structures render it difficult to comply with the security-by-design paradigm. In many cases, project partners responsible for security are not tightly enough involved in development activities carried out by other partners. Strict distribution of different responsibilities in different work packages and tasks often complicates collaboration and the consideration of security in all relevant parts of the project.

The typical characteristics of development-oriented collaborative research projects, along with the related challenges in adequately considering security, often result in software developed within these projects falling short of meeting essential security requirements. Even if this is not an issue for the respective research project, e.g., because the project operates on test data only, this is a severe problem, if project results are later reused outside the project in more critical application scenarios. To address this concern, in Sect. 4, we present a method for appropriately considering security in development-oriented collaborative research projects. Before delving into the details of this method, the following subsection introduces the H2020 research project mGov4EU as a concrete use case. This project exemplifies the typical characteristics outlined above and provides an ideal scenario for testing and evaluating the proposed method described in Sect. 4.

3.3 Use Case: H2020 Project mGov4EU

Between January 2021 and December 2023, the EU-funded H2020 project mGov4EU has developed solutions to enhance mobile government services in Europe. The project has put a special focus on technical solutions implementing provisions of the EU eIDAS Regulation [1] and the EU SDG Regulation [2]. Accordingly, enabling cross-border user authentication and cross-border data retrieval while using mobile end-user devices has been the core concept followed by the project.

A closer examination of mGov4EU's project structure and content reveals its alignment with typical characteristics found in development-oriented collaborative research projects.

- **Software as main project result:** mGov4EU's main goal has been the development of software building blocks to leverage eIDAS-based and SDG-based e-government processes on mobile end-user devices. In addition, mGov4EU has developed three pilot applications to test its building blocks in real-world scenarios. Accordingly, software has been a main project result of mGov4EU.
- **Evaluation through piloting:** Software building blocks developed by mGov4EU have been tested and evaluated by means of three pilot applications, which have integrated developed building blocks and have applied them in different real-world scenarios.

- **Agile development:** While functional and other requirements have been defined upfront in the first project year, the actual software development process has also followed agile development paradigms. For instance, for all software building blocks, initial prototypes have been developed first and have then been gradually extended and refined.
- **Complex project structure:** With ten consortium partners and one linked third party, mGov4EU can be regarded an average-sized H2020 project. With 8 work packages in total and 28 tasks distributed over these work packages, mGov4EU still has come up with a rather complex project structure. As a result, development activities and security-related activities have also been spread over various tasks and work packages. The mGov4EU work-package structure and basic dependencies between the different work packages are illustrated in Fig. 1.
- **Limited TRL:** It has become clear early during the project that most developed software components (building blocks, pilots) will operate on test data only. This was mainly due to the lack of project partners (public-sector organizations, trust service providers, etc.), who could have managed to connect developed components to production systems.

In summary, mGov4EU can be considered a prime example of a development-oriented collaborative research project, exhibiting all typical characteristics of such projects and consequently facing related security challenges. To address these challenges, mGov4EU has applied a comprehensive method to integrate security seamlessly into the project. This method is detailed in the following section.

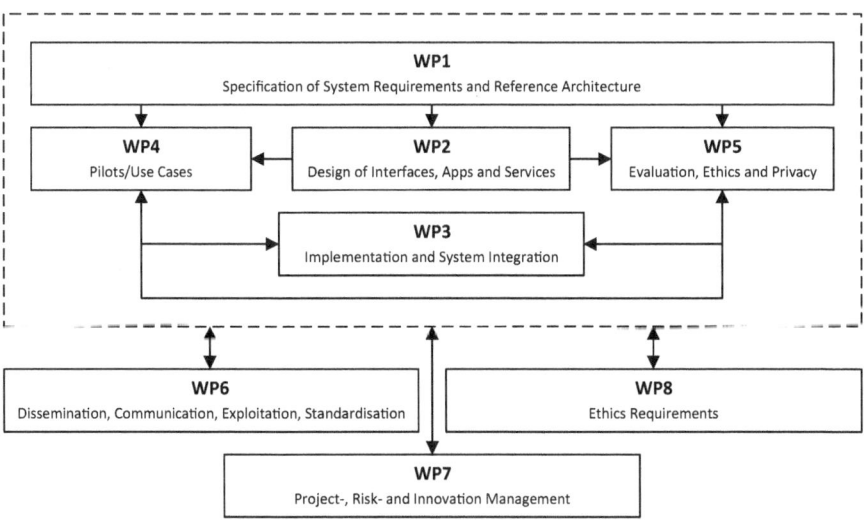

Fig. 1 mGov4EU work-package structure

4 Integration of Security into Collaborative Research Projects

Making security an integral part of all development-related activities in a collaborative research project is a crucial but challenging task. This section proposes and introduces a method to achieve this goal. The proposed method is designed to be generic, applicable to a wide range of development-oriented collaborative research projects. This adaptability is achievable because, despite their differences, these projects share common characteristics. The proposed method builds on these common characteristics but also takes into account varying properties of different research projects.

The proposed method is illustrated in Fig. 2. The method consists of five steps in total. While the first two steps can be carried out in parallel, the subsequent three steps are to be carried out in sequential order only after the first two steps have been completed successfully. The five steps comprising the proposed model are described in the following subsections in more detail. Each subsection reflects one of the five steps.

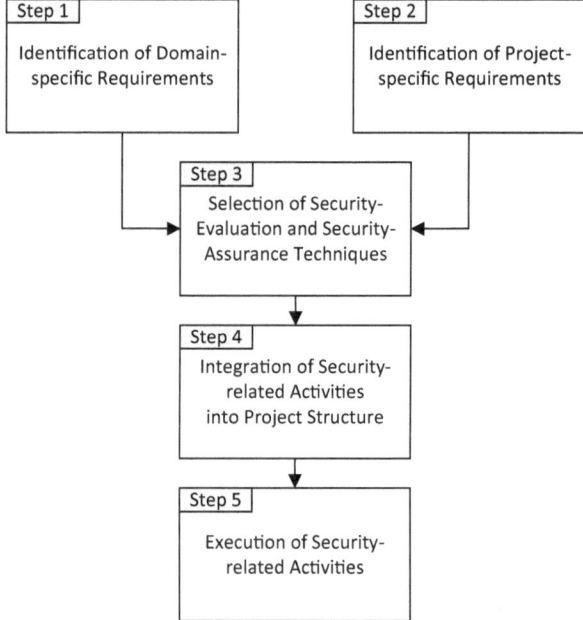

Fig. 2 Proposed model

4.1   Step 1: Identification of Domain-Specific Requirements

In the first step, domain-specific requirements of the project are identified. In general, development-oriented collaborative research projects operate on different domains. The domain basically refers to the area for which the project develops software components. As a matter of fact, each domain comes with its own specific requirements. For instance, depending on the respective target domain, different legal requirements stemming from relevant legal provisions can apply. Therefore, it is crucial to be aware of the project's target domain and of all relevant requirements associated with that domain.

In a typical project setting, the project consortium is composed of domain experts. Consequently, the consortium is usually well aware of the respective target domain and its associated domain-specific requirements. The main challenge in practice is hence to make efficient use of the consortium's expertise and to turn the consortium's implicit knowledge into a set of explicit and well-documented domain-specific requirements. Application of approved requirement-engineering techniques leverages these efforts.

4.2   Step 2: Identification of Project-Specific Requirements

In the second step, which can optionally be carried out in parallel to the first step, project-specific requirements are identified. Accordingly, this second step complements Step 1. While Step 1 focuses on the identification of domain-specific requirements, this second step complements domain-specific requirements with project-specific requirements. Project-specific requirements identified in this step largely depend on the project's type, structure, and organization. These project properties define and potentially limit possible ways to integrate security-related activities into the project.

Similar to domain-specific requirements, project properties and related requirements are in most cases implicitly known to the project consortium. Again, in practice, the main challenge is to transform this implicit knowledge into explicit knowledge and to derive a set of well-defined and documented requirements.

4.3   Step 3: Selection of Security-Evaluation and Security-Assurance Techniques

While Step 1 and Step 2 can optionally be carried out in parallel, their output serves as direct input for Step 3. Accordingly, Step 3 can be carried out only once Step 1 and Step 2 have been completed successfully. The main goal of this third step is to select appropriate security-evaluation and security-assurance techniques based on the domain-specific and project-specific requirements identified in the preceding steps. These techniques include but are not limited to methods for the identification of security threats, methods for the mitigation for identified threats, etc.

In literature, a plethora of security-evaluation methods and security-assurance techniques can be found. In most cases, it is hence not necessary to reinvent the wheel. Instead, security-related activities can be based on existing and approved methods. In practice, the challenge is in identifying those existing methods that are most suitable for the given domain and project. Consideration of results obtained from Steps 1 and 2 is hence crucial to select those methods most appropriate for the specific domain and project requirements.

4.4   Step 4: Integration of Security-Related Activities into Project Structure

Once appropriate security-evaluation and security-assurance techniques have been identified, they must be integrated into the project structure by means of concrete security-related activities. This is the main goal of Step 4 in the proposed method. Ideally, this step and hence also the preceding steps are carried out already during project setup, when, e.g., the project's work package structure is still to be defined. Ex-post integration of security-related activities into an already final project structure can be difficult and should therefore be prevented. The ideal integration depends on the chosen methods and techniques and on the derived security activities. Also, the overall project structure needs to be taken into account. Accordingly, the method proposed in this section does not further define details on how to integrate security-related activities into the respective project. This is intentionally delegated to the consortium of the respective project.

4.5   Step 5: Execution of Security-Related Activities

In the first four steps of the proposed method, relevant requirements have been identified (Step 1 and Step 2), appropriate security-evaluation and security assurance techniques have been identified (Step 3), and derived security-related activities have been planned and integrated into the overall project structure (Step 4). In the fifth and final step, integrated security-related activities must finally be executed as planned during the project's run. Details regarding the execution of planned activities depend on the respective activity and its integration into the project structure. Accordingly, the proposed method does not make any concrete provisions on the execution of security-related activities. In general, this last step typically has the longest duration of all steps. While Step 1 till Step 4 are typically carried out during project setup, Step 5 often comprises the entire project lifetime.

5   Evaluation

In the previous section, a generic method to identify relevant security-related activities for development-oriented collaborative research projects and to integrate them into the project structure has been proposed. To ensure applicability to a wide range of different projects, the proposed method has been defined intentionally on a rather generic and abstract level. This raises the question whether such a generic method is applicable in practice to concrete projects. To evaluate its applicability and usefulness, the proposed method has been applied to the EU-funded H2020 project mGov4EU.

A brief overview of the H2020 project mGov4EU has been provided in Sect. 3.3. In the following subsections, we show how the proposed method has been applied to this project. Again, each subsection reflects one of the five steps comprising the proposed method.

5.1   Step 1: Identification of Domain-Specific Requirements

Identification of relevant domain-specific requirements is the first step according to the proposed method. From a high-level perspective, mGov4EU can be assigned to the e-government domain. To further narrow down the project domain, cross-border user authentication, cross-border data retrieval, and the use of mobile end-user devices in public-sector services can be identified as main focus areas of the mGov4EU project. Relevant domain-specific requirements are hence mainly derived from underlying legal frameworks like the EU eIDAS Regulation [1] and the EU SDG Regulation [2]. Additional domain-specific requirements are imposed from technical restrictions that emerge from the project's goals to make developed solutions applicable on mobile end-user devices.

As shown in Fig. 1, the project structure of mGov4EU has supported a systematic identification of domain-specific requirements. In work package 1 (WP1), which was carried out in the first project year, all relevant requirements (technical, legal, etc.) have been collected and categorized. This way, a comprehensive set of requirements has been available early, including domain-specific requirements as demanded by the method evaluated in this section.

5.2   Step 2: Identification of Project-Specific Requirements

According to the method proposed in Sect. 4, identification of project-specific requirements has constituted the second step to be carried out. Since this step is independent from Step 1, the first two steps have actually been carried out in parallel.

Identification of project-specific requirements has been straightforward, since mGov4EU can be considered a classical development-oriented research project with only few project-specific characteristics. For instance, mGov4EU—like many other projects of this type—has followed a rather intuitive work-package structure, which (on a high level) perfectly reflects the different phases of a software development process. Accordingly, mGov4EU's first four work packages have reflected the development of a reference architecture (WP1), the derivation of detailed technical architectures from this reference architecture (WP2), the implementation of required software components (WP3) defined by the technical architecture, and the development and execution of several pilot applications to test and evaluate the developed software components (WP4).

This high-level project structure has made it apparent that mGov4EU aimed to develop two types of software, i.e., software building blocks and pilot applications. Accordingly, the project-specific requirement has been derived to appropriately consider security for both of these. The overall project structure has also reflected the project's goal to develop innovative technical solutions to make eIDAS-based cross-border user authentication and SDG-based cross-border data retrieval applicable on mobile end-user devices. The resulting requirements from this goal have been perfectly aligned with domain-specific requirements derived for this project. From the defined project goals and structure, it has also become apparent that in addition to functional and related security requirements, also usability and user experience are crucial aspects to be considered. These aspects have had at least an indirect impact on security-evaluation and security-assurance techniques to be applied in the project, due to the well-known trade-offs between security and usability requirements.

Similar to the identification of domain-specific requirements, also the identification of project-specific requirements has been at least partially supported by mGov4EU's project structure. This becomes apparent from Fig. 1. Again, the systematic collection and categorization of all relevant requirements in WP1 have helped to identify all relevant project-specific requirements with an direct or indirect impact on necessary security activities.

5.3 Step 3: Selection of Security-Evaluation and Security-Assurance Techniques

Mainly targeting the e-government domain and following a straightforward structure for development-oriented research projects, mGov4EU has not shown any extraordinary domain-specific or project-specific characteristics or requirements. This has been the main result and finding of the preceding requirement-identification processes. Accordingly, it has been expected that established norms and standards with regard to security-evaluation and security-assurance techniques should be applicable to mGov4EU. Consequently, mGov4EU has carried out a thorough

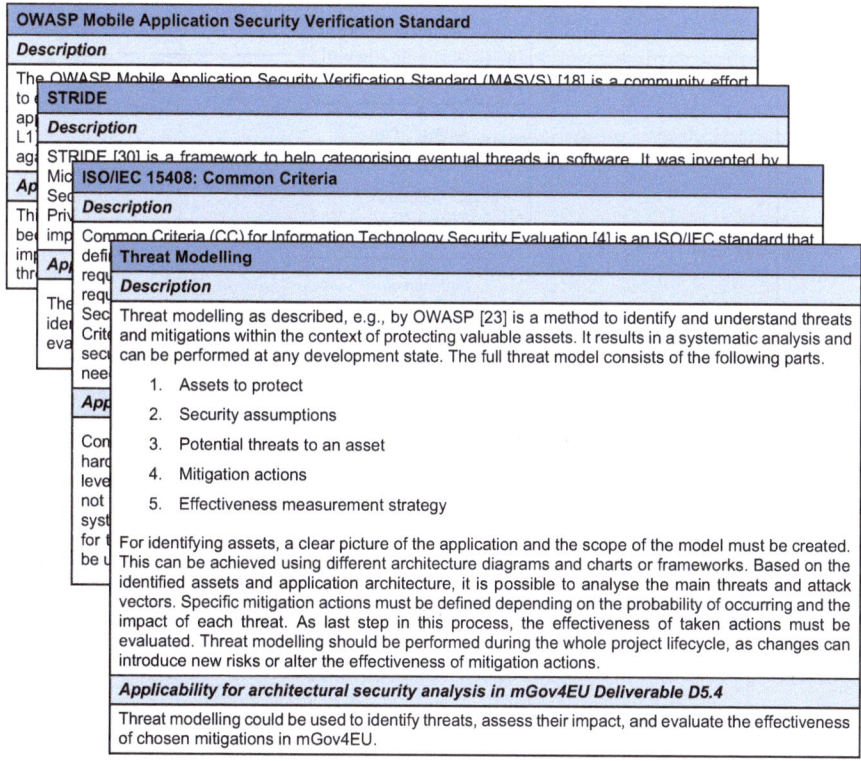

Fig. 3 Example fact sheets created during survey of relevant norms, standards, tools, and techniques

survey on these standards and has assessed them by means of defined evaluation criteria. The survey has collected information on relevant norms, standards, tools, and techniques in fact sheets. Figure 3 shows a small subset of the created fact sheets. In total, more than 30 items have been surveyed and assessed.

From the results and findings of the conducted survey, mGov4EU-specific security-evaluation methods have been derived. Many of the surveyed standards, norms, and techniques share some common concepts and approaches. These approaches are also reflected in the derived mGov4EU-specific security-evaluation methods. For instance, this includes the systematic identification of assets, threats, and relevant threat agents, as well as the derivation of countermeasures to mitigate the threats identified. In addition, the derived mGov4EU-specific security-evaluation methods contain various elements specifically tailored to mGov4EU. This, for instance, applies to the initial input (e.g., technical specifications and architectures, pilot descriptions, etc.), from which assets, threat agents, etc. are

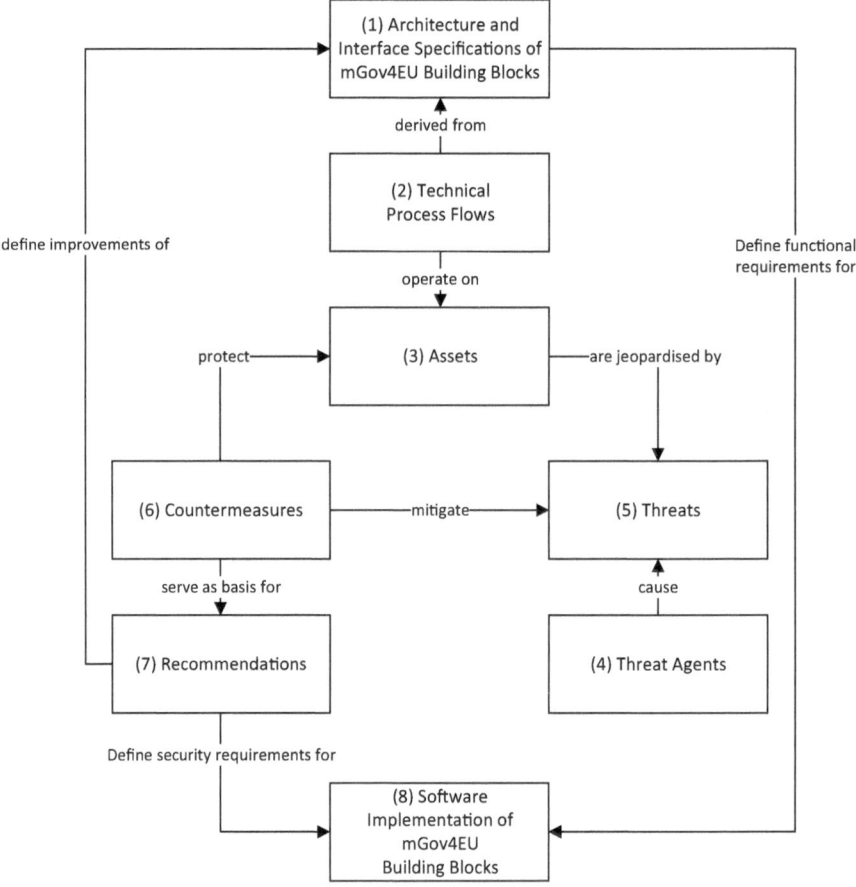

Fig. 4 Evaluation method for mGov4EU building blocks

derived. These mGov4EU-specific elements have ensured that the derived evaluation methods integrate seamlessly into the project.

Overall, two mGov4EU-specific evaluation methods have been defined, specifically tailored to the evaluation of mGov4EU building blocks and mGov4EU pilot, respectively. The two evaluation methods are depicted in Figs. 4 and 5. Numbers used in the two figures indicate the order in which the single steps are to be executed.

These figures show that evaluation of mGov4EU building blocks and mGov4EU pilots have shared a common approach and hence show several similarities. This is rather intuitive, as both methods rely on similar established norms and standards. Still, the two methods differ in terms of their input data serving as starting point for the conducted evaluation, as well as in terms of their output.

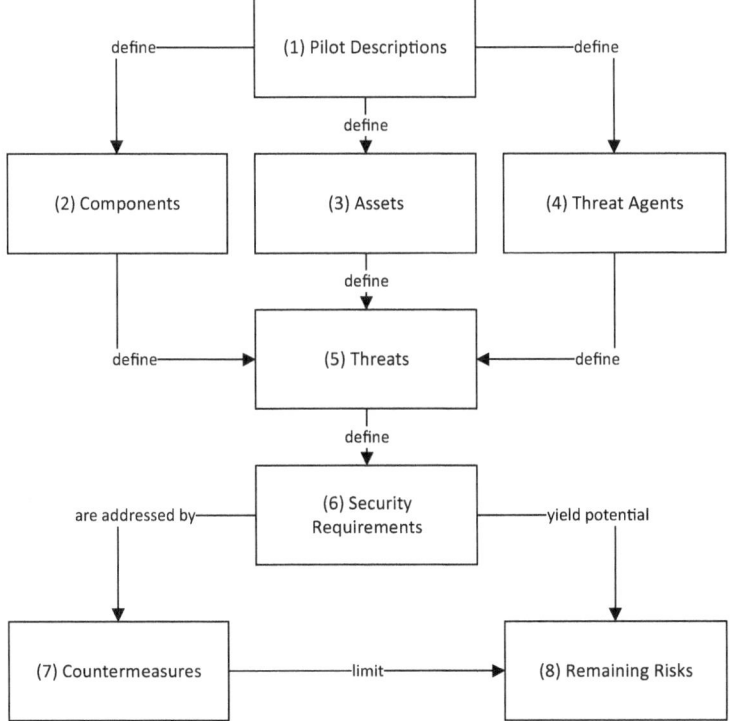

Fig. 5 Evaluation method for mGov4EU pilots

The evaluation method for mGov4EU building blocks (Fig. 4) takes as initial input the building blocks' architecture and interface specifications. From these specifications, technical process flows are derived. The derived technical process flows serve as input for the systematic derivation of assets and their threats, which are, in turn, leveraged by respective threat agents. For all threats identified, appropriate countermeasures are then conceived. Based on the set of derived countermeasures, concrete recommendations for the implementation of the building blocks based on their architecture and interface specifications are derived. In summary, the evaluation method hence pursues the goal to improve an initial version of architecture and interface specifications to improve the security of the resulting software building block. The rationale behind the evaluation method shown in Fig. 4 has also been discussed in more detail by Zefferer et al. [7].

In contrast, the evaluation method for mGov4EU pilot applications follows a slightly different approach (Fig. 5). In this evaluation method, a more generic and hence less technical pilot description serves as initial input and starting point. From this initial input, relevant technical components, assets, and potential threat agents are derived. By systematically combining these three factors, a complete set of relevant threats can be derived. In the next step, security requirements are defined to counter all of these threats by means of appropriate countermeasures. Depending on the fulfillment degree of defined security requirements, certain risks can remain, which are not adequately addressed by any countermeasures. The main goal of the conducted security evaluation according to the methodology shown in Fig. 5 hence is to assess whether the mGov4EU pilots meet all relevant security requirements or if there are any remaining risks that are not addressed adequately.

5.4 Step 4: Integration of Security-Related Activities into Project Structure

The selection of appropriate security-evaluation and security-assurance techniques has yielded two main security-related activities to be carried out in the project: the security evaluation of mGov4EU building blocks according to the methodology shown in Fig. 4 and the evaluation of mGov4EU pilots according to the methodology shown in Fig. 5. These two activities have hence been integrated into mGov4EU's project structure so that they are adequately covered and aligned with mGov4EU's defined work packages and tasks.

According to the initial project structure, all security-related activities have been assigned to a single task within one work package. However, in practice, security-related activities such as security evaluations typically cannot be carried out in an isolated way but require tight collaboration with other tasks and work packages. In the case of mGov4EU, close alignment and collaboration were needed especially with those tasks and work packages responsible for the design, implementation, and integration of mGov4EU building blocks and pilots. This was mainly due to the fact that results of conducted security evaluations were expected to serve as input for design, implementation, and integration activities.

To address adequately this need for close collaboration between security-related activities and activities related to design, implementation, and integration, a thorough plan has been conceived. This plan identifies crucial dependencies between the different activities and defines a schedule for necessary security-related activities. A graphical representation of the conceived plan is shown in Fig. 6.

Figure 6 depicts all relevant work packages, among which appropriate collaboration and alignment need to be ensured. This applies to WP2 (responsible for the design of technical architectures), WP3 (focusing on the development of mGov4EU software building blocks), and WP4 (in charge of pilot development and operation). For each work package, Fig. 6 also depicts relevant activities within the work package and dates of associated milestones to be reached.

Security-related activities carried out within WP5 have been scheduled based on relevant activities and milestones defined for WP2, WP3, and WP4. As shown in Fig. 6, this has led to the following schedule of security-related activities.

In the first 10 months of the project, focus has been put on the definition of initial technical architectures and interfaces and on the preparation of the security

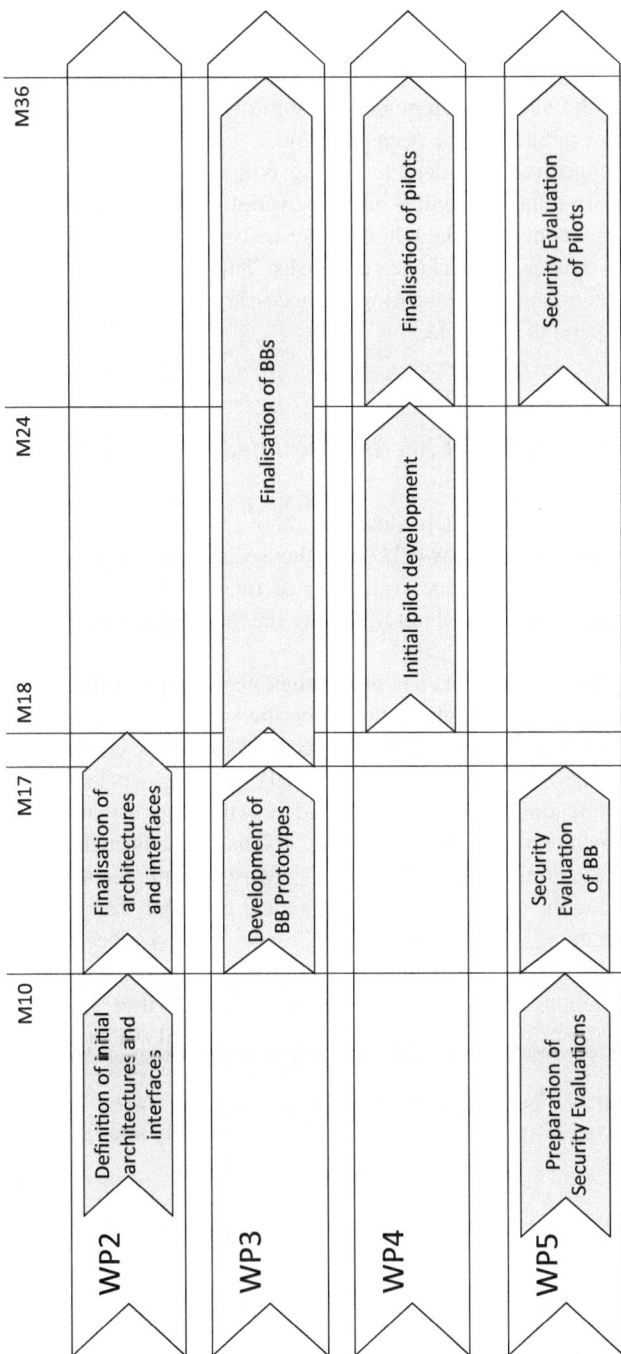

Fig. 6 Integration of security-related activities into project structure

evaluations. Based on the outputs of these activities, the security evaluation of the mGov4EU building blocks has then started along with the finalization of the architectures and interfaces and the development of the first building-block prototypes. The security evaluation of mGov4EU pilots could start only later in M25. Only then, the initial development of the pilots had started and required input for their security evaluation have been available.

Overall, the conceived plan depicted in Fig. 6 has ensured a suitable integration of relevant security-related activities into the overall project structure. The plan has not only made the concrete schedule of these activities clear but also highlighted dependencies to other work packages and tasks. This way, the conceived plan has also ensured a common understanding of necessary security activities and their impact on other parts of the project.

5.5 Step 5: Execution of Security-Related Activities

According to the preparatory steps described above, two security-related activities had to be carried out in mGov4EU, i.e., the security evaluation of mGov4EU building blocks and the security evaluation of mGov4EU pilots. In the project, these activities have been carried out following the methodology and plan described above.

Execution of the two analyses has shown the effectiveness of the defined evaluation methodologies. Both evaluations have identified potential threats and associated risks. From these risks, several concrete recommendations could be derived to further improve the security of both mGov4EU building blocks and mGov4EU pilots. All recommendations have been provided to the responsible project partners in written form by means of evaluation reports and have also been discussed through established project communication channels. Most recommendations have been followed, removing the majority of the threats identified. Only few threats remained unaddressed. Acceptance of these threats and associated risks (because of their low probability or impact) has been a deliberate decision.

Overall, execution of the two security-related activities has considerably improved the security of software produced in mGov4EU. This applies to both mGov4EU building blocks and pilots. Furthermore, the successful completion of this final step of the method proposed in Sect. 4 has shown that this method can—despite its intentional generic nature—be successfully applied in practice.

6 Conclusions

This chapter has introduced a generic method designed to ensure the effective consideration of security aspects in development-oriented collaborative research projects. The method's successful application to the H2020 project mGov4EU has demonstrated its practical effectiveness. The generic nature of the proposed method positions it for broader applicability across diverse projects. Reflecting on the achievements witnessed in the mGov4EU project, we have observed notable enhancements in security measures. While challenges were encountered and addressed during the application, the method has proven its aptitude to elevate security in development-oriented collaborative research projects.

As we move forward, the proposed method holds promise for influencing methodologies and approaches in similar projects. Acknowledging the dynamic nature of this field, future work involves the application of the method to other projects and potential fine-tuning to address specific contexts. This chapter concludes with the anticipation that the proposed method, already in its current form, can significantly elevate the security posture of collaborative research projects, paving the way for more resilient and secure outcomes.

References

1. European Parliament and the Council of the European Union: Regulation (EU) No 910/2014 on electronic identification and trust services for electronic transactions in the internal market (eIDAS) (2014). https://eur-lex.europa.eu/legal-content/EN/TXT/?uri=CELEX:32014R0910
2. European Parliament and the Council of the European Union: Regulation (EU) 2018/1724 of the European Parliament and of the Council of 2 October 2018 establishing a single digital gateway to provide access to information, to procedures and to assistance and problem-solving services and amending Regulation (EU) No 1024/2012 (Text with EEA relevance) (2018). https://eur-lex.europa.eu/legal-content/EN/TXT/?uri=celex%3A32018R1724
3. Keramati, H., Mirian-Hosseinabadi, M.-H.: Integrating software development security activities with agile methodologies. In: 2008 IEEE/ACS International Conference on Computer Systems and Applications, pp. 749–754. IEEE, Piscataway (2008)
4. Sonia, Singhal, A.: Development of agile security framework using a hybrid technique for requirements elicitation. In: International Conference on Advances in Computing, Communication and Control, pp. 178–188. Springer, Berlin (2011)
5. ben Othmane, L., Angin, P., Weffers, H., Bhargava, B.: Extending the agile development process to develop acceptably secure software. In: IEEE Transactions on Dependable and Secure Computing, pp. 497–509. IEEE, Piscataway (2014)
6. Firdaus, A., Ghani, I., Jeong, S.R.: Secure feature driven development (SFDD) model for secure software development. In: Procedia-Social and Behavioral Sciences, pp. 546 553. Elsevier, Amsterdam (2014)
7. Zefferer, T., Prünster, B., Kollmann, C., Corici, A.A., Alber, L., Czerny, R., Podgorelec, B.: A security-evaluation framework for mobile cross-border e-government solutions. In: Proceedings of the 24th Annual International Conference on Digital Government Research, pp. 536–543. Association for Computing Machinery, New York (2023)

Sustainability and Governance of the mGov4EU Project

Carsten Schmidt ⓘ and Stefan Dedovic ⓘ

Abstract Sustainability and governance of the mGov4EU project are critical for its long-term success, particularly in transforming public services and streamlining administrative processes. The mGov4EU project, aiming to design user-centric solutions and enhance cross-border digital public services, places sustainability and governance at the forefront. This involves meticulous outcomes analysis, focusing on pilots and architecture, considering legal frameworks, stakeholder involvement, financial models, and developmental status. The exploration of cross-border mobile government factors reveals consistent determinants across various typologies, encompassing technology, innovation, public officials, citizens, organisations, institutions, public sector context, and broader environmental factors. The multifaceted influences on digital governance initiatives underscore the complex nature of the mGov4EU project. This chapter delves into the piloting impact assessment, analysing design and execution phases. The assessment is crucial for shaping a sustainability plan, recognising core results requiring sustained focus, and identifying areas for improvement. The GOFA model (Governance, Operations, Finance, and Architecture) and Objectives and Key Results (OKR) methodology are applied for a detailed analysis of project outcomes, ensuring a thorough understanding of challenges and requirements for long-term success. The goal is to establish a robust foundation for sustainability and governance, introducing the GOFA model and OKR analysis to navigate the complex landscape of mGov4EU outcomes. The integrated approach ensures a thorough understanding of challenges and requirements essential for long-term success. Challenges across pilots and architecture are addressed, focusing on stakeholder involvement, take-up, flexibility, and continuity. Co-creation principles are integrated into different project stages, fostering collaboration and engagement with various stakeholders. A transdisci-

C. Schmidt (✉)
University of Tartu, Tartu, Estonia

S. Dedovic
University of Tartu, Tartu, Estonia

KU Leuven Brussels Campus, Brussels, Belgium
e-mail: stefan.dedovic@kuleuven.be

V. Homburg et al. (eds.), *From Electronic to Mobile Government*,
https://doi.org/10.1007/978-3-031-64471-9_10

plinary context is integrated into the impact assessment, and the GOFA model is employed for sustainability and governance. The co-creation principle is a recurring theme, engaging stakeholders in ongoing project development and execution. In general, the mGov4EU project, emphasising sustainability and governance, presents a holistic approach to address the complexities of cross-border digital public services, ensuring long-term success and impactful outcomes.

Keywords SDG · Once-only principle · GOFA · eIDAS · EUID Wallet

1 Introduction

During the last decades, sustainability has become of utmost importance to every work and project, especially if they are co-financed by public money. The sustainability and governance of the mGov4EU project constitute essential pillars in ensuring the project's long-term viability and successful outcomes. As the project aims to transform public services by designing user-centric solutions and streamlining administrative processes, addressing the broader context within which these innovations will operate becomes imperative. The introduction of sustainable practices and effective governance frameworks not only guarantees the continued functionality of the project's results but also fosters collaboration among diverse stakeholders, including public sector organisations, businesses, and citizens. This introductory exploration sets the stage for a comprehensive analysis of how the mGov4EU project aligns with the dynamic landscape of public administration, emphasising the crucial role that strategic governance and sustainable practices play in shaping the project's lasting impact on cross-border digital public services.

The mGov4EU project has, during its lifetime, delivered several outcomes. Based on this, one of the main tasks was to identify the results that must be sustained and the best way to fulfil the needs and expectations. As the results produced within the mGov4EU project have a particular focus on pilots and architecture, the analysis of the sustainability requirements was done with particular attention not only to sustainability but also to governance.

mGov4EU results pose several challenges and requirements that have to be taken into account when drawing up future sustainability and governance models for each of the results due to several reasons, e.g., legal frameworks, involvement of different stakeholders, difficulties in developing concrete financial models, and current status of development/implementation. Furthermore, specific national and supranational, mainly European, aspects must be considered. When looking at the identified needs and requirements, a few common key challenges across the pilots and architecture can be highlighted—the involvement of stakeholders, take-up, flexibility, interoperability, and continuity.

This chapter on sustainability and governance delves into the fundamental aspects of the mGov4EU project. It focuses explicitly on comprehending the broader context of public sector organisations and the intricate structural, organisational, and cultural facets inherent to them. At the heart of the mGov4EU project lies the ambitious aim of crafting public services with a user-centric approach. This dual-pronged objective seeks to alleviate the administrative burdens citizens and businesses bear while simultaneously streamlining administrative processes, conserving resources, and reducing costs for public administrations.

Within these aspirations, this chapter serves as a comprehensive platform that harnesses and scrutinises the non-technical dimensions of the mGov4EU implementation and its pivotal elements. Its central scope extends to separating the overarching landscape of public sector organisations, meticulously examining their structural, organisational, and cultural attributes. To fulfil these overarching objectives, the mGov4EU project diligently addresses the alignment and appraisal of drivers and barriers, conducts an ex-post impact assessment of piloting efforts, and undertakes the weighty topics of governance and sustainability vis-à-vis the project's outcomes.

The structure of this chapter is designed along these guiding parameters. It encompasses an inventory and proposal for the methodology and structure that can be enriched and expanded upon in subsequent iterations for other projects.

As such, this book paves the way for a more comprehensive exploration of the multifaceted intricacies at play within not only the mGov4EU project but also other projects, facilitating an in-depth analysis that will provide invaluable insights for both current and future undertakings.

2 Drivers and Barriers of the mGov4EU Project

The objective of the mGov4EU project is to streamline interactions among citizens, businesses, and governments. The primary motivation behind this initiative is to create public services centred around user needs, focusing on lowering the administrative burdens faced by citizens and businesses operating across borders in meeting government-mandated requirements and accessing public services. In an effort to alleviate this administrative load, public administrations aspire to minimise the frequency with which citizens and businesses are required to furnish data to the government.

To achieve this objective, public administrations aim to transition from soliciting data from citizens or businesses to implementing automated data exchange systems. The intention is to leverage data that is already digitally stored in public sector databases or registers, thereby adhering to the principle of providing data to the government "only once" [1].

While the OOP concept is currently being implemented in Europe, the European Commission, Member States, and affiliated countries have made substantial strides to advocate for and embrace the OOP at the European level. This collective effort is geared towards the development of cross-border e-government services for European citizens and businesses [2–4].

This sub-chapter describes and categorises, based on a comprehensive analysis, the various factors influencing the success of other initiatives. These factors encompass aspects recognised as drivers or barriers in the existing body of literature. They also serve as criteria at the conclusion of the mGov4EU project for validating the achieved outcomes.

2.1 Impacting Factors

2.1.1 Exploring Cross-Border Mobile Government Factors

This section digs into the drivers and barriers influencing cross-border mobile government services, employing various typologies to categorise these factors. Initially proposed by Gil-Garcia and Pardo [5], the classification includes five categories: (1) information and data, (2) information technology, (3) organisational and managerial, (4) legal, and (5) institutional and environmental. The first two pertain to data and technology quality, while the latter three extend beyond technology, encompassing the organisational, legal, and institutional landscape impacting digital service provisioning.

Subsequent works followed a comparable approach in categorising factors affecting e-government, m-government, and ICT adoption. Germanakos et al. [6] identified technical, legal, social, and institutional factors in the European Union. Gascó et al. [7] distinguished between "outer context" and "inner" factors, emphasising the relevance of the latter, particularly in the context of e-procurement.

Across studies, whether scrutinising e-service provisioning, ICT adoption, or e-government maturity, the frameworks consistently identify determinants. Olesk [8] emphasised factors influencing collaborative digital government initiatives, ranging from technology and innovation to stakeholder characteristics, organisational context, public sector peculiarities, and broader environmental developments. Notably, factors like innovation championship and a supportive regulatory environment drive innovation, while others, such as stakeholder beliefs, organisational resistance, and resource limitations, act as barriers to adopting and institutionalising innovative public governance practices. An overview of influencing factors is given by the table below.

In summary, exploring cross-border mobile government factors reveals a consistent set of determinants across various typologies and studies, emphasising the multifaceted nature of influences on digital governance initiatives.

Technology	Innovation characteristics	Public officials	Citizens
Availability of hardware and software	Ease of use Cost	Characteristics of individual innovators	Motivation to engage with the government
Features of specific technologies (e.g. security)	Compatibility	Attitudes, beliefs	Interests
	Trustworthiness	Knowledge and competences	Knowledge and competences
Interoperability	Relative advantage	Trust in citizens	Trust in government
		Leadership	Time constraints
		Human error in innovation management	Perceptions (e.g. usefulness of the innovation)

Organisations	Institutions	Public sector context	Broader environment
Capabilities	Regulations and legal constraints	Influence of politics and political will	Public attention
Incentives	Informal norms		Media attention
Financial resources	Institutional histories	Stakeholder complexity, different agendas	Mimetic pressures
Human resources	Legal and administrative culture		Technological development
Organisational structures	Coordination and governance mechanisms	Multi-rationality	
Organisational cultures	Existing power relations	Bureaucratic and democratic principles	
Resistance to change		Organisational competition for power and legitimacy	
Top management support		Expanding the domain of public intervention	
Participation in networks			

Influencing Factors based on Leosk and Poder (2021), Angelopoulos et al. (2010), Anthopoulos et al. (2016), Chadwick (2011), Cinar et al. (2019), Cordella and Tempini (2015), De Vries et al. (2016), Dwivedi et al. (2015), European Commission (2013a), Janssen et al. (2012, 2015), Meijer (2015), Nasi et al. (2015), Osborne and Brown (2011), Susha and Grönlund (2014), Van Veenstra et al. (2011), Weerakkody et al. (2016)

Examining the European landscape, the obstacles to m-government implementation can be categorised into five distinct groups: (1) legal, (2) organisational, (3) semantic, (4) technical, and (5) other. The latter, a more loosely defined category, encompasses elements such as political will, user awareness, or the existence of bilateral or multilateral agreements. Notably, two key points emerge from this comprehensive examination focusing on the OOP. Firstly, there exists a divergence in perspectives among individuals, businesses, and civil servants regarding perceived barriers. Secondly, the analysis underscores the significance of semantic aspects, specifically highlighting the imperative need for establishing comprehensive semantic interoperability [9]. In this context, the analysis emphasises the dimensions of interoperability and cross-border considerations. The subsequent paragraphs elaborate on each dimension and its individual contributing factors.

2.1.2 Technological Factors: Navigating Cross-Border Challenges

The significance of technological factors lies in their dependence on diverse information and process models. Notably, interoperability, particularly in the context of cross-organisational information systems, emerges as a pivotal challenge. Interoperability, defined as the capability to exchange data between different organisations and their ICT systems, necessitates collaborative interaction for mutual and shared objectives. This becomes especially crucial at the semantic level when fostering cooperation between different countries.

In the cross-border context, alongside interoperability, factors such as data quality, database peculiarities, and the technical government architecture of countries become relevant. Recognising these challenges, the European Commission underscores the need for organisations to collaborate to establish technical and semantic interoperability. Achieving technical interoperability involves adopting common specifications and building infrastructures for secure data exchange. Semantic interoperability requires consensus on standard data formats and the development of core vocabularies, ensuring a shared understanding of data meaning among communicating systems. Addressing technological challenges is pivotal for successful cross-border data exchange and cooperation.

2.1.3 Organisational Factors

The organisational dimension encompasses factors tied to organisational structures, highlighting the profound changes induced by mobile government implementation. Barriers at the national level involve governmental silos, communication gaps between departments, complexities in structural changes, and concerns about implementation costs. Similar constraints persist at the cross-border level, emphasising the need for effective collaboration and adaptation across organisations. The literature underscores the importance of adaptability, innovation, organisational culture, networks, and cross-organisational knowledge transfer in successful implementation. Financial and human resources are crucial for adopting and implementing electronic services, with capacity constraints posing significant obstacles.

2.1.4   Institutional Factors

This dimension focuses on laws, rules, and principles shaping digital governance. External factors, such as legal culture and administrative traditions, affect public sector organisations. Regulations can drive change and innovation, with the political environment influencing government transformation. In the realms of OOP and electronic ID (eID), institutional and legal rules play a critical role in data sharing and personal data protection. Resolving legal obstacles is critical for implementation, and intergovernmental and supranational institutions play a fundamental role.

2.1.5   Actors

The role of various actors, including public and private stakeholders, is fundamental. Political will, public demand, and business requirements strongly influence the modernisation of services. Resistance to OOP may arise if certain groups benefit from service inefficiencies, and privacy concerns can impact support for m-government services. The expected benefits of m-government include increased efficiency, user-friendliness, and service quality across organisations and countries involved in service provisioning.

2.1.6   Other Factors

Additional factors, not fitting neatly into previous dimensions, can significantly impact implementation success. User group characteristics (gender, age, education, technology experience) and ICT skills are vital in the adoption process. These challenging-to-specify factors are crucial considerations for a successful m-government service implementation.

In essence, a comprehensive understanding of the aforementioned dimensions is essential for navigating the complexities of mobile government implementation, ensuring effective collaboration, and addressing barriers to innovation.

3   Piloting Impact Assessment

The assessment of pilot impacts is pivotal in shaping the project's sustainability plan, identifying areas for future enhancement, and recognising core results requiring sustained focus. Drawing on data from the transdisciplinary pilot evaluation, the sustainability plan is informed by two distinct phases of pilot assessment.

3.1   Phase I: Design Phase Evaluation

This phase centres on the design of pilots, with a primary focus on transdisciplinarity, emphasising six pillars outlined in the chapter "Evaluating Digital Government Projects: Emphasizing Process and Relevance through Transdisciplinary Research" of this book:

Real-world context: maintaining connection with practitioners and considering legal and policy constraints

Interdisciplinarity: crossing disciplinary boundaries to address complex problems comprehensively

Beyond science: engaging a heterogeneous range of stakeholders beyond scientific disciplines

Interaction: adopting relevant communication approaches and reflecting on their usage

Integration: emphasising continuous learning processes and developing solutions through stakeholder interaction

Relevance: providing meaningful results to various domains and stakeholders

The project identified indicators for each pillar, assessing project partners' experiences in planning and designing pilots. Feedback and assessment involve group discussions and individual partner perspectives, resulting in further insights and recommendations for sustainability outcomes.

3.2   Phase II: Pilot Execution Evaluation

This phase followed a classical piloting approach, evaluating building blocks, piloting scenarios, and defining requirements. The assessment considered security and complements results with remaining requirements in business and usability domains. Pilot-specific indicators guided the evaluation, offering a comprehensive impact perspective. Focus areas include I-Voting, e-Signature, Smart Mobility, and the underlying architecture.

In summary, the impact assessment phases holistically analyse the design and execution of pilots, ensuring a nuanced understanding of successes, challenges, and areas for improvement. The resulting documentation becomes integral in shaping a robust sustainability plan for the project's future .

4   Sustainability and Governance

In this sub-chapter, the mGov4EU project underlines the importance of sustainability and governance in delivering results. During the project phase, the attention was directed toward identifying sustainable results and determining the optimal means to meet ongoing needs and expectations. The focus centres on the mGov4EU pilots and architecture, necessitating a detailed analysis of sustainability requirements, considering legal frameworks, stakeholder involvement, financial models, and progressive status.

4.1 Challenges and Requirements

Several common challenges emerge across pilots and architecture, affecting stakeholder engagement, take-up, flexibility, and continuity. Stakeholders, encompassing citizens, businesses, and governments, introduce diverse needs and requirements. Successful take-up pivots on the readiness of key stakeholders to integrate existing systems with mGov4EU outcomes. Flexibility is crucial, given variations in pilot maturity levels, and continuity depends on well-considered deployment factors, including governance, operations, financing, and architecture.

4.2 GOFA Model

Introducing the Governance, Operations, Finance, and Architecture (GOFA) model, the sub-chapter outlines its acceptance as a framework for classifying activities and assessing needs. Recognising the multifaceted nature of sustainability, the GOFA model, as displayed in Fig. 1, serves as a structured approach to guaranteeing long-term viability. It is particularly relevant in managing project results, ensuring solutions' availability and continuous development, and preserving the developed architecture. The model facilitates analysis across the four main dimensions: governance, operations, finance, and architecture.

Recognising and pursuing the goals outlined in the Tallinn Declaration on eGovernment and the Digital Single Market (DSM) is crucial [10, 11]. This can be achieved by implementing a tool that aids digital transformation and supports solution development, as exemplified by projects like mGov4EU. Hence, monitor-

Fig. 1 GOFA model

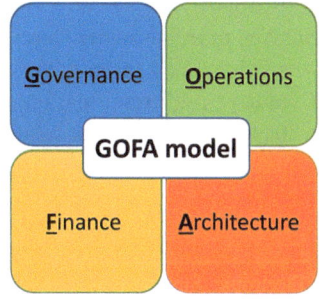

ing key project elements such as stakeholders, services, legislative specifications, and standards is essential [12].

For the sustainability of a project, ongoing monitoring is necessary to adapt to changing developments, such as evolving stakeholder needs or ensuring the continued relevance of services. Appropriate governance and management structures guarantee that your value proposition evolves in response to changing requirements. The European Commission has introduced the GOFA model, encompassing governance, operations, financing, and architecture, which has been refined through various European projects (e.g. e-SENS[1]) [13]. Each dimension of the GOFA model is further detailed in sub-dimensions.

The governance model establishes the principles, organisational structures, and decision-making processes guiding the creation and management of digital services at both individual and collective levels. The three crucial aspects of governance are discussed next.

4.2.1 Principles of Governance: High-Level "Rules" Shaping Organisational Structures and Governance Processes

Organisational structures: Defining roles and responsibilities of governance bodies and determining participants and influencers.
Governance processes: Defining the activities of each governance body, including inputs and outputs, outlining their functions, and interactions.
Governance body: Deciding which governance body can make specific decisions is a significant part of governance. The impact and importance of a decision determine the appropriate governance body. High-level policy decisions set the overall direction, while lower-level decisions are made frequently to support daily operations.

4.2.2 Operational Dimension of GOFA

The operational dimension of GOFA concerns the day-to-day provision of services. Operations involve processes to ensure high-quality service delivery, and four key aspects should be defined and monitored:

Service management: Describing how services are provided and setting expected service levels through Service Level Arrangements (SLAs)
Evolutive maintenance: Identifying and implementing improvement opportunities based on feedback or quality monitoring

---

[1] Electronic Simple European Networked Services, https://cordis.europa.eu/project/id/325211 (Accessed: 19.01.2024).

Control and monitoring: Measuring quality, performance, and potential risks related to service offerings to ensure compliance and identify improvement opportunities.

4.2.3 Financial Dimension of GOFA

The financial dimension addresses the financing of governance, operations, and architecture. Digital solutions may need initial funding, but developing a self-sustainable funding model over time is encouraged. Two key aspects of financial management include:

Cost model: Understanding setup and maintenance costs and potential cost savings through solution reuse

Funding model: Ensuring sufficient funding or a steady revenue stream for service setup and provision.

4.2.4 Architecture Dimension of GOFA

The architecture dimension is crucial for strategic alignment and interoperability among different digital building blocks. Two key aspects include:

Strategic architecture: A formal description of the common digital platform and guiding its design and evolution through an architecture meta-model, standards, guidelines, and principles.

Solution architecture: Ensuring compliance with architectural standards and principles for each digital building block of the common digital platform.
Architecture is vital for aligning digital building blocks with user needs. An overarching governance structure ensures collaboration and interaction between parties, and interoperability principles defined in the European Interoperability Framework are crucial for sharing data between common digital platforms.

4.3   Objective and Key Results

The Objectives and Key Results (OKRs) methodology incorporates a goal-setting framework that has been continuously developed since the 1970s [14, 15]. OKRs are set and evaluated constantly and are future references for monitoring project execution. This framework, applied subsequently to the GOFA model, enhances the detailed analysis of project outcomes. OKRs involve setting objectives and defining two to five key results—measurable actions leading to objective achievement. The framework is utilised to analyse mGov4EU artefacts, pilots, or architecture from governance, operations, finance, and architecture perspectives.

In conclusion, this sub-chapter describes establishing a robust foundation for sustainability and governance, employing the GOFA model and OKR analysis to navigate the complex landscape of mGov4EU outcomes. The integrated approach ensures a thorough understanding of the challenges and requirements essential for long-term sustainability.

5 Co-creation and Business Model Canvas

Throughout its life cycle, the mGov4EU project is set to yield multiple outcomes, necessitating a dedicated focus on sustainability and governance. The primary objective is to pinpoint results requiring sustained support and determine the most effective means of meeting ongoing needs and expectations. With a focus on the mGov4EU pilots and architecture, this chapter delves into the analysis of sustainability requirements, considering diverse challenges and requirements arising from legal frameworks, stakeholder involvement, financial modelling complexities, and the current status of development/implementation. Additionally, this sub-chapter introduces the Business Model Canvas [16] for the mGov4EU mobile application, emphasising the pivotal role of business stability in governance and sustainability. Another sub-chapter details the mGov4EU project's approach to co-creation, aiming to co-design an ecosystem facilitating cross-border services and contributing to further result implementation.

5.1 Challenges and Requirements

Several common challenges resonate across the various pilots and architecture components. Notably, stakeholder involvement poses a challenge due to the diverse stakeholders in each pilot, including citizens, businesses, governments, and others, each bringing unique needs to the table. Successful take-up is contingent upon key stakeholders' development level and readiness, both in integrating existing systems with mGov4EU outcomes and adopting and implementing the results across borders. Flexibility becomes crucial to accommodate differences between pilots and architecture, considering the varying maturity levels of mGov4EU solutions. The continuity of solutions relies on how well these factors are considered during deploying mGov4EU solutions for cross-border public services.

5.2   Co-creation Principles of mGov4EU

Within the mGov4EU project, the principles of co-creation are respected through diverse approaches that consider different levels and stages of involvement. These stages encompass project phases such as requirement and use-case definition, solution development, implementation and piloting, and evaluation. Inclusivity is fostered by engaging experts from various domains, including businesses, public administrations, and academia. This occurs internally through representatives and experts from project members and externally through consultation with stakeholders via the project's stakeholder board or support from related projects from the same co-financing cluster (eGov cluster, inGOV[2] or INTERLINK[3]), which emphasises co-creation [17].

The overarching goal of co-creation in the project is to collaboratively design an ecosystem that facilitates cross-border services, ultimately contributing to the broader implementation of project outcomes [18]. To achieve this, the project envisions strengthening the dialogue with internal and external stakeholders and users, employing various communication modes, including unidirectional (one-way communication) and bidirectional (two-way communication) information flows.

5.2.1   Co-creation Workshop Concepts

The conceptualised forms of communication and co-creation include seminars and workshops incorporating unidirectional and bidirectional communication. Specifically, distinct workshops are planned for experts, decision-makers, and potential users and consumers of the solutions to construct a comprehensive understanding of pilots. Taking the I-Voting pilot as an example, three workshops are anticipated at this stage of project deployment:

The *first workshop* focused on a feasibility assessment and the expansion of pilot platforms involving the Information System Authority, Danube University Krems, and Graz University of Technology following the co-implementation principle.

The *second workshop* addressed electoral concerns, inviting the Estonian Ministry of Interior, the Estonian State Electoral Office, and electoral experts to participate, adhering to the co-implementation principle.

During implementation, the third workshop aimed to engage students, the primary target group, presenting preliminary results and collecting non-technical feedback to adjust the user experience based on the co-design principle.

---

[2] inGov, Grant Agreement 962563, https://ingov-project.eu/ (Accessed: 19.01.2024).

[3] Innovating goverNment and ciTizen co-dEliveRy for the digitaL sINgle market, Grant Agreement 959201, https://interlink-project.eu/ (Accessed: 19.01.2024).

5.3 *Business Model Canvas for mGov4EU*

The business model canvas for the mGov4EU project addressed the business innovation model aspect of sustainability and governance. In this model, the partners co-created a favourable approach for the business model's sustainability by addressing aspects that include the customer segments and value prepositions, channels and customer relationships, revenue streams and key resources, key activities, and cost structure. Detailed elaboration and discussion of the business model canvas can be found in the chapter "Cross-Border Mobile Government Services: Business Model Dynamics in mGov4EU" of this book.

6 Summary and Conclusions

This book chapter comprehensively examines the non-technical facets encompassing the mGov4EU project, addressing the complexities associated with cross-border digital public services delivered through mobile devices. A keen understanding of the project's non-technical dimensions, including organisational, institutional, and cultural features, is imperative for its success.

The mGov4EU ecosystem incorporates building blocks developed within the project, interlinked with national building blocks, and operates within the public sector context. These building blocks ensure a sturdy interoperability between the diverse legacy systems employed by national administrations. However, during the development of these building blocks, non-technical dimensions were essential in sustaining and governing these outcomes and solutions. Thus, we identified several factors in the literature also grounded in empirics which affect the sustainability and governance of such endeavours.

In this chapter we explored which factors influence and drive the mGov4EU project, considering elements such as political will, user awareness, and bilateral agreements. Various factors, such as perceived barriers, influence the development of cross-border mobile government services in a transdisciplinary context. These barriers, which can differ among individuals, businesses, and civil servants, are broadly categorised into four main dimensions: technical, organisational, institutional, and actors. Collectively, these dimensions play a significant role in shaping the progress of mobile government services across borders.

The evaluation of mGov4EU pilots involves a comprehensive approach that considers the transdisciplinary context in two distinct phases. The first phase involves assessing the design phase, while the second phase involves evaluating the execution phase based on the previous assessment. To ensure that the pilots are sustainable and governed properly, the GOFA model is used. This model encompasses governance, operations, finance, and architecture dimensions, allowing a holistic view of the pilots. To establish and monitor business objectives and outcomes, the OKRs methodology is employed within the GOFA framework. This ensures that the pilots are aligned with the overall goals and objectives of mGov4EU.

In addition to the existing strategies, the mGov4EU mobile application utilises the business model canvas ("Cross-Border Mobile Government Services: Exploring Business Model Dynamics in mGov4EU" chapter of this book), a strategic management template for developing new or documenting existing business models. This canvas is a visual chart with elements describing a firm's value proposition, infrastructure, customers, and finances, providing a comprehensive view of the business operations. The business model canvas is not used in isolation. It harmoniously aligns with the OKR methodology, a goal-setting framework that helps organisations set challenging, ambitious goals with measurable results. OKRs are designed to align the goals of individuals and teams with the companies, prioritise actions, improve teamwork, and focus on results. Integrating the business model canvas with the OKR methodology in the mGov4EU mobile application serves a critical role. It facilitates the development and continuous refinement of innovative business models. This approach allows the application to adapt to changing market dynamics, user needs, and technological advancements. It fosters a culture of innovation and agility within the organisation, ensuring the application remains relevant, competitive, and valuable to its users. This strategic combination of the business model canvas and OKR methodology underscores the commitment of the mGov4EU mobile application to deliver superior value to its users, continually innovate, and achieve its business objectives. It is a testament to the application's robust strategic planning and execution capabilities.

The successful completion of any project requires the involvement of experts, public administrators, and academics at different stages. To ensure internal co-creation and co-design, it is important to involve various stakeholders in the project's ongoing development and execution. Using a transdisciplinary evaluation framework helps facilitate the co-creation principle by promoting collaboration and knowledge sharing [19]. As the project progresses, the co-creation principle will evolve, enabling the engagement of stakeholders from diverse backgrounds to contribute to its success.

References

1. Krimmer, R., Prentza, A., Mamrot, S. (eds.): The once-only principle (TOOP). Springer (2021)
2. Mamrot, S. and K. Rzyszczak, Implementation of the 'once-only' principle in Europe – national approach. 2020
3. Prentza, A., et al.: TOOP pilot experiences: challenges and achievements in implementing once-only in different domains and member states. In: Krimmer, R., Prentza, A., Mamrot, S. (eds.) The once-only principle: the TOOP project, pp. 191–207. Springer International Publishing, Cham (2021)
4. Krimmer, R., et al.: European interoperability landscape report 2022 public report (2022)
5. Gil-Garcia, J.R., Pardo, T., Pardo, T.A.: E-government success factors: mapping practical tools to theoretical foundations. Gov. Inf. Q. 22(2), 187–216 (2005)

6. Germanakos, P., Christodoulou, E., Samaras, G.: A European perspective of E-government presence – where do we stand? The EU- 10 case. In Electronic Government. Berlin, Heidelberg: Springer (2007)
7. Gascó, M., et al., Determinants and barriers of e-procurement: a European comparison of public sector experiences. 2018
8. Olesk, M.: Challenges of collaborative digital government: e-participation, open government data and cross-border interoperability. Tallinn University of Technology (2020)
9. Leosk, N., et al.: Drivers for and barriers to the cross-border implementation of the once-only principle. In: Krimmer, R., Prentza, A., Mamrot, S. (eds.) The once-only principle: the TOOP project, pp. 38–60. Springer International Publishing, Cham (2021)
10. European Union, *Tallinn Declaration on eGovernment*. 2017. p. at the ministerial meeting during Estonian Presidency of the Council of the EU on 6 October 2017
11. Schmidt, C., et al., "When need becomes necessity" - the single digital gateway regulation and the once-only principle from a European point of view. 2021
12. Schmidt, C., Krimmer, R.: How to implement the European digital single market: identifying the catalyst for digital transformation. J. Eur. Integr. **44**(1), 59–80 (2022)
13. Commission, E, et al.: Long-term sustainability of digital service infrastructures: final report. Publications Office (2017)
14. Niven, P.R., Lamonte, B.: Objectives and key results: driving focus, alignment, and engagement with OKRs. Wiley, Hoboken, NJ (2016)
15. Stray, V., et al.: Using objectives and key results (OKRs) and slack: a case study of coordination in large-scale distributed agile (2021)
16. Diehl, A., Business Model Canvas – Geschäftsmodelle visualisieren, strukturieren und diskutieren (2018)
17. Vargo, S., Maglio, P., Akaka, M.: On value and value co-creation: a service systems and service logic perspective. Eur. Manag. J. **26**, 145–152 (2008)
18. Torfing, J., Sørensen, E., Røiseland, A.: Transforming the public sector into an arena for co-creation: barriers, drivers, benefits, and ways forward, p. 51. Administration & Society (2016)
19. Eibl, G., et al.: Towards a transdisciplinary evaluation framework for mobile cross-border government services. In Electronic government. Springer International Publishing, Cham (2022)

Cross-Border Mobile Government Services: Exploring Business Model Dynamics in mGov4EU

Thomas J. Lampoltshammer ⓘ, Rachelle Sellung ⓘ, and Stefan Dedovic ⓘ

Abstract The mGov4EU project represents an ambitious effort to revolutionise European mobile government services. It aims to develop an ecosystem that integrates state-of-the-art digital wallet approaches within the framework of eIDAS and SDG. This initiative is pivotal in fostering a seamless interface between citizens, businesses, and public administrations, enhancing the efficiency and user experience in accessing government services. Despite its potential, the mGov4EU project confronts many challenges, including legal compliance, technical interoperability, user acceptance, and the formulation of viable and sustainable business models. These challenges are particularly pronounced in the public sector, where traditional business strategies may not align seamlessly with innovative digital service models. This chapter focuses on examining the business model aspects of the mGov4EU project. It explores the strategies and priorities of the project's partners, particularly in the context of sustaining and scaling the project outcomes within the European framework. It reflects on decisions, as well as challenges accordingly.

Keywords mGov4EU · eIDAS · SDG · Digital government services · Business model innovation · Public sector · Interoperability · User-centric services

T. J. Lampoltshammer (✉)
University for Continuing Education Krems, Krems an der Donau, Austria
e-mail: thomas.lampoltshammer@donau-uni.ac.at

R. Sellung
Fraunhofer IAO, Stuttgart, Germany
e-mail: rachelle.sellung@iao.fraunhofer.de

S. Dedovic
KU Leuven, Leuven, Belgium

University of Tartu, Tartu, Estonia
e-mail: stefan.dedovic@kuleuven.be; stefan.dedovic@ut.ee

1 Introduction

The core objective of the mGov4EU (Mobile Cross-Border Government Services for Europe) project is to design, implement, and evaluate innovative solutions toward an ecosystem for secure and user-centric mobile government services [1], particularly in integrating digital wallet approaches. An essential part of this ecosystem is extending the development and use of technological building blocks within the domains of eIDAS (Electronic Identification, Authentication, and Trust Services) and SDG (Single Digital Gateway) via the realisation of three different piloting domains, i.e. mobile signature, smart mobility, as well as electronic voting. The overall vision is that the mGov4EU approach will ultimately foster the interaction between citizens, businesses, and public administrations while significantly reducing the associated burden concerning complicated processes and administrative overhead in general [2].

Before this backdrop, the success and sustainability of such an ecosystem and its included building blocks face not only legal challenges, challenges of technical interoperability, and challenges concerning usability and user acceptance [3] but also business-related challenges. These business-related challenges are faced from both sides, the public sector side and the business sector side [4]. Besides others, these challenges include securing sustainable funding sources, balancing short-term costs vs. long-term benefits, or integrating within existing business models and strategies [5–7].

Given this scenario of challenges, this chapter investigated the perspective of mGov4EU's business partners concerning initial business model venues for their developed building blocks and pilot artefacts. This contribution aims to explore the focus points of developing partners in the context of a European project concerning perceived priorities for sustaining their project outcomes.

The remainder of this chapter is structured as follows: Section 2 discusses related work concerning business model concepts in general, as well as current developments of business model innovation within the public sector. Section 3 then continues with the description of the project setting, the chosen methodology for exploring business model dynamics within the project, as well as the data used within this chapter. Section 4 then presents a summary of the business model dynamics, followed by Sect. 5, which discusses interesting findings and some initial thoughts on touching points with current developments in the public sector. Finally, Sect. 6 closes the chapter with our conclusions, alongside starting points for future work.

2 Background

The focus of this section is twofold. A brief overview of business model concepts from a general perspective is provided on the one side. Conversely, the current state of play within the public sector is briefly summarised. This information combined shall enable readers to put the results of the workshops into perspective.

2.1 Business Model Concepts

The concept of the business model, originally coined in 1957, encompasses a range of definitions that encapsulate its elements and capacity to generate value [8]. Most definitions explain business models as concepts that describe and define how businesses work and the value generated by stakeholders [9]. In addition, Osterwalder's widely known definition of a business model states that a business model describes the rationale of how an organisation creates, delivers, and captures value [10].

Research has been conducted in various fields regarding concepts or approaches to business models. Three perspectives that have shown an interesting intertwining of approaches for business models are the following [11, 12]: (i) information technology, (ii) organisational management, and (iii) strategic management.

First, from an information technology perspective, business model concepts took an approach that eventually evolved into an organisational theory approach, and strategic management approaches for business models were more of a management tool [12]. This perspective eventually developed tools and technologies that would help assist in faster and more efficient processes regarding documentation and analyses. In [13], the authors presented a business model concept that is separated into three steps:

1. The CEO and/or responsible managers determine the available resources and business objectives.
2. The system developer designs the structure and the business process, including the appropriation of the resources, thus presenting the business model as a simplified business process.
3. Development of an information system based on the business model.

Second, the work of [14] highlights that organisational theory views a business model as more of an abstract depiction of the company's architecture. This architecture would aim to achieve high results by optimising its organisational regulations. Further, this interpretation sees that the business model is no longer reduced to the first stages of technology development and includes a wider range of services. Regarding organisational theory, it is assumed that some business model goals are to understand key business methods better, identify outsourcing opportunities, and try out new business concepts [12].

Third, the strategic management approach to business models shows how to incorporate strategic components in the conception. The approach is based on resource-based and market-based views. It relies on strategic approaches to allow flexibility to shape and change current business models and tailor them to the situation. In addition, there is an introduction of innovation factors that can also impact business models [11, 12].

2.2   Business Model Innovation in the Public Sector

The public sector, encompassing various governmental and semi-governmental organisations, has traditionally been viewed as rigid and slow to adapt compared to its private sector counterparts [15]. However, recent literature indicates a significant shift toward innovation and adaptability in public sector management.

Within the strive for innovation, public sector organisations face similar challenges regarding alignment and anticipation of stakeholder perspectives [16]. By their very nature, public organisations cater to a broad spectrum of stakeholders, including citizens, policymakers, and other governmental entities. The complexity lies in the diverse and sometimes conflicting expectations of these groups. Unlike private companies primarily focusing on customer needs and shareholder value, public organisations must juggle multiple, often competing, interests. This necessitates a delicate balance between delivering public value (i.e. social good and sustainability) and maintaining operational efficiency [17]. While private sector organisations increasingly embrace such values within the business models as well [18], their focus is still more towards profit orientation [19].

Within this context, [20] advocates an innovation-based approach as a key strategy for public sector organisations. Public institutions must evolve continually to remain relevant and effective in rapidly changing societal and economic landscapes. This perspective encourages public sector organisations to adopt more dynamic and flexible business models similar to those in the private sector. This approach allows public entities to respond more swiftly to today's multi-faced changes and emerging stakeholder demands, enhancing their ability to serve the public effectively.

An excellent example of a framework approach towards public sector business model innovation can be found in the work of [21]. This comprehensive framework can be used by public sector organisations as a strategic planning tool, reflecting the necessity for reflexive actions in highly dynamic environments, as well as the necessity for revisited (value) negotiation with the relevant stakeholders.

3   Methodology

To assess the initial business model venues of the mGov4EU developing partners, the Business Model Canvas (BMC) was used to plan and assess potential business model approaches and solutions based on the developed building blocks and pilot artefacts. A BMC is a strategy tool used for visualising, evaluating, and, if necessary, changing business models of organisations or solutions [22].

The model comprises a single-page document consisting of nine boxes, each representing a fundamental element of a business. The BMC is split into two sections: one emphasises the customer or the market (external factors beyond organisational control) and one focuses on the business (internal factors primarily within the organisational control). This is tied with the value propositions, highlighting the value exchange between business and customer. The nine central elements are:

1. Customer segments: The different groups of people or organisations that a business aims to reach and serve
2. Value propositions: The products or services a business offers its customers
3. Channels: The ways through which a business delivers its products or services to its customers
4. Customer relationships: The types of relationships that a business establishes with its customers
5. Revenue streams: The ways through which a business generates revenue from its customers
6. Key resources: The most important assets that a business needs to operate
7. Key activities: The most important things a business must do to deliver its value proposition
8. Key partnerships: A business must work with other businesses or organisations to deliver its value proposition
9. Cost structure: The costs that a business incurs to operate

To populate this strategic instrument, a co-creation workshop was facilitated during a project meeting in Barcelona in October 2022 with the partners of the mGov4EU project. The approach involved a detailed examination of each section, with ample time allotted for partners to address the pertinent questions associated with each unit. The workshop analysis followed a thematic synthesis approach [23] and gained a common theme for each proposed business model aspect.

For better reference, Table 1 outlines the questions posed by our partners during the workshop.

4 Results

The following section summarises the thematic synthesis for each cluster of aspects within the BMC, i.e. the customer segments and value propositions, the distribution channels and customer relations, the revenue streams and key resources, as well as key activities and cost structures.

4.1 Customer Segments (Key Partnerships) and Value Propositions

The principal group or organisations that the mGov4EU solution aims to reach predominantly comprises entities within the public service domain, encompassing both providers and consumers of public services. Within the public service providers' side is a heterogeneous cohort containing local, national, and supranational public

Table 1 Set of supporting inputs during the workshop

Customer segments	Value propositions	Channels	Customer relationships	Revenue streams	Key resources	Key activities	Key partnerships	Cost structure
For whom do we provide a solution?	What customer problem do we solve?	How can we reach out to our "customers"?	What do our customers expect from us? Relationships are established through channels	You must ask yourself, for what value is each customer segment genuinely willing to pay?	What kind of resources do we need for our solution/project?	How do we plan to fulfil our value proposition? What key activities must we conduct after our project ends to sustain the solution?	The key partners are entities that might/must be involved in our project/specific solution without whom our solution doesn't have a purpose	What are the most important costs inherent in our business model?
Who are our most important customers?	Why does our project/solution matter?	How do we reach our customers (e.g. EC, public administrations, businesses)	Examples and types of relationships: transactional (on an occasional basis), personal assistance (customer representative), self-service (no help)	How would they prefer to pay?	Intellectual (brand patents, copyrights), human resources for maintenance, financial resources, data inputs	These activities include research development, marketing, patenting, selling, updating, and maintenance		Which key resources are most expensive?
Who do you think will use/buy our solution (eSignature, eID Wallet, etc.)?				How much does each revenue stream contribute to overall revenues in percentages of the total?				Which key activities are most expensive?

administrations alongside private sector enterprises, each delineated by distinct responsibilities and requirements. Particularly noteworthy is the imperative faced by public service providers who embark on the digitisation of their procedures. This transformative process needs the integration of electronic identification (eID) solutions, with such solutions commonly sourced from central governmental authorities or endorsed by supranational institutions, notably directorates engaged in proposing a unified solution (such as DG DIGIT, DG CNECT, DG GROW). Depending on Member States' (MS) public administration organisational structure and culture, providers may extend to private sector organisations that offer public services and operate transnationally within the European Union (EU).

From the public service consumer perspective in digital governmental interactions, the stakeholders are diverse, comprising public administrations, businesses, and citizens. From the standpoint of consumers engaged in digital governmental interactions, the stakeholder landscape is characterised by digital government service relationships, including public administrations, businesses, and citizens. The efficacy of mGov4EU solutions in meeting the needs of these diverse stakeholders hinges on the strategic alignment of the sustainability and governance paradigms relevant within the mobile government domain.

The mGov4EU project offers a solution to target users that presents a range of essential values that can enhance the primary missions of the target organisations. The project partners have envisaged values promoting digital democracy and digital sovereignty, thereby increasing EU values and benefiting citizens' and public administration's efficiency and effectiveness. Digital democracy encompasses the values of trust, authenticity, and security. In the case of Internet voting use, the project demonstrates that voting can be carried out across borders with a higher level of security and trust, including the main parts of electronic authentication and identification. In addition, digital sovereignty over data empowers citizens and public administrations to control data exchange through various mechanisms, including consent forms and user acceptance. Moreover, with the mobile-first approach, citizens benefit from the ease of use and user experience. The mGov4EU solution represents the first integrated eID/SDG mobile-friendly solution, offering citizens an increase in public service consumption efficiency. For public administrations, the solution is expected to increase efficiency, efficacy, and effectiveness in exchanging data and documents across borders.

Furthermore, the mGov4EU solution enhances EU values by increasing possibilities of digital access to public services across borders, following and supporting policy developments in the EU. Respective MSs and European Commission (EC) directorates may reuse the building blocks developed by mGov4EU. Specifically, with the policy development of the new European Digital Identity Wallet (EUDI) proposed by the EC, the mGov4EU artefacts may already be reused. Thus, the mGov4EU advantage lies in its novel and innovative approach, developed for the first time in the EU, and may help existing developments in the EU policy cycle.

4.2 Channels and Customer Relationships

The partners presented a variety of ways to promote the mGov4EU solution for the channels section of the BMC, approaches on communicating the solution to the target groups, primarily public administrations and the private sector.

First, it includes presentations at events such as, inter-alia, scientific and technical conferences and startup competitions. Second, existing contacts from partners' networks could be utilised to reach out to respective countries' public administrations. Third is reaching out to the general public by promoting the solution through public and social media, word of mouth, and general dissemination (newsletters). Last, the partners would reach out through scientific publications in respective journals and conference proceedings to the specific public in the technical and knowledgeable field.

For the customer relationships, the focus of the mGov4EU project would be based on the transactional, dedicated personal assistance and self-service type of relationships. The transactional model includes individual interactions without a long-term commitment; this includes using the mGov4EU solutions, primarily based on the customer. However, in case of need and unforeseen issues, the partners would have dedicated personal assistance to help overcome issues. Last, the self-service approach will also be used as an extensive knowledge base, frequently asked questions (FAQs), and tutorials that may allow users to address the issues, learn new features, and make the most of the mGov4EU solution without requesting personal assistance.

4.3 Revenue Streams and Key Resources

The mGov4EU project is driven by a non-profit agenda, primarily supported by public funding. Additional revenue avenues may be explored by providing consultancy services and licensing for commercial purposes. The partners identified several important approaches towards revenue streams based on the types of partners involved in the project. While not considering licensing a favourable option, the legal partner deemed consultancy fees for integration and customisation more viable. Technical partners have delineated revenue streams encompassing both non-profit and profit options. While the solution remains proprietary, certain modules of mGov4EU could be made an open source. Customers remit payments per service utilised, independent of the code license. Partners involved in technical aspects have also indicated a lack of specific revenue interest in the non-profit budget context. Alternative revenue streams under consideration include consulting, support, operational contracts, and indirect sources such as added value through extended use by private service providers. Profitable prospects include the solution as a foundational enabler for future endeavours, fostering synergies with related activities, attracting additional clients, and securing public funding. Partners not involved in the technical aspects advocate for an open-source model for public administration and citizens, coupled with licensing for commercial entities. They emphasise customer payment for utilised services. Additional revenue streams include tailored solutions with supplemental license fees, dual licensing, support services for foundational components, base funding from the EC, customer subscription fees, and, notably, charges based on usage.

The successful execution of this project business model necessitates both human and financial capital. Licensing is a pivotal resource; however, the partners have also underscored the importance of legality, data, technical considerations, research and development (R&D) funding, maintenance and marketing, and intellectual resources within their respective business models. The legal partner indicated that a dedicated budget for producing a high-quality demonstration video (akin to the Once-Only Principle Project [24]) would be instrumental in facilitating active promotion. Furthermore, partners proposed that an ownership strategy and licensing arrangements are integral resources. The partners should reach a consensus on a unified strategy if they decide to proceed. From the viewpoint of the technical partners, human and financial resources are indispensable for carrying out the key activities outlined earlier. Expertise in technical and legal domains is also a prerequisite. Partners have additionally highlighted the need for more researchers and developers as key resources and the acquisition of grants for R&D. Mirroring the sentiments of the technical partners, the non-technical partners have cited financial and human resources as necessary for maintenance, support, marketing, and development. They perceive the key resources as contributions to standards and sustainability through new research grants or licensed products at no cost. Data and trust also play crucial roles as key resources.

4.4   Key Activities and Cost Structure

Key activities involved in the business model of the solution are the following. Primarily, the principal activities encompass human resources and R&D activities. Engaging the target demographic facilitates the integration of innovative solutions and ideas, thereby ensuring continuous performance enhancement, maintenance, and support for the updates that need to be provided for the mGov4EU solution. The legal partner indicated the provision of an out-of-the-box demonstration promotion of the resolution and consistent support as their primary activities. The majority of the technical partners identified technical maintenance, development, and marketing activities aimed at disseminating the solution as their main activities. Additional activities include research on usability and privacy aspects and continuous customer support. One technical partner emphasised the importance of communicating with relevant key partners and testing and piloting modules beyond the mGov4EU pilot scope to gain confidence in its broader applicability. Non-technical partners have listed activities such as code stewardship, incorporating the solutions and knowledge into subsequent projects, and publishing the results and repositories. Other activities include R&D, stakeholder engagement, organising and attending fairs, and marketing. Maintenance and support, marketing and information campaigns, continuous improvements and developments, and patenting were also key activities.

The allocation of resources, both human and infrastructural, constitutes a significant portion of the overall expenditure. This is followed by costs associated with marketing and the organisation of events and workshops. Expenditures for R&D, patenting, and legal consultancy will span several years. Lean cost structure is achieved through establishing an expert network and maintaining an online presence for a few years. The need for a Web site and promotional activities is anticipated to persist for a similar duration. The cost structures identified encompass infrastructure, maintenance, marketing, and human resources. This includes developers and senior architects with knowledge of the national/EU environment (eIDAS, SDG), advertising, and support for additional R&D. One technical partner suggested that organising workshops and fares could incur in high costs. By contrast, fare tickets could range from low to medium expenses. Cloud infrastructure is expected to incur medium charges, with human resources being the costliest. In comparison, non-technical partners highlighted human resources, patenting, representation costs (e.g. symposia, events), and technical hardware costs. Additional charges include maintaining an online presence, training on how to use or integrate the building blocks, sandboxing services for demonstrations, and legal consultancy. It was also noted that costs are covered up to a certain technology readiness (TR) level, and as the TR level increases, additional revenue sources will be required.

5   Reflection

This section aims to reflect on a selection of challenges within the respective aspects of the BMC and the associated workshop results to raise awareness for similar development activities and projects and to share the lessons learned.

1. Customer Segments and Value Propositions
   The mGov4EU project targets a broad spectrum of public service stakeholders, including providers and consumers. This dual focus on public service providers (local, national, supranational administrations, and private sector enterprises) and consumers (public administrations, businesses, and citizens) demonstrates a comprehensive approach to digital governance.
   While the project ambitiously addresses a wide range of stakeholders, the challenge lies in catering to these different groups' diverse needs and technical capabilities. Sustainable, digital solutions are required to be accessible and user-friendly for all, especially for citizens who might not be technologically adept. This challenge is further amplified, as building blocks and the underlying technology need to be compatible with existing infrastructure and service ecosystems, which consequently can limit design decisions and would occasionally require a fundamental redesign of either the digital building block or the service ecosystem at its core.

2. Channels and Customer Relationships

The varied communication strategies, including presentations, media promotion, and scientific publications, indicate a thorough approach to outreach and engagement. The focus on transactional, personal assistance and self-service in customer relationships is commendable.

However, relying on transactional relationships might not foster long-term user engagement or loyalty. Implementing strategies must incorporate the promotion of ongoing engagement and feedback loops with its users. Again, this requires a high level of alignment, as direct interaction without an intermediary might be limited depending on who the users are, e.g. public administration vs. citizens.

3. Revenue Streams and Key Resources

The non-profit nature of the project, supported by public funding and supplemented by consultancy services and licensing, reflects a commitment to public service. The consideration of open-source components is a positive step towards transparency and collaboration.

The challenge will be maintaining financial sustainability and balancing the need for revenue generation with the project's non-profit ethos. Additionally, reliance on public funding can be precarious, requiring the exploration of more diverse and stable revenue streams. However, the dual use of developed technologies, i.e. in the public and the private sector, might be limited due to the high degree of specialisation of the provided service or building block. Furthermore, this dual-use strategy needs to be embraced from the very beginning, as changing such fundamental aspects later might introduce insurmountable obstacles.

4. Key Activities and Cost Structure

The emphasis on R&D, technical maintenance, marketing, and legal considerations showcases a well-rounded approach to project development. The allocation of resources to these activities is critical for the project's success.

There is a risk of resource allocation being spread too thin across the various building blocks to be sustained. The cost structure also raises concerns about long-term financial sustainability, especially given the reliance on external funding.

6 Conclusions

The mGov4EU project represents a significant stride towards realising a digitally empowered European Union, where cross-border government services are accessible, efficient, and user-centric. This initiative, as explored in this chapter, aligns with the broader goals of eIDAS and SDG, fostering an ecosystem that is not only technologically advanced but also secure and trustworthy.

The project's emphasis on integrating digital wallet approaches and developing technological building blocks has contributed significantly towards the future of digital governance and service provision. By focusing on mobile platforms, mGov4EU addresses a critical aspect of modern communication and service delivery, acknowledging the ubiquitous nature of mobile technology in everyday life. This approach ensures that government services are not only more accessible but also aligned with the contemporary user's expectations of convenience and immediacy.

Throughout the various stages of development and implementation, the project has demonstrated a keen understanding of the complex landscape of public service provision in the EU. The heterogeneity of stakeholders, including public administrations, businesses, and citizens, presents unique challenges in terms of requirements, expectations, and technical capabilities. The mGov4EU project has addressed these challenges, showcasing a model of inclusiveness and adaptability. One strong aspect, in particular, is the project's commitment to digital democracy and sovereignty, which resonates deeply with the core values of the European Union. By emphasising principles like trust, security, and data empowerment, mGov4EU reinforces the democratic foundations upon which the EU is built.

The project's business model approach, which encompasses diverse revenue streams and resource allocation strategies, reflects the need for a nuanced understanding of the financial landscape. The non-profit nature, supplemented by consultancy services and licensing, balances public service commitment and financial viability. Moreover, the open-source components of the project promote transparency, collaboration, and innovation, setting a precedent for future initiatives in the public sector.

However, as with any innovative venture, the mGov4EU project faces its set of challenges. While a strength, the diversity of the stakeholder base also poses the risk of diluting the focus and impact. Financial sustainability remains a concern, especially given the reliance on external funding sources. Furthermore, the technological landscape is rapidly evolving, and future trustees of the project results need to carefully but swiftly follow these developments and act upon them.

References

1. Eibl, G., Lampoltshammer, T., Temple, L.: Towards identifying factors influencing mobile government adoption: an exploratory literature review. eJ eDemocr Open Gov. **14**, 1–18 (2022)
2. Eibl, G., Temple, L., Sellung, R., Dedovic, S., Alishani, A., Schmidt, C.: Towards a transdisciplinary evaluation framework for mobile cross-border government services (2022). doi:https://doi.org/10.1007/978-3-031-15086-9_35
3. Schmidt, C., Krimmer, R., Lampoltshammer, J., T.: "When need becomes necessity"-The single digital gateway regulation and the once-only principle from a European point of view. Open Identity Summit. **2021** (2021)
4. Kaplan, S.: Business models aren't just for business. Harv. Bus. Rev. **19** (2011)
5. Vasilescu, L.: Accessing finance for innovative EU SMES key drivers and challenges. Econ. Rev. J Econ. Bus. **12**, 35–47 (2014)
6. Eniola, A.A., Entebang, H.: SME firm performance-financial innovation and challenges. Procedia Soc. Behav. Sci. **195**, 334–342 (2015)
7. Eggers, F.: Masters of disasters? Challenges and opportunities for SMEs in times of crisis. J. Bus. Res. **116**, 199–208 (2020)
8. Bellman, R., Clark, C.E., Malcolm, D.G., Craft, C.J., Ricciardi, F.M.: On the construction of a multi-stage, multi-person business game. Oper. Res. **5**, 469–503 (1957). https://doi.org/10.1287/opre.5.4.469

9. Geissdoerfer, M., Savaget, P., Evans, S.: The Cambridge business model innovation process. Proc. Manuf. **8**, 262–269 (2017)
10. Osterwalder, A., Pigneur, Y., Tucci, C.L.: Clarifying business models: origins, present, and future of the concept. Communications of the association for. Inf. Syst. **16**, 1 (2005)
11. DaSilva, C.M., Trkman, P.: Business model: what it is and what it is not. Long Range Plan. **47**, 379–389 (2014)
12. Wirtz, B.W.: The business model concept. In: Wirtz, B.W. (ed.) Business model management: design - process - instruments, pp. 7–17. Springer International Publishing, Cham (2020). https://doi.org/10.1007/978-3-030-48017-2_2
13. Eriksson, H.E., Penker, M.: Business modeling with UML. New York. 12 (2000)
14. Al-Debi, M.M., El-Haddadeh, R., Avison, D.: Defining the business model in the new world of digital business. AMCIS 2008 proceedings. 300 (2008)
15. Windrum, P.: Innovation and entrepreneurship in public services. Innovation in public sector services: Entrepreneurship, creativity and management. 3–20 (2008)
16. Bernier, L., Hafsi, T., Deschamps, C.: Environmental determinants of public sector innovation: a study of innovation awards in Canada. Public Manag. Rev. **17**, 834–856 (2015). https://doi.org/10.1080/14719037.2013.867066
17. Wirtz, B.W., Weyerer, J.C., Kohler, J.: Public business model management: a literature review-based integrated framework. IJPSPM. **11**, 1 (2023). https://doi.org/10.1504/IJPSPM.2023.128533
18. Lampoltshammer, T.J., Albrecht, V., Raith, C.: Teaching digital sustainability in higher education from a transdisciplinary perspective. Sustain. For. **13**, 12039 (2021)
19. Ricciardi, F., Zardini, A., Rossignoli, C.: Organizational dynamism and adaptive business model innovation: the triple paradox configuration. J. Bus. Res. **69**, 5487–5493 (2016)
20. Talbot, C.: Paradoxes and prospects of 'public value'. Public Money Manag. **31**, 27–34 (2011). https://doi.org/10.1080/09540962.2011.545544
21. Wirtz, B.W., Kubin, P.R.M., Weyerer, J.C.: Business model innovation in the public sector: an integrative framework. Public Manag. Rev. **25**, 340–375 (2023). https://doi.org/10.1080/14719037.2021.1972703
22. Osterwalder, A., Pigneur, Y.: Designing business models and similar strategic objects: the contribution of IS. J. Assoc. Inf. Syst. **14**, 237 (2013)
23. Creswell, J.W.: Educational research: Planning, conducting, and evaluating quantitative and qualitative research. Pearson Higher Ed. (2020)
24. Lampoltshammer, T.J., John, K., Helger, P., Piswanger, C.-M.: Connectathons-a sustainable path towards development in European large-scale pilots. In: Proceedings of ongoing research, practitioners, posters, workshops, and projects of the international conference EGOV-CeDEM-ePart. pp. 207–214 (2019)

Future Outlook and Research Ideas

Thomas J. Lampoltshammer ⓘ, Herbert Leitold, Carsten Schmidt ⓘ, and Thomas Zefferer ⓘ

Abstract This chapter uses the lessons learned from technical work and piloting of the mGov4EU project, as well as experience made so far in developing the Single Digital Gateway (SDG) Once-Only Technical System (OOTS) and the European Digital Identity Wallet (EUDIW). These are our basis, and we dare to look into the future. The two European flagship policy initiatives OOTS and EUDIW are meant to facilitate citizens' journey through European public services but also are meant as tools to navigate private services in the Digital Single Market. It, however, would be naïve to assume that setting such complex systems into production is the end of an endeavour. We might only learn through first experience where pitfalls lie but in particular what opportunities are given that haven't been seen before. We, therefore, give authors' views on where this road might lead us and what research might be essential to get there. The chapter, thus, aims at anticipating what might be needed to reap the benefits of OOTS and EUDIW in a mobile world from a governance perspective, a privacy and data protection perspective, a services perspective and a mobile technologies perspective. Therefore, each section first sets the scene by outlining the status. This is followed by addressing some challenges and gives an outlook by indicating how research might address these challenges.

T. J. Lampoltshammer
University for Continuing Education Krems, Krems an der Donau, Austria
e-mail: thomas.lampoltshammer@donau-uni.ac.at

H. Leitold (✉)
Secure Information Technology Center - Austria A-SIT, Graz, Austria
e-mail: Herbert.Leitold@a-sit.at

C. Schmidt
University of Tartu, Tartu, Estonia
e-mail: carsten.schmidt@ut.ee

T. Zefferer
A-SIT Plus GmbH, Wien, Austria
e-mail: thomas.zefferer@a-sit.at

© The Author(s) 2025
V. Homburg et al. (eds.), *From Electronic to Mobile Government*,
https://doi.org/10.1007/978-3-031-64471-9_12

Keywords eIDAS · SDG · EUDI Wallet · OOTS · AI · Blockchain · Once-Only

1   The Basis: eIDAS, SDG and Synergies Between These

The two EU Regulations SDG [1] and eIDAS [2], the ongoing eIDAS revision [3], respectively, address citizen and business needs in the Digital Single Market with a particular focus on cross-border services. SDG and electronic identity provisions of the original eIDAS Regulations are primarily directed to the public sector. This is due to Member State (MS) obligations to integrate in their services. The eIDAS revision enhances such mandatory support to the private sector, in particular for the European Digital Identity (EUDI) framework—commonly referred to as the EUDI Wallet or EUDIW [4]—in case such private sector services legally or contractually require strong authentication.

The SDG OOTS [5] and the EUDI Wallet have in common that the provision of citizen or business data shall be facilitated. Such citizen or business data are referred to as evidence in SDG and as electronic attestations of attributes (EAA) or qualified electronic attestations of attributes (QEAA) in eIDAS, respectively. For simplicity, we refer to both evidence and EAA as "attributes". While the common goal of providing attributes is shared by both regulations, its implementation follows quite different paradigms: OOTS aims to relieve a citizen or business from providing needed attributes whatsoever, as with OOTS, a system is established where (public) service providers can, based on citizen consent, request attributes (i.e. evidence in SDG-terminology) from the competent authority that is authoritative for such data, usually some form of register. The eIDAS Revision, however, puts the citizen or business into the centre of data provision, as the EUDI Wallet is meant to be a mobile tool that can hold and provide attributes (EAA or QEAA in eIDAS terminology), and thus, the citizen is somehow a carrier of her data and in control of it.

These two paradigms are conceptually different: With OOTS, evidence is requested at the very moment it is needed by a service. Provided the citizen consents to do so, the evidence requester needs to learn which competent authority is holding and is authoritative for such attributes. This needs quite some core platform services like directories or semantic mappings of different evidence MS hold to a service's information needs and requires common protocols and interfaces—this is what OOTS essentially is about and what has been enshrined in an Implementing Act [5] and accompanying technical specifications. The OOTS infrastructure comes with relieving the citizen or businesses from taking care of who can provide which information about them but is currently limited to public sector services and public sector attribute providers. With the EUDI Wallet, on the other hand, the service requests information it requires directly from the citizen or business as EAA or QEAA through the Wallet. Thus, less core services are involved in the very moment when the citizen or business wants to get service but comes with the need to anticipate what the actual information demand of this service is and has to get these attributes as EAA or QEAA with the EUDI Wallet in advance. Note, that therefore some MS aim to provide EAA also synchronously by the EUDI Wallet, retrieving attributes from authentic sources only when required. However, for the general case of an EUDI Wallet storing data asynchronously in advance, one could argue that the EUDI Wallet is better suited for attributes that are frequently needed and that are not too dynamic, as outdated information is of little use when asynchronously stored ahead. Address and age being somehow atomic attributes are simple examples, but the Wallet is also meant to hold complex EAA like a mobile driving licence. OOTS seems superior, in particular with complex processes where citizens may not know what the service's actual information need is, where information needs are not static but dependent on context or simply where citizens do not want to manage their data on their own. Examples of SDG evidence would be register excerpts like a professional qualification certificate. These are, however, just examples where OOTS and the Wallet might be seen serving different situations and needs, and a clear-cut borderline is not given—to the contrary, OOTS and the EUDI Wallet may both serve a particular service on the same information need; hence, the objectives are similar despite conceptual differences.

Taking such conceptional differences aside, there are dependencies between SDG and eIDAS, as well as obvious similarities. On the one hand, service access via OOTS requires authentication, which eIDAS provides. On the other hand, for providing EAA to the EUDI Wallet, some common interfaces for retrieving data are needed, which OOTS is developing. Further synergies exist, and in an attempt to exploit these, the European Commission has established an OOTS-EUDI Contact Group of MS experts so that investments in OOTS and EUDI can cross-fertilise and lead to even better user experience.

Being directed to public services a communality is that mobile government (mGovernment) is still in its infancy. Governments have of course not overlooked the trend of using mobile phones and, in particular, smartphones to access the Internet and services. Those MS that already have a mobile first strategy are ahead and provide various mGovernment apps. Still, eGovernment services are long-term investments and procedural rules that have grown from traditional ways of interacting with government-defined service needs. Mobile services, however, often follow different paradigms like being transaction-based rather than conventional session-based services with browsers. A main difference is of course the devices' form factor, where filling forms or attaching documents in many conventional eGovernment processes give questionable user experience. This is where both OOTS and EUDIW can make a difference in no longer bothering users with filling data, provided that services make intensive use of it aiming at a user experience as convenient as the many commercial apps have that we all use daily, where ordering goods or booking travels is at one's fingertip.

The remainder of this chapter addresses exactly these challenges, namely, how synergies between the SDG OOTS and the eIDAS EUDIW can be best exploited and how these basic infrastructures are best to prepare for seamless mobile user experience. The focus is on giving an outlook and identifying research challenges that are to be addressed to make that happen. We therefore structure this chapter into sections viewing current challenges from a governance angle, a privacy and data protection perspective, a services view and from mobile technology constraints. Each of these sections first sketches the current state in relation to SDG and eIDAS, then highlights challenges or potential pain points and finally elaborates on research questions that might be worthwhile solving to overcome these. The chapter takes the findings of the mGov4EU project into account, complemented by the authors' own experiences and views. Such personal views in excess of common project findings are justified, taking into account that research by its heart is a creative process where excellent results can be driven by a consensual view on a challenge but often even more by individual ideas.

2   Governance Outlook

At the time of writing this chapter, the legislative process on the eIDAS revision has not yet been completed, as well as the launch of OOTS in December 2023 being close ahead. Still, the political agreement reached in the trilogue and the status of the EUDIW toolbox process [4] gives a first glance of what lies ahead for eIDAS. Moreover, the public OOTS launch in December 2023 was a few days ahead when these lines where written, so practical experience with SDG was limited to a few Connectathon events where the European Commission and Member States got together for interoperability events and did their first practical tests with the OOTS components.

With the legal basis of the SDG Regulation [1], the existing eIDAS Regulation [2] and its revision [3], the top-level governance structure is defined. An SDG Coordination Group governs OOTS, and a similar role is taken by the eIDAS Coordination Network and its successor, European Digital Identity Cooperation Group (EDICG), under the eIDAS revision, respectively. In these governance groups, the European Commission works together with Member States to shape OOTS and the EUDI Wallet, respectively. This includes preparing the comitology of the Implementing Acts as secondary legislation.

With SDG primarily directed to the public sector— it binds public services in requesting evidence from public sector competent authorities cross-border—the public sector-led SDG Cooperation Group seems suitable in governing OOTS. At first sight, the same holds for EDICG in relation to the EUDI Wallet, as obligations are directed to Member States like to issue a Wallet, to provide person identification data (PID) and to provide interfaces to competent authorities so EAA and QEAA can get issued to the EUDI Wallet. Thus, the public sector-led EDICG is a suitable vehicle to represent public sector interest.

However, when taking a closer look at the eIDAS revision, the stakeholder landscape is much broader. Private sector services have a right to integrate with the EUDI Wallet. Some sectors even have an obligation to do so. The latter include sectors as important as banking and financial services, telecommunications, health or social security, as well as gatekeepers under the Digital Markets Act

(DMA) [6]. In September 2023, the European Commission announced the six big companies as first gatekeepers under DMA: Alphabet (Google), Amazon, Apple, ByteDance (TikTok), Meta (Facebook) and Microsoft. Aside from these sectors and organisations that will act as relying parties making use of the Wallet, further stakeholders exist like qualified trust service providers (QTSP) that will offer citizens provision of QEAA, the software industry that might want to provide integration components for the EUDI Wallet or develop Wallets on their own, qualified consumer protection organisations or privacy advocates.

It is not realistic and would be naïve to assume that EDICG, which likely will be recruited from Member State electronic identity and trust services experts, can alone cover requirements of such a diverse stakeholder grouping or can represent their interest. Drivers, barriers and opportunities of policy initiatives are to be considered for cross-border governance [7].

We argue that stakeholder engagement needs to be broadened to best reap the benefits of OOTS and EUDI Wallet and the synergies between them. Policy-led initiatives like the EUDI-OOTS Contact Group are a good first step but at most scratch the surface on what these infrastructures can deliver. Public consultation on the outcomes should be a step to get the various interests heard but shall be further intensified by community building to have stakeholders engage themselves.

3   Privacy and Data Protection Outlook

OOTS and the EUDI Wallet process personal data in order to facilitate citizens' service needs and, thus, with the purpose to serve citizens. Still, trust needs to be earned so that citizens feel that their data stays protected and does not get misused. Both eIDAS and SDG have data protection at their core. The implementation of the SDGR is set to streamline and simplify the provision of cross-border digital services within the European Union. This regulation aims to create a unified digital environment, making it easier for citizens and businesses to access and utilise public services across borders. Mobile solutions will play a crucial role in realising the objectives of the SDGR, enabling users to seamlessly interact with government services through their smartphones. The harmonisation of digital processes under the SDGR will reduce bureaucratic barriers, enhancing the efficiency of cross-border transactions and fostering a more interconnected European digital landscape. A complementing key aspect shaping the future landscape of cross-border mGovernment services is the emphasis on data privacy and security, with the General Data Protection Regulation (GDPR) [8] playing a pivotal role. Member State governments are obliged to ensure that cross-border services adhere to stringent data protection standards, safeguarding the personal information of individuals. The GDPR acts as a cornerstone, fostering trust among users and encouraging the adoption of mGovernment services by addressing concerns related to privacy and data security.

The main measures taken by OOTS are that citizen consent is required before a service can issue an evidence request and data preview must be seen by the citizen before such evidence actually gets delivered. The EUDI Wallet has a couple of privacy measures as well. First and upfront, users have to consent to the release of their attributes and, through selective disclosure provisions, can de-select data they do not want to release. This is complemented with the fact that relying parties need to register and declare their information needs. Moreover, the EUDI Wallet shall provide unobservability of the user so citizens cannot be tracked.

While these measures provide basic privacy protection, there are a number of challenges that ask for future research. Firstly, the class of services the Wallet is meant for requires unique identification. This, for instance, holds true for public services or for banking services under "know your customer" (KYC) and anti-money laundering rules. Unique identification shall be supported by eIDAS provisions on identity matching where Member States shall assist in matching to user accounts. However, the provision for unique and persistent person identifiers that the original European Commission proposal [3] and the Council's general approach have foreseen for this class of services has been turned down in the trilogue—the interinstitutional negotiations of the co-legislators Parliament, Commission and Council. While the lack of persistent identifiers can be seen as privacy enhancing, when in combination with the identity matching requirement it essentially means that the latter may need a bigger set of attributes than when supported by unique identifiers. Further research may be needed on how identity matching can best be implemented under data minimisation principles.

A further source of future research related to the EUDI Wallet relates to the use of pseudonyms versus their recovery. The eIDAS revision foresees pseudonymous identifiers as a privacy measure, and one approach commonly followed is to have these pseudonyms device-bound and device-generated, i.e. to have the Wallet create pseudonyms. A user requirement, however, will be that these pseudonyms can get recovered, if the Wallet device that created it gets lost or is defunct. This allows for the user to continue to use accounts that these pseudonyms are linked to, like a social media service. The Wallet foresees backup functions for user data, which can also be seen as questionable. On the one hand, it renders the user in charge to manage their data, which creates efforts or at least needs awareness that such data management is needed. On the other hand, smartphones use hardware-backed secure elements to protect sensitive data. This gives challenges when pseudonyms shall get protected at this level, as they can no longer easily get backed up. Research may be needed on how to best assist citizens in managing their Wallet data like their pseudonyms.

Finally, further work is suggested on how the stringent privacy measures of both OOTS and the EUDI Wallet, such as user consent and selective disclosure, match with usability goals. Authentication and attribute provision as provided by eIDAS and SDG are no goal in themselves but are needed to fulfil the service the citizen is seeking for. Each additional step may be seen as a hurdle in getting these services. This asks for research on how to best align privacy measures with usability.

4 Electronic Services Outlook

Citizens and businesses expect a seamless integration experience when using OOTS and their EUDI Wallet when requesting a service. Public services are, however, still document-based in asking particular evidence like a birth certificate. SDG OOTS does the first step to dematerialise a service's information need from a particular document, in mapping a certain information need to various evidence attributes. To give a simple example, age could either be proven by a birth certificate as well as by a proof of citizenship as OOTS evidence but also by the minimum data set of an eIDAS authentication or an age claim of the EUDI Wallet. Using OOTS and the Wallet seamlessly to provide attributes is also one of the synergies identified by the OOTS-EUDI Contact Group.

Taxonomies of public service requirements could, however, go far further in describing the actual information need rather than evidence or documents. To achieve this, it would need further research on how typically rule-based public services that are tailored to information available in the same state can best handle other states' data. The Wallet poses a particular challenge in that context, as EAA and QEAA need to be provided in advance, unless synchronously retrieved from authentic sources.

We also envision that the sole availability of OOTS and the EUDI Wallet will influence future service design. The current limitation of OOTS to public services and competent authorities does not mean that its concepts cannot be transformed to or be taken up by other sectors. Consider, for instance, a short weekend vacation where the air carrier asks the user for identity card data in its booking app, as the travel will be outside the Schengen area. The car rental app needs driving license data and information about the insurance policy that the user claims providing additional waivers. Finally, the hotel advance room check-in asks for the client's home address and—again—identity card data. These are just some data that may be requested already before the vacation starts. Users currently may employ browser form filler extensions to get these tasks facilitated. This has the downside that the user needs to trust the browser vendor in storing their personal data, as sensitive as the home address. Imagine how the same use case can be carried out when using the home address and identity card data held and safeguarded by the user's EUDI Wallet and where data from the insurance company can be provided by services similar to what OOTS does. Such an approach, however, would need research on how OOTS could get transposed to private sector services in a trustworthy way so that private data providers do not learn user traits. Combine these with advanced cryptographic methods like zero knowledge proofs and the various actors like in our simple example of an air carrier, a car rental company and a hotel can get information they need in a privacy-enhanced manner and without the user having to fetch the data or to entrust other services on managing these.

Public services can be complex and may involve various authorities. With the advent of the EUDI Wallet promising authentication that is supposed to work cross border and with introducing identity matching to serve all public services, research on service redesign is advisable so that citizens' life situations can get better addressed without having them to approach various authorities. The concept of a single point of contact (SPOC) in cross-border public services where a SPOC is meant as a hub orchestrating the process with several authorities was introduced as early as 2006 with the EU Services Directive [9]. With unique high-quality authentication the EUDI Wallet provides, it can be used further beyond businesses that provide services. An example for citizens is the Digital Babypoint that has been introduced as a mobile service in Austria: making massive use of once-only principles and of public registers, the various administrative procedures after birth, such as registering at the parent's home and getting official documents delivered, can be done in one step. The unique identification of a parent in an eGovernment app and the civil status register proving custodianship serve as key to trigger the processes at the various authorities. Several such examples exist nationally, where the public register ecosystem and administrative culture is homogeneous. It however soon grows complex cross border. Research is advisable how life situations involving many competent authorities and different processes can be orchestrated in a service design that works across the EU and get best facilitated by OOTS.

5 Mobile Technologies Outlook

A shift to mobile devices and services is clearly seen but already showing a trend of being "conservative" in the sense of assuming a tablet or smartphone as the primary user device. Personal computing environments are increasingly amended by wearables with less user interaction capabilities but more sensors, as well as edge and cloud services, smart vehicles, etc. with unprecedented computing capabilities. Thus, complementing traditional service offerings by a user's life situation in a privacy-friendly manner can benefit the user with personalised service offerings, as long as their control and privacy are well protected.

Delivering public services electronically has, however, grown from traditional procedural laws and often started from simply transforming these to an electronic replica of the very same process, i.e. have the user fill an application form, enclose the documents needed to prove claims and have the application signed. Carrying out such a process on the smartphone already gives challenges, where just using responsive design alone to match the form factor does not do the job: filling out large forms on a mobile phone, while possible, is cumbersome, and we hardly ever carry electronic copies of official documents like birth certificates with us on the mobile device. That is where the EUDI Wallet and OOTS come into play and can benefit mobile service design: data usually collected through forms and accompanying evidence can be provided as QEAA through the Wallet, which at the same time are already an authentic representation of facts, and making use of OOTS allows one to not bother the user about collecting documents at all. OOTS is meant to have the service take care of this, and based on the consent given by the user, the service can take care of collecting the information needed from the various competent authorities. Thus, constraints given to mobile devices ask for a service design that makes massive use of information provisioning through OOTS and the Wallet.

Also when using OOTS with mobile devices, they can suffer constraints. OOTS foresees the preview of evidence before these are being delivered. Preview seems easy with simple documents or atomic attributes. For complex documents, however, the display form factor can be a challenge. Research is advisable on how information provided by SDG evidence providers can be transformed from paper-inspired documents to a structured representation where rather the actual facts, which the evidence requester needs, gets asserted, not a lengthy document. For example, services granting building permits may only need to know that the applicant is a master builder and prefer that as structured information over a full diploma with nice visual seals.

The EUDI Wallet, while meant to be in production in only a few years—indicatively end of 2026 to early 2027—will require extensive research. A pain point is that the high information security and data protection requirements would ask for support by hardware security elements to operate the Wallet self-contained on the mobile device. Such hardware elements exist on modern smartphones with secure enclaves or trusted execution environments (TEE), but requirements of the Wallet may well exceed their standard functions, like their needed resistance against attacks or the strength of function or the support of novel cryptographic primitives. Mobile devices and their operating systems, however, rarely originate from within the EU, and it remains to be seen how the market will support such needs. Even if the eIDAS Revision will ask gatekeepers under the Digital Market Act [6] to grant Wallet issuers access to the operating system, hardware or software features, some of the desired features may simply not exist on some devices. Think, for instance, of a Wallet issuer that plans to implement zero-knowledge proofs for advanced privacy features and would hope for hardware support of cryptographic primitives for better protection of the processing. Research may be needed how to make the EUDI Wallet broadly available based on technology provided on the market—and some variants are already enshrined in recitals of the eIDAS Revision like making use of external secure elements or remote hardware security modules (HSM)—and gradually advanced as more advanced technology appears.

The EUDI Wallet is mainly thought from technology available and broadly used today, i.e. smartphones. This is pretty limiting for two main reasons:

1. On one hand, services for citizens need to be inclusive and accessible. It should also serve citizens who do not want to or cannot use a smartphone—for whatever the reason may be. Think, for instance, of persons with special needs like visually impaired or persons who need financial aid and cannot afford an expensive phone to file for such subsidy.
2. On the other hand, technology evolves quickly, and we may not yet know the devices we will have in only 5 years, which is when the EUDI Wallet will be set into production. Consider how fast traditional PCs were complemented by tablet computers with different physical interfaces and introducing apps as

a paradigm different to office software, not to mention the smartphone wave and cloud computing. This asks for research on how to complement smartphone Wallets already now so we are ready for such technological progress.

Finally, the EUDI Wallet—while pretty innovative—still can be seen as just an evolution of electronic identity to be used with services as we know them now. With the user holding an electronic identity device that has various other sensors and is already connected to other computing components either in the cloud or in close proximity, we can think further. The very same physical device that holds the Wallet is playing music via the car's entertainment systems and knows my exact location and even the route I will be using through the navigation app. Why should my surrounding full of various computing not mesh and the smart car suggest to me the best road-toll package when approaching the first toll station in another country so I can use the fast lane? The car registration certificate stored as QEAA in my Wallet anyhow can fill the application; OOTS might need to deliver the license number and maximum weight of the boat trailer, and that needs an extra toll; and finally, the payment can be made through the upcoming Digital Euro that I authorise through the EUDI Wallet. It seems obvious that such a scenario needs loads of research and engineering to fill the gaps before such a scenario can become a reality in a secure, privacy-friendly, usable and, in a particularly not distracting way, hands-free via voice biometry while one drives safely. But that is what this chapter was about, to identify future research to advance OOTS and EUDIW. Such research may also well be challenging.

A paradigm shift towards efficiency, security and user-centricity marks the future outlook of cross-border mGovernment services. This is fuelled by innovative approaches such as the OOTS and the EUDIW, in conjunction with disruptive technologies like blockchain and artificial intelligence (AI). OOTS represents a key enabler for the seamless provision of cross-border government e-services. This principle ensures that citizens only need to provide their information once to the government, and this information is then securely shared across various public administrations. OOTS streamlines bureaucratic processes, reduces data redundancy and enhances the overall user experience for citizens and companies engaging in cross-border services. Implementing OOTS in mobile applications can significantly reduce administrative burdens, allowing citizens to access government services effortlessly, regardless of their location.

The EUDIW is another pivotal element shaping the future of cross-border government services. EUDIW aims to provide citizens with a secure and interoperable digital identity that can be used across EU Member States. This digital identity wallet ensures reliable means of authentication, enabling them to access government services seamlessly. The integration of EUDIW with mobile applications enhances the convenience of cross-border transactions, offering citizens a unified and secure platform for interacting with various government agencies. Complementing these advancements, disruptive technologies like blockchain and AI play crucial roles in fortifying the future of mobile cross-border government services.

With its decentralised and tamper-resistant nature, blockchain technology ensures the integrity of cross-border transactions. Implementing blockchain in mobile applications can enhance the security and transparency of data exchange, providing a robust foundation for cross-border collaboration. Additionally, blockchain can facilitate smart contracts, automating and executing predefined conditions in a trustful manner and further streamlining cross-border processes.

AI contributes to the evolution of cross-border government services by enabling advanced data analytics, natural language processing and automation. AI-powered chatbots can enhance user interactions, providing users with instant assistance in multiple languages. Machine learning algorithms can analyse vast datasets to identify trends, supporting decision-making processes for government agencies involved in cross-border initiatives. The combination of AI and mobile cross-border services creates a dynamic and responsive ecosystem that adapts to citizens', companies', and governments' diverse needs.

6 Conclusions

The Single Digital Gateway Regulation (SDG) that defines the Once-Only Technical System (OOTS) and the revision of the eIDAS Regulation introducing the European Digital Identity Wallet (EUDI Wallet) are European flagship policy initiatives that address the Digital Single Market, and both aim to facilitate providing information that citizens and businesses need to deliver when accessing public sector or private services. The paradigms are different. The EUDI Wallet can be seen as an identification means and as an information storage under the user's control, while OOTS frees the user from the hassle of collecting such information whatsoever. Still, the overall purpose is argued targeting similar goals.

The European Commission-funded mGov4EU project was meant to get these concepts together in making SDG and eIDAS fit for the mobile computing environment we meanwhile live in. It complements policy initiatives like the OOTS-EUDI Contact Group that addresses synergies in a dialogue between the European Commission and Member State experts. mGov4EU was meant to carry out research on how to best implement such synergies. Such research and the successful completion of the project, through proofing its concepts in its three pilots i-voting, smart mobility and e-signatures, are, however, not to be seen as the end of a journey but rather an opening to even further research questions.

We gave an outlook on what SDG and the eIDAS Wallet might bring and discussed research potential we see. This covered various dimensions: In the governance dimension, we argue that an environment as complex as and involving as many stakeholders as SDG and the EUDI Wallet cannot just be governed by expert groups defined in the policy basis. It needs community building and stakeholder engagement to cover various interests, diverse service requirements and user needs. The privacy dimension we discussed acknowledges that data protection is at the heart of both SDG and eIDAS. Still, some future research is suggested like how the objective of citizen unobservability when using the Wallet can cope with the services' need of identity matching that both eIDAS and OOTS have. In the electronic services dimension, we argue that with the new paradigms OOTS and EUDI Wallet introduced, research on new service designs is needed so as to best make services fit for the mobile environment. Finally, we discussed the mobile computing dimension where constraints of mobile devices or dependency on the non-European market players providing smartphones and mobile operating systems ask for research on how the EUDI Wallet can be broadly deployed with the technology we currently have without getting in compromises on security and privacy. We also argue that research is needed on how to implement with alternatives to smartphones, particularly for accessibility and inclusiveness considerations but also to prepare for future devices we now even cannot imagine.

Mobile cross-border government services are characterised by a convergence of innovative frameworks like OOTS and EUDIW, possibly aligned with the transformative power of blockchain and AI. These advancements on the one side promise a future where citizens and companies can seamlessly access government services across borders, fostering greater collaboration and efficiency in the globalised digital landscape. On the other side, some challenges and considerations must be addressed and continuously monitored. Issues related to data privacy, security and international regulatory frameworks need careful attention to ensure the responsible implementation of these technologies. Governments must collaborate on standards for cross-border data exchange and establish trust frameworks to build confidence in using disruptive technologies.

References

1. Regulation (EU) 2018/1724 of the European Parliament and of the Council of 2 October 2018 establishing a single digital gateway to provide access to information, to procedures and to assistance and problem-solving services and amending Regulation (EU) No 1024/2012.
2. Regulation (EU) 2018/1724 of the European Parliament and of the Council of 23 July 2014 on electronic identification and trust services for electronic transactions in the internal market and repealing Directive 1999/93/EC.
3. European Commission Proposal for a Regulation of the European Parliament and of the Council amending Regulation (EU) No 910/2014 as regards establishing a framework for a European Digital Identity.
4. European Commission Recommendation of 3.6.2021 on a common Union Toolbox for a coordinated approach towards a European Digital Identity Framework.
5. European Commission Implementing Regulation of 5 August 2022 setting out technical and operational specifications of the technical system for the cross-border automated exchange of evidence and application of the 'once-only' principle in accordance with Regulation (EU) 2018/1724 of the European Parliament and of the Council.
6. Regulation (EU) 2022/1925 of the European Parliament and of the Council of 14 September 2022 on contestable and fair markets in the digital sector and amending Directives (EU) 2019/1937 and (EU) 2020/1828 (Digital Markets Act).

7. Krimmer, R., Dedovic, S., Schmidt, C., Corici, A.-A.: Developing cross-border E-governance: exploring interoperability and cross-border integration. In Electronic participation. Springer International Publishing (2021)
8. Regulation (EU) 2016/679 of the European Parliament and of the Council of 27 April 2016 on the protection of natural persons with regard to the processing of personal data and on the free movement of such data, and repealing Directive 95/46/EC (General Data Protection Regulation)
9. Directive 2006/123/EU (EU) 2018/1724 of the European Parliament and of the Council of 12 December 2006 on services in the internal market

Summary

Carsten Schmidt ⓘ, Thomas J. Lampoltshammer ⓘ, and Vincent Homburg ⓘ

Abstract The preceding chapters present lessons from 3 years of work in the mGov4EU project. This chapter summarises and synthesises the key findings and takeaways based on experiences gathered in 3 years of working with pilots in the mGov4EU project. Concerning the mGov4EU reference architecture, it is concluded that technical challenges could be addressed with a dedicated eID app to allow for app-to-app interaction, tighter integration between mobile applications and service provider applications and alternative wallet-based authentication protocols. Studies of mobile government users identified users' lack of awareness and reluctance to use biometric functionalities in mobile devices, highlighting the critical role of a well-designed user interface. It was also found that identity wallets come with accessibility risks and data protection concerns, for which solutions are proposed. Overall, it is concluded that mGov4EU's results are reusable and sustainable.

Keywords Once-only principle · Single digital gateway · SDGR · Digital single market · mGov4EU · Building blocks · OOTS · eID · eIDAS · Co-creation

1 What Can We Learn from 3 Years of Transdisciplinary Research in the mGov4EU Project?

In the preceding chapters, mGov4EU participants have presented the findings of 3 years of practice-oriented transdisciplinary research in the mGov4EU project. In this chapter, the findings are summarised, and key takeaways are synthesised. As one of the key motivations of mGov4EU was to study practical implementations

C. Schmidt · V. Homburg (✉)
University of Tartu, Tartu, Estonia
e-mail: carsten.schmidt@ut.ee; vincent.homburg@ut.ee

T. J. Lampoltshammer
University for Continuing Education Krems, Krems an der Donau, Austria
e-mail: thomas.lampoltshammer@donau-uni.ac.at

© The Author(s) 2025
V. Homburg et al. (eds.), *From Electronic to Mobile Government*,
https://doi.org/10.1007/978-3-031-64471-9_13

of the ongoing eIDAS regulation and SDGR once-only principle by developing and testing mobile cross-border services, we will first present takeaways from using eIDAS and SDGR layers in mobile government applications and reflect on how eIDAS and SDGR principles relate to mobile government architectures and business models. In the subsequent section, we will present lessons learned from studying users' experiences and reflect on how studying user journeys and focusing on user experiences can help elevate mobile government applications. Then, Sect. 4 will synthesise key takeaways on how to deal with safety, ethics and privacy considerations. In Sect. 5, we will present relevant insights for future research endeavours and European digital government policy initiatives and, more generally, reflect on the sustainability of the mGov4EU deliverables. We end this chapter with a short epilogue.

2   Takeaways from Using SDGR and eIDAS Layers in Pilots

Throughout the various project phases and during the development, implementation and validation of the internet voting, mobile signing and smart mobility pilots, a cohesive mGov4EU reference architecture was developed with which challenges of 'mobile-first', secure user identification across borders and efficient cross-border data exchange could be addressed in the various pilots. The mGov4EU reference architecture aligns reasonably well with eIDAS nodes, and it was concluded that the architecture allows for cross-border authentication, cross-border data exchange and document/evidence retrieval. Challenges that had to be dealt with were that eIDAS nodes use Security Assertion Markup Language (SAML) protocols that were incompatible with many native mobile applications. In order to resolve these compatibility challenges, two solutions were developed. The first was to develop dedicated eID apps to allow for app-to-app communication, and the second was to develop a mobile app software development kit (SDK) for tighter integration between mobile applications and service provider applications. OpenID Connect (OIDC) and OAuth open authentication protocols were implemented as alternatives to the SAML protocols.

Another lesson learned was that the EUDIW standards proved difficult to work with, and throughout the project, a specific wallet solution was developed as a transitional bridge between the current and upcoming eIDAS Regulation iterations. Wallet-based authentication was realised using Verifiable Credentials and Self-Issued Open ID Provider v2-to-Open ID Connect translation.

In conclusion, especially the 'mobile-first' principle central to the mGov4EU project made it necessary to implement alternative technical solutions for identification and wallet-based authentication. With these modifications, the mGov4EU project resulted in a comprehensive solution for mobile-first, digital identity and cross-border evidence retrieval within the eIDAS and SDGR frameworks, and these solutions demonstrate the potential of mobile-first public service delivery in a European context.

3 Findings Derived from Mobile Government Users' Experiences

Studies of mobile government users revealed that especially smartphones' biometric functionalities pose challenges. Partly this is so because some users are unaware of identification by fingerprint, and partly this is because some users are reluctant to use biometric solutions. These findings underline the importance of accommodating diverse user preferences in the design of mobile government applications. Furthermore, it was found that well-designed, inclusive user interfaces and seamless user experience reduce the need for user training and are generally conducive to adoption of mobile government adoption across various types of users.

4 Security, Ethics and Privacy

Continuous reflection on the pilots' experiences and ongoing political development revealed that the EU Digital Identity Wallets trigger general accessibility and digital divide concerns. Furthermore, it was concluded that security is a critical concern in collaborative research projects like mGov4EU, and in order to remedy these concerns, a five-step method is proposed and tested in the mGov4EU project. Application of the method in the mGov4EU showed its strength in identifying security risks and integrating security measures into work packages. The proposed method, with its generic nature, holds the potential for broader applicability across various collaborative research projects.

5 Sustainability Beyond the Project

mGov4EU is a project and, by definition, has an end date. An important ambition, however, was to produce relevant insights and deliverables for cross-border mobile government services beyond the pilots central to the project. A vital goal for mGov4EU was to develop sustainable results. Reflection on the development process, testing and validation and lessons learned resulted in the identification of four crucial insights that allow for sustainability beyond the project's end date.

First, from a technical point of view, it can be stated that decoupling the eID interoperability system, the Digital Wallet system, the SDG interoperability system, the eSignature system and the architecture allows for maximum reusability of the deliverables beyond the project itself. This resulted in reusable and extensible technical building blocks.

Second, policymakers and developers of future cross-border mobile government services may also use the five-step security risk assessment method that is generic in its ability to detect and remedy risks in other initiatives as well.

Third, the usage of co-creation in the project was valuable for its outcomes; it has resulted in an analysis of business model dynamics within the context of the mGov4EU project, enabling future policymakers and mobile government developers to create innovative mobile government initiatives. The earlier and stronger co-creation elements are incorporated into the process, the more beneficial they are.

Fourth, from a non-technical point of view, on the one side, the mGov4EU project has taught us in detail that achieving semantic operability is both a key challenge and a critical factor for any future European mobile government initiative. On the other side, it has used the GOFA (Governance, Operational, Finance and Architecture) model to develop a sustainability plan. Furthermore, the project has showcased that the GOFA model itself is sustainable and extensible; it can be used for large-scale projects and projects on a smaller scale and beyond.

6 Epilogue: Some Famous Last Words

With the summary of findings and identification of lessons learnt throughout the mGov4EU project, this chapter marks the end of a project that has not only brought together scholars and practitioners from ten participating organisations and five countries but has also invited participants with backgrounds in computer science, law, political science and public administration to embark on a transdisciplinary journey. The pilots in internet voting, smart mobility and mobile signing provided engineering challenges and opportunities to record users' experiences and also allowed for ethical reflection and, above all, for lessons learned and concrete deliverables that are most likely relevant, valid and usable, beyond the end date of the project. We are quite confident that policymakers and developers in future European mobile government initiatives can make fruitful use of the insights reported in the various chapters of this book, and we would like to wish them gute Reise, turvalist reisi, buen viaje, *safe travels*.